SLAVE TO BEAUTY

Estelle Jussim

SLAVE

TO

BEAUTY

The Eccentric Life and Controversial
Career of ❖ F. HOLLAND DAY ❖

Photographer
Publisher
Aesthete

David R. Godine, Publisher, Boston

First published in 1981 by
David R. Godine, Publisher, Inc.
306 Dartmouth Street
Boston, Massachusetts 02116

LIBRARY OF CONGRESS CATALOGING IN PUBLICATION DATA
Jussim, Estelle.
Slave to beauty.
Bibliography: p. 301.
Includes index.
1. Day, Fred Holland, 1864-1933.
2. Photographers – United States – Biography.
I. Title.
TR140.D37J87   770'.92'4 [B]   80-66460
ISBN 0-87923-346-X

Manufactured in the United States of America

Acknowledgments

A few years ago, Jerome P. O'Neill, Jr., a Rochester, New York, historian of photography, sent me some newspaper clippings and a letter from Charles Lennon of Norwood, Massachusetts. The letter remarked it was a shame that no one had written about F. Holland Day, whose letters and other memorabilia were awaiting biographical research at the Norwood Historical Society. As I was geographically closer to Norwood than he, O'Neill suggested that I look into it. 'Looking into it' has been the most fascinating project of my career, and I can never thank Jerry O'Neill sufficiently for passing along what proved to be a unique opportunity.

Charles and Miriam Lennon at the Norwood Historical Society were the most amazingly energetic and devoted assistants in my pursuits. William L. Hyland, former President of the Norwood Historical Society, originally granted me permission to publish materials from their collection, and I thank him and the present President, Mrs. Bettina Cottrell, for their encouragement. Other Norwood residents or associates who were most kind were William A. Gifford, Mary Dean, and Freeman N. Chadbourne.

Two useful sources already existed as starting points for further investigation of Day's photographic and publishing careers: Ellen Fritz Clattenburg's catalog of the exhibition of Day's photographs at Wellesley College, and the fine doctoral dissertation by Professor Stephen Maxfield Parrish of Cornell University, to which Harvard University graciously granted me access.

Without the painstaking and pioneering work of Joe W.

Kraus, Director of Libraries, Illinois State University, in his bibliographical studies of Copeland and Day, much time would have been lost and many leads overlooked. His thesis and his subsequent book on the publishing partnership were invaluable.

Jerald Maddox, Curator of Photography of the Prints and Photographs Department, Library of Congress, manifested extraordinary patience with this project. Thanks, too, to Jerry L. Kearns, Head of Reference of the Prints and Photographs Department, Leroy Bellamy, Reference Librarian of that department, and the staff of the Library of Congress Department of Photographic Reproduction for their generous assistance.

Dr. William Inness Homer, Chairman of the Art History Department, University of Delaware, not only shared information from his vast store of knowledge about the pictorialists and Alfred Stieglitz, but undertook to read a draft of the manuscript and made many clarifications and suggestions. The same courtesies were graciously provided by another specialist in the Photo-Secession, Robert 'Mac' Doty, Curator of the Currier Gallery of Art, Manchester, New Hampshire. Any errors which remain in the book are, of course, my own.

Many individuals at the International Museum of Photography at George Eastman House gave unstintingly of their time and energies: Martha Jenks, former Director of the Archives, and Susan Wyngaard, Director of the Photographic Prints Department and the Library, as well as her assistant, Mary Widger. This book could not have been written without the periodical holdings of the IMP-GEH Library. The Photographic Reproduction Department of the Museum provided swift and excellent service, and I thank George Eastman House for permission to reproduce from their extraordinary collections.

Overseas, thanks go especially to Errol Jackson, who took time from his work for Henry Moore to obtain several of F. Holland Day's unpublished photographs and Keats materials at the Keats House in Hampstead. Mrs. C. M. Gee, Assistant Curator, Keats House, was both encouraging and helpful. At the Royal Photographic Society in London, Valerie Lloyd and Katherine Di Giulio gave useful assistance, and special thanks go to Professor Margaret Harker of the London Polytechnic for introductions and suggestions. The *British Journal of Photography* kindly granted permission to quote extensively from their publication.

I am deeply grateful to Georgia O'Keeffe for granting permission to quote from the extensive correspondence of Alfred

Stieglitz in the collection of the Beinecke Rare Book and Manuscript Library, Yale University, and thank Donald C. Gallup for his assistance.

Dr. Maynard P. White, Jr. was most kind in sharing information about Clarence White and his circle in Maine.

The Metropolitan Museum of Art, New York City, granted permission to reproduce the rare Day materials in their outstanding Stieglitz Collection.

Dr. Susan Otis Thompson, Columbia University, was most liberal with permissions to use her materials on the publishing activities of Copeland and Day.

Among many other individuals and institutions that merit special gratitude: the Rare Books and Fine Arts Departments of the Boston Public Library; the Reference Librarians and the Print Department of the Boston Athenaeum; Eugene J. Harrington, S.J., Curator of Special Collections, Dinand Library, College of the Holy Cross in Worcester, Mass.; the Prints and Photographs Department of the Museum of Fine Arts, Boston; the Archives of American Art; and Boyd Edmonston, Reference Librarian, Simmons College.

My publisher, David R. Godine, deserves much credit for his many significant editorial suggestions, and I thank him for his dedication to fine books. I will always be indebted to his hard-working staff and associates, among them Kathleen Riley, production manager, Sarah Saint-Onge, managing editor, and Ann Schroeder, designer, who organized the complexity of illustration with patience, skill, and intelligence.

There is yet another level of appreciation owed to the example of scholars like Philippe Jullian, a biographer of Oscar Wilde and author of brilliant works on Symbolist and Decadent artists of the late nineteenth century. His creative syntheses spurred my search for interconnections among the arts of the nineties. To Morse Peckham I also owe vast intellectual debts.

Dr. Elizabeth Lindquist-Cock, art historian and historian of photography at the Massachusetts College of Art, proved invaluable as a most knowledgeable resource, and another friend and colleague, Dr. Heinz Henisch, Pennsylvania State University, offered both encouragement and solace during the many difficulties which this project involved, especially by his belief in the importance of F. Holland Day.

If by some unintended oversight I have neglected to seek permission or to acknowledge assistance, I offer my sincerest apologies.

Contents

SLAVE TO BEAUTY

F. Holland Day in London,
1900, by Alvin Langdon
Coburn.

1 An Introduction

He was a most unusual human being, an extraordinary genius with the camera, an eccentric in dress and habits, generous to poets, impoverished women writers, Boston bohemians, and young immigrant boys, especially his protégé, Kahlil Gibran. Proud of his affiliation with the 1890s Decadents – a term of vastly different meaning to his generation than to ours – he worshipped John Keats and Honoré de Balzac, collected one of the most impressive private libraries in the United States, and was the confidant of the English and French æsthetes. With his good friend, Gertrude Käsebier, he experimented with thought transference; with William Butler Yeats and other adherents of the Rosicrucian cults, he dabbled in spiritism, séances, and the occult.

As a publisher of fine books, he helped to introduce the design and printing influence of William Morris to America. Under the imprint of his firm – Copeland and Day – appeared that scandal of the 1890s, *The Yellow Book*. He brought over from England the tainted hyperboles of Oscar Wilde's *Salomé*, and shocked Boston (while entertaining the rest of America) with Aubrey Beardsley's drawings. With John Lane, his publishing associate in London, he presented the talents of unconventional young poets.

As a photographer, F. Holland Day ranked among the very first, most influential, and most successful American proponents of photography as fine art. Lauded both here and in Europe, recognized as an equal to Alfred Stieglitz, and one of the first American members of the Brotherhood of the Linked Ring, Day was more famous by far than most of his competitors. He enjoyed a brief decade of great achievement – essentially from 1895 to 1905 – but continued working privately afterwards. He was fêted and acclaimed in the capitals of Europe and the great cities of the United States. Then his reputation plummeted to the depths of an obscurity from which it is only now recovering.

This obscurity resulted partly from a catastrophic fire that destroyed his Boston studio in 1904, and with it perhaps two thousand glass negatives, hundreds of magnificent prints, dozens of pictures by his contemporaries, Japanese paintings and Oriental objects, and a priceless collection of original Beardsley drawings. But there are other, less conspicuous but far more important, reasons for his obscurity, reasons this book will attempt to uncover.

The primary cause was the unremitting competition between F. Holland Day and Alfred Stieglitz. Although their relationship began amicably, and Stieglitz published both Day's articles and his photographs in *Camera Notes*, Stieglitz was unwilling to share his own leadership of the American pictorialists. In 1899 and 1900, Stieglitz actually attempted to block Day's exhibition in London of 'The New School of American Photography.' Convinced that he alone was the messiah of the new group, Stieglitz nevertheless behaved ambivalently. Even as he resented Day's legitimate claims to leadership, he admired Day's photographs sufficiently to collect a considerable number of superb examples. In fact, Stieglitz was so impressed with Day's work that he collected two different prints of the same negative, the only time he so indulged his fancy. In the 1977 exhibition of the Stieglitz collection at the Metropolitan Museum in New York City, Day's mysterious subjects and his controversial *Seven Last Words of Christ* of Day attracted substantial attention even among superlative works by his good friends, Clarence White, Gertrude Käsebier, Edward Steichen, and Frederick Evans.

Well after Day's own establishment of the 'New School,' Stieglitz began in 1902 to organize the Photo-Secession. But

Three views of F. Holland Day
as publisher, 1894 or 1895.

Stieglitz's egocentric manipulation of his colleagues eventually
led to the dissolution of that extraordinary group. When Stieglitz came to produce that most influential of photographic journals, *Camera Work* (1903–1917), he invited F. Holland Day
to be the first to have his work reproduced in its magnificent
photogravure pages. But by then he had alienated Day so completely that Day declined. It was Day's most serious mistake as
an artist. If he had hoped to preserve his own image, to achieve
a kind of immortality, he should have participated in *Camera
Work,* for many photographers who appeared there have received the benefits of scholarship and criticism, often far beyond
what their work merited.

Had Day's subtle, sophisticated, and haunting pictures appeared in *Camera Work,* the present generation would be familiar with his work, his reputation would be brighter, his
sequestered prints evaluated, and attention finally paid to his
development as an artist. As it is, this volume is the first major
attempt[1] to present a complete survey of his life and work, an
effort to weave together the many strands of his personality, his
literary and artistic interests, his sometimes bizarre affiliations
and practices, his generosities and loyalties, and his final mystifying seclusion. For, oddly, those writers who have addressed
F. Holland Day's outstanding contributions to American publishing dismiss his photography in one or two sentences, while
those who admire his photography often seem unaware of any
other activity, least of all his major contribution as a controversial publisher and *littérateur.*

If there are any underlying hypotheses that serve as a

focus for this book, they are concerned with the fascinating interconnections between Day's bibliomania and his photography, between his continual search for mystical experience and the spiritual revolutions of his generation. Several writers have elucidated Day's obsession with John Keats, yet none has attempted to evaluate the impact of Keatsian imagery and philosophy on Day's approach to photography, nor has any book documented or explained Day's simultaneous obsession with Balzac. Not only Keats and Balzac, but Maeterlinck and almost-forgotten exotics like Edgar Saltus influenced Day's thinking and his imagery.

One of the unifying and most essential strands in Day's complex life was an æsthetic ideal borne of Keats's passionate belief in the supremacy of art over all other activities. The idea that poetry (and literature), rather than painting alone, might be a major influence on a visual art has not been sufficiently explored in its relation to the development of photography. Histories of the Pictorialist movement of the 1890s and the first decade of the twentieth century have tended to emphasize photography's competition with painting, especially in terms of its imitation of the effects of the traditional graphic arts. We are only beginning to explore the classic ideal of *ut pictura poesis* – a picture is like a poem – as that ideal relates to photography. Dante Gabriel Rossetti had prophesied that the next Keats would be a painter; it was too early in the history of photography for him to have prophesied that the next Keats would be a photographer. This is not to imply that Day's sole preoccupation was with Keatsian imagery. He was as devoted to the psychological and occultist perspicacities and sensibilities of Balzac. It may be that Day was so possessed by literature that its influence on him was largely unconscious.

Day's articles in *Camera Notes* and elsewhere point to his belief that his excellence as a photographer came from a decade of study of the great painters: Guido Reni, Mantegna, Rembrandt, Hans Holbein, Velásquez, and ultimately James McNeill Whistler. Whistler himself had relied not only on Oriental decorative approaches to composition – approaches also widely used by Day, Clarence White, and Käsebier – but on the close tonal values of Velásquez in particular. No matter how significantly the masters of painting influenced F. Holland Day, his psychological set, his interest in symbolism, and his fascination with certain images of pagan mythology and arcane rit-

F. Holland Day as a French dandy, Paris, 1889.

Day in costume for a medieval
dinner party at Norwood, 1893.

ual substantially emanated from his passion for literature and for
the Keatsian romanticism that pervaded not only Pre-Raphælite
ideology but the æstheticism of Oscar Wilde. In this romantic
æstheticism, Day allied himself with all the other artists, poets,
and novelists who decried the popular rage for realism as a de-
humanizing and despiritualizing materialism. He was a leader
among image makers who longed for a return to the metaphysi-
cal manifestations of human life and objected to the very accuracy of photography as catering to the demands of the masses
for representationalism; he agreed with Baudelaire's rejection
of verisimilitude for its own sake.

That photography could rise above a mechanical recording of nature to rival the fine arts was hardly an acceptable
proposition in the 1880s. For forty years, the primacy of photography as a literal transcript of reality had seemed both its
greatest virtue and its most demeaning handicap. If photography was admired for its documentary capabilities, it was be-
littled as incapable of producing art. The camera was nothing
more than a machine, an aid to memory. Only the manipulations of the human hand could produce a visual product worthy
of the label 'art.' Thus the painterly imitations by Henry Peach
Robinson and Oscar Rejlander, who created composite pictures
mimicking sentimental tableaux, demonstrated the need to
document the presence of the human hand and human decision making. Then came the 'soft-focus' adherents, who insisted that the presence of the artist could be determined by the
choice of a particular focus selected for a specific artistic effect.
Under the leadership of Peter Henry Emerson, photographers
began to claim an equal place in the pantheon of the fine arts.

Selection of focus, the determination of what was or was
not to be included in a picture, the magnification of certain
graphic-arts qualities of the print in the photogravure process –
all of these were now guarantees that the artist had taken control of the camera. Special new processes were introduced –
gum bichromate, for example – that permitted the direct manipulation of the print by the photographer while providing
effects closely imitative of etching, lithography, aquatint, mezzotint, charcoal drawing, and ink washes. It seemed as if the
struggle to ally photography with the fine arts had indeed resulted in triumph. In fact the triumph was fleeting, for the
imitation of other graphic arts seemed to indicate that photography was a secondary invention, hardly worth consideration

on its own merits. It was not until the more rapid emulsions, faster lenses, and smaller cameras made possible the so-called snapshot that the radically different characteristics of photography began to be recognized as evidence that the camera produces a unique product.

Until very recently, 'straight' photography has been regarded as springing as spontaneously from the brow of Stieglitz as Athena did from the head of Zeus. Much as Stieglitz deserves credit, straight photography had gained other adherents as influential as Frederick Evans, master of architecture, and F. Holland Day, master of nuance – each of them claiming to leave the negative 'pure,' unretouched and uncropped. This pure photography turns out not to have been quite so pure; even Stieglitz sometimes enjoyed the use of manipulated gum bichromate and glycerine prints. What straight photography demanded, however, was that the composition and all other effects of the picture be conceived by the photographer prior to snapping the shutter. For Stieglitz, this led to magnificent moments of time on film: icy storms, snowy city streets, steam rising from a horse's flanks, a primitive aeroplane, like a giant butterfly, gliding on the wind almost out of the rectangle of the frame, and, much later, the moody cloud forms of 'Songs of the Sky.' For F. Holland Day, it produced a series of superbly dramatic portraits, among the first in this country to ennoble black people (sometimes under the guise of 'Ethiopian Chiefs'). The faces of exotics, young women in Moorish costumes, Syrians, Greeks, Japanese, Chinese, were all handsomely composed and viewed in an often mysterious chiaroscuro. Ultimately, Day sought to modify the pure images of reality by using a specially manufactured lens for a series of allegories. It created an aura of light, a diffused image unmanipulated in the negative but distinctly different from daguerreotype precision, perfect for romanticizing the male nude.

F. Holland Day could never have become a Paul Strand or an Edward Weston, nor even an Alfred Stieglitz. His fin-de-siècle æstheticism, his admiration for Clarence White and Gertrude Käsebier, his literary romanticism, even his intoxication with male beauty, all led him on different paths. A superficial analysis might indicate that, while Stieglitz and his disciples worshipped form, Day remained entranced by subject. Yet the philosophers and theorists of photography are still struggling to express a perfect equation, a more accurate description

Solitude, Edward Steichen's portrait of Day, as it appeared in *Camera Work,* April 1906.

Father, Forgive Them, the first in Day's series, *The Seven Last Words of Christ,* 1898.

of the nexus between form and content. F. Holland Day consciously and studiously pursued what he believed to be form. It may be that his later allegorical and religious subjects tend to confuse the discussion.

It has been said that you can tell a man by the company he keeps. It has also been said that you cannot tell a man by the books in his library. As we shall see, the former statement held true for Holland Day, but since the writers of the books in his spectacular library were as real to him as living friends – indeed, many of them were his friends – they *can* be taken as a reliable indication of his interests and predilections. His lifelong relationship with the Catholic poet Louise Imogen Guiney was most mystifying. This book attempts to uncover the major developments in that friendship, and therefore hopes to correct some seriously misleading impressions formulated by Guiney's biographers. Day has been accused by writers, who apparently did not seek access to his notebooks, of being sexually impotent or freakishly willful with Guiney. The truth proves to be both ludicrous and pathetic, although many details of their relationship were lost forever in the bonfire that Guiney's friend, the writer Alice Brown, made of Day's letters to her.

Even more mysterious than his relationship with Louise Guiney was Day's final seclusion. No longer a world leader in photography, he confined himself to bed for sixteen years, depending on servants and male friends to help him pursue genealogical studies, horticulture, and the secrets of his Keats collection. Regarded as mad by his Norwood neighbors of the 1920s, he nevertheless continued to be the kindest of men – and the most generous, as the letters of the Clarence White family attest. New information about these last years helps to evaluate Day's eccentric hypochondria from a medical and psychological viewpoint. The contradictory statements about his burial have also been clarified.

F. Holland Day epitomizes the elegant, uninhibited artist of the decadent nineties. We can imagine him working in his Turkish robes and Chinese silk shirts, planning the secret panels in his Norwood library, attiring himself in loincloth and crown of thorns and fastening himself to a wooden cross – imported from Syria – so that he could pose as Jesus crucified. We can see him bantering with Bernard Berenson or Yeats; dining with Lord Alfred Douglas and Oscar Wilde; obsessively photographing every spot Keats or Balzac ever inhabited, visited, or even mentioned; meticulously dressing his black chauffeur in leopard skin and feathered cap for portraits; lecturing boldly to an irate group of English photographers; knocking about Algerian streets on a wild spree with Alvin Langdon Coburn; or lighting the thirteen candles of cabalistic ritual in his incense-fragrant studio on Beacon Hill.

A superb portraitist, a photographer willing to take risks, an early leader in the Pictorialist movement, an image maker whose pictures were startling in their originality and breathtaking in the subtlety and intensity of their execution, F. Holland Day has been sadly neglected. It is hoped that this book will begin to rectify that negligence, and to return a master photographer to his rightful place.

F. Holland Day in his London darkroom, 1900, by Alvin Langdon Coburn.

2

Bibliomaniac with a Camera

For her diary entry of Saturday, July 23, 1864, Anna Day dutifully recorded all the significant events, including the birth of a son. In a minuscule, almost illegibly cramped hand, she noted 'The advent of a little Day all the Smiths away weather cool but very dry dry dry clear and very windy . . .'[1] Victorian proprieties did demand the suppression of the awesome details of birth and all bodily processes, but there was not even the smallest hint of any spontaneous enthusiasm for the baby. Anna's prim excesses of gentility earned her the private nickname of 'Lady Day.'

A frail, sometimes sickly but skillfully domineering woman, she was twenty-eight when she bore her husband, Lewis, their first and only child. Lewis was outgoing and energetic, with the wits to increase an inherited fortune until he became a millionaire in the 1890s. Between his real-estate ventures, cattle ranches, and various leather enterprises spread as far as Florida and Wisconsin, he often had reason to be away. Lively and playful, young Fred Holland Day lacked for nothing, except, perhaps, some respite from his mother's overprotective ministrations.

Their home town exemplified everything about American

Lewis and Anna Day, and Fred
when he was about six years old.

materialism that Fred and his friends came to detest, although
he chose to retire to the family mansion at the end of his career.
Norwood was a thriving industrial town, twenty miles south of
Boston, a major stop on the railway. The Day property was
known as 'Bullard Farm,' and from their hill lawns they could
look down at the tanneries, ink factories, paper mills, and book
manufactories. Across the rail line were the tenements for the
Irish, Italian, and French-Canadian workers whose labors en-
riched the Plimptons, the Winslows, and the Days. With so
many industries in Norwood connected with books and printing, it seems almost inevitable that young Fred would take a
strong interest in the production of books.

The miracle was that he ever learned to read and write,
considering his early schooling. Writing was late in coming,
and his spelling and syntax, to put it charitably, remained idio-
syncratic most of his life. That may have been less the result of
his mother's insistence on private tutors and a local private
school than of some minor form of dyslexia. Despite this early
difficulty, Day became an avid correspondent, trading eager
notes with his school chums, all of whom, in the fashion of the
day, were assigned nicknames like 'Fly,' 'Spider,' and 'Bumble-
Bee.' When he came to regard 'Fred,' the name by which he
had been christened – not 'Frederick' – as beneath the dignity
of an artist, he signed himself 'F.H.D.,' and later he even short-
ened 'Fred' to the 'F.' in 'F. Holland Day.'

His first artistic adventure came during his fifteenth year.

'Bullard Farm' – the Day mansion before the renovations of 1892.

In the spring of 1879 Anna Day became ill with a lung disease. The purer air of the mountains was prescribed, and so she took Fred, now a lanky adolescent with rather big ears, with her to Denver, Colorado. There he had the opportunity to study ethnic and racial groups which he had barely seen in his brief visits to Boston neighborhoods. What struck him with lasting impact was the large colony of Chinese then in Denver. He was enchanted by their looks, fascinated by the fact that the Chinese women wore the same clothes as the men, 'only the cloth was nicer, and the way they comb their hair was greesed [sic] with something sticky.'[2] Almost all of his allowance went for Chinese inks and brushes, paints, papers, and artifacts.

None of his early sketches and watercolors has survived, but in his dutiful letters to his father, he revealed his great attraction to the physical surfaces of objects, commenting in detail on their textures and shapes. There can be no question that he was vastly influenced by this first sustained contact with Oriental culture. He had been born the same year that Whistler painted his famous *The Little White Girl, Symphony in White, No. 2,* and completed his other Oriental canvases, *La Princess du Pays de la Porcelaine* and the odd *Lange Lijzen of the Six Marks.* But Day was too young to be paying much attention to the flamboyant Whistler, who had already created a revolution in the composition and subject matter of painting, and would influence photography as well.

Indeed, by the time Fred was in Denver, not only Whis-

Portrait of James Abbott Mc-
Neill Whistler.

Fred Day on February 8, 1878,
thirteen and a half years old.

tler but Oscar Wilde, Dante Gabriel Rossetti, and other trend-
setters had made it quite the fashion to sigh over Chinese porcelains, especially the famed blue-and-white china, which became
a collecting craze. The *japonisme,* as it was called, was so fever-
ish that *Punch* published cartoons of intense young men fon-
dling teapots while their wives swooned over lilies. It was all
part of the mid-century Cult of the Beautiful, of which Whistler
and Wilde became the major prophets. If it was occasionally
ludicrous, it was always sublime. Day grew into it like a hot-
house orchid.

The fascination with Oriental art was perhaps the single
æsthetic constant in his life. When he was old and too ill to
travel, he would confess that he had been frustrated by a lifelong ambition to travel to China in pursuit of objets d'art.[3] His
friends found him a compulsive collector at an early age. From
Denver, he wrote to his father that he was picking up exotic
rock samples, Oriental fabrics, Indian headdresses, and Chinese
blue silk overshirts. He was also enjoying splashing about in
high rubber boots as he hunted for insect specimens in the cold
mountain brooks. His father responded affectionately: 'You
must go fishing and see if you can catch some trout but don't
try to catch any Bears as they hug too tight for comfort. . . . Be
good.'[4] Poor Fred could hardly help but be good; he was never
allowed to venture out of doors, for example, without Lady
Day deciding if he should wear his overcoat. Even when Fred
was a celebrity, in his early thirties, Anna Day fussed over him
without mercy. While his father's letters made the logical pro-
gression from avoiding bears to the principles of running a
publishing business, his mother's were frequently long ha-
rangues about how often he should wash his hair, or how he
should celebrate the Fourth of July when he went to Europe.

When they returned to Norwood from Denver, Anna decided that young Fred must now go to the Chauncy Hall School
in Boston, a preparatory school with high academic standards
and a liberal-arts curriculum well suited to future gentlemen
and ladies. It may have been at this time that the Days began
to winter regularly in Boston, going down to Norwood for
weekends and during the spring and summer. Norwood remained the center of their lives, not only because Lewis Day
supervised the tannery there, but because it offered all the pleasures a large house, with acres of greenery, could afford. Winters in Boston were difficult, to be sure, but Lewis had a busi-

Left: *Madame Sadi Yaco with Parasol;* right: *Portrait of a Chinese Man,* both by F. Holland Day, about 1896.

ness office there, and, besides, it was the height of fashion to live in the 'Athens of America,' where all forms of culture were readily accessible.

At the Chauncy Hall School, which Fred entered at the age of sixteen, he made several lifelong friends, and through these friends, contacts at Harvard University. He was popular with both sexes, and he blossomed almost immediately into a debonair young man, well-dressed, well-groomed, with a dash of the Whistler dandy already suggested in his poses for commercial studio portraits. Madame Day, as he often called her, had already persuaded Fred – or so she thought – that he was very special, and he must seek out people who were 'good enough' for him. It was not long before he totally rejected this narrow-minded advice, not so subtly tinged with racism. For much of his life he shocked family and friends by consorting with precisely the ethnic and racial company which he preferred and they avoided.

When Chauncy Hall organized its annual tour to Europe in the summer of 1883, Fred Day was nineteen. Travel to Europe was considered mandatory in achieving a cultivated mind, and so he gaped reverentially at all the required sights: the

Fred Day with two young women at school, about 1880.

Fred Day at nineteen, en route to Europe in 1883.

Blarney Stone in Ireland, the castles of Scotland, England, and Belgium, the mountains of Switzerland, the canals of Venice, the museums of Paris. The young man who had experienced such difficulties in learning how to write was now serving as correspondent for the *Norwood Review*. He had studied his Washington Irving, and in his long letter of July 29, published in the *Review* on August 18, he was enthusiastic about the many literary shrines which Irving had described. From his ensuing correspondence, it was clear that he was especially fascinated by the haunts of one of his favorite authors, Honoré de Balzac.

To his family's great surprise, when he graduated from Chauncy Hall in 1884 Fred received a special gold medal for 'the best scholarship in English literature,' and he made enough of an impression as an actor in the closing festivities to warrant notice in a newspaper:

> . . . *It is hard to pass over one of the best bits of character acting the school has seen for years, by Fred Holland Day, entitled 'A Piece of Red Calico,' admirably descriptive of a man's difficulties in a dry goods store amidst a bewildering maze of inefficient 'sales ladies.'*[5]

A predilection for recitation, declamation, and stagecraft, and a general sense of the theatrical, would form a crucial foundation for many of his achievements in photography. Indeed, one British critic of his Royal Photographic Society Exhibition of 1900 remarked acidly that Day would have made a fine stage manager, as he knew so well how to pose both himself and his other camera subjects.

Day dabbled briefly in travelogue lectures illustrated with lantern slides,[6] but he was already deeply immersed in the activities of his own literary society, 'a small group of ten or twelve members calling themselves "Athenes Therapes," among whom we count a nephew of Louisa Alcott, a daughter of Rev. J. Minot Savage, with other bright people young and old – this association I helped to establish and keep up the enthusiasm since 1884.'[7] Reverend Savage's daughter Gertrude became one of his closest friends and lifelong correspondents, and her brother Philip was responsible for introducing him to Herbert Copeland, the young man who would become Day's partner in publishing.

The 'Monday Nighters,' as they sometimes called them-

Above: 'Madame Day' in 1883; below: offices of A. S. Barnes and other Boston book dealers, 1885.

selves, were devoted to the theatre, traveling en masse to see the many notable stage performances in Boston: Sir Henry Irving, Edwin Booth, and the Italian actor Salvini, whose Othello reportedly was thrilling. At their own meetings, they read and enacted Shakespeare's plays, another great passion of Fred's. Simultaneously, he was devouring the Russian authors in translation, as well as the prodigious œuvre of Balzac. He complained from time to time of his slow pace in French, and he feared he would never master another language.

In 1885, his obsession with books seduced him into accepting an appointment as a 'depositary' for A. S. Barnes & Company in Boston. This book-selling initiative was certainly encouraged by Lewis Day, who had a strictly puritanical outlook on the virtues of earning one's own way in life. Still, it was a commitment that gave Fred, now twenty-one, considerable pause. On February 10, he wrote to a friend,

> *Did I really write 'My days of frivolities are gradually coming to a close, I do not care for dancing now?'*

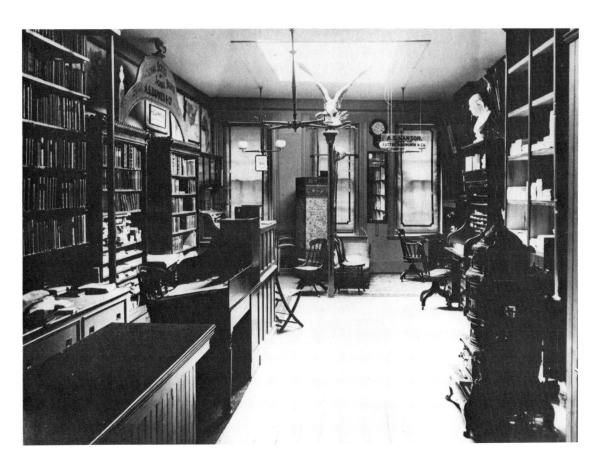

*Well all I can say is that it must have been written
in one of my blue days. You didn't know I had such
days? Well, I don't often. 'I begin to feel the weight
of my years.' That is solemn truth – I do – for 'I'm
not as young as I used to be' nor are any of us.*[8]

After the freedom, even indulgences, he had enjoyed for
so very long, his coming into his majority was not quite
what the son of a successful merchant might have expected. Yet
he did not despair long over his vanishing youth. Within the
month, he had cheered himself up by spending most of his salary on Oriental art objects. His favorite among these was an
antique Persian lamp of brass, inlaid with silver, which he
hung in his library.

In 1886 the Days rented apartments in Boston at 24
Boylston Street, a location Fred described delightedly as 'two
doors this side the Second Church and opposite Trinity – well
located but a little far uptown to get home to lunch. The Club
meet with us as usual and are doing fine work – *twenty* members.'[9] They were reading ancient Greek drama in translation,
then went on to Ralph Waldo Emerson. The group was dominated by Fred Day, who was not above chiding members for
not having prepared properly. He took it all seriously – probably as a substitute for the kinds of discussion which occur in
college classrooms. For, despite receiving a gold medal in English literature from Chauncy Hall, he carried with him all of
his life that sensitive chip on the shoulder of the self-educated
man. His parents, apparently, thought college a luxury.

When Fred was first coming to know Philip Savage, who
was attending Harvard, he wrote a long confession:

*Had I been fortunate enough to have had the right
sort of advice when I left school and entered business,
my progress would not have been so slow I fancy. But
I think I may be pardoned for saying that I have
pulled my own weight up by my own strength alone
and that all I have and am in that distinction is due
to my own, no doubt, often misguided judgment.
None of my family are students or even readers.
What books I have, have been gotten without advice
and what reading I have done has been accomplished
on my own responsibility.*[10]

With photography, too, it would once again be a question of

pulling himself up by the bootstraps. Yet in photography there were precious few who could have taught him anything valuable, for he was an instinctive pictorial innovator and never inclined to technical details.

Day's circle of friends was not confined to the Athenes Therapes, nor was that the only literary club he helped to establish. Another was the Club of Odd Volumes, an esoteric society whose wealthy acolytes pursued rare books like big-game hunters. Armed with Eppie Sargent's book, *The Scientific Basis of Spiritualism*, Fred was also beginning to make the rounds of séances and lectures given by noted mediums whose patrons included some of the most respected Boston intellectuals, among them William James. Thanks to a young poet, Louise Imogen Guiney, he was introduced to the aristocratic literary salons that included George Santayana and Bernard Berenson.

Yet of all these sometimes dazzling acquaintances, he seems to have fixed a particularly passionate devotion on one of the 'Monday Nighters,' a somewhat elusive fellow by the name of Jack. Jack was strong with the ladies, and Fred worshipped his manliness. When Jack went off and married without notice, Fred reacted with the cold bitterness that characterizes spurned lovers; his had been a serious and painful adolescent crush, one of the first symptoms of his later fixation on the ideal male. Fortunately, he had other sources of affection. He was greatly attached to Gertrude Savage, to whom he wrote many humorous and punning letters, complete with zany sketches.

More important, perhaps, he was possessed by books and thoroughly devoted to authors. By his twenty-first year, he had already amassed nine hundred volumes, many of them first editions, all examples of fine printing. A rich man's hobby, definitely. Curiously enough, it was through his bibliomania that he was led to the camera.

In the 1880s, when bibliomania was just becoming fashionable, book collecting involved not only the hunt for the fine specimen, the rare edition, or the autographed copy, but prints and pictures associated with authors and their works. In March 1885, Fred wrote to a friend about a current preoccupation:

> . . . *illustrating two very rare books, one the story of the 'State Prisoner commonly called The Man of the Iron Mask,' which will take 43 portraits altogether, Dr. Akins letters on literature which will take 84 portraits so you see I have set myself up in business . . .*[11]

What Fred called 'illustrating' refers to what Victorian bibliophiles knew as the process of 'extra-illustrating,' 'extending,' or 'grangerizing' a book. The practice consisted of collecting images in any graphic medium, of people and places mentioned as characters or locations in either fiction or nonfiction. These could be prints or photographic copies of paintings, pictures of the authors themselves supplied by commercial portrait houses, or sketches, sometimes pasted directly into the bound copy of a book. More frequently, the literary work was purchased in unbound signatures. When the extra-illustrating was completed, the proud owner could have the entire collection bound up in his favorite style and color of morocco, usually to match the rest of his leather-bound library of rarities. Any book so treated increased enormously in value.

For an edition of Balzac, Fred committed himself to collecting four hundred prints of the writer's friends and haunts, along with forty portraits of the man himself, photographic cartes de visite, and other memorabilia. He wrote directly to contemporary authors, asking for 'the address of some artist of whom I may procure a photograph of yourself.'[12] But his passionate pursuit of pictures grew obsessive in the case of his greatest hero, Keats. In 1886, he wrote to Dodd, Mead, the New York publishers, to make a typical request.

An early photograph by F. Holland Day, probably taken to 'extra-illustrate' a volume, about 1886.

> *My Dear Sir: –*
> *The liberty I take in addressing you is rather forced upon me by my anxiety to possess a copy, in plaster, of the death mask of him who nearer can be truly no dearer to you than myself. Since my boyhood days the name of 'Keats' has chimed such melodies in my heart as scarcely another has awakened. Anything pertaining to him or his, has ever had a tender charm for me like the thrills of Chopin.*[13]

All this was simply a prelude to requesting the name of the firm in London which manufactured casts of Haydon's death mask of the poet. Fred also asked for a photograph of the Severn portrait of Keats. He importuned friends to do little commissions for him by way of obtaining pictures. Writing to Bernard Berenson, who was living in Paris during the winter of 1887, Fred spoke of his deep envy.

> *For I can but think of that wonderful Balzac who dwelt on the Rue Leodiguieres on his first long so-*

*journ in Mecca. Only he lived rather more poorly
than you or I should wish to. . . . Alas what I
would not give . . . to tread one short day out in
those worn shoes of his over his cobbled ways!!!*[14]

This somewhat convoluted rhapsody on Balzac was just the
preliminary, again, to asking his friend for a photograph of
Balzac's bust in the lobby of the Théâtre Français, along with
whatever news there was of Sarah Bernhardt.

While Day did not see the magnificent Sarah until 1890,
he did have the pleasure of enjoying the Boston visit of another
great actress, Madame Helena Modjeska, in 1888. Excusing
himself for having been prevented from meeting her at a dinner party arranged by friends, he wrote begging a photograph –
and, incidentally, urging her to consider adapting a Balzac story
as a play with a grand part for herself. With the ingratiating
thoughtfulness which characterized so many of Day's transactions with the famous, he sent along an English translation of
the Balzac novella, as well as this comment: 'I am personally
one of those "queer" specimens of humanity who like the man
in the play finds "sermons in stones, books in running brooks,
and good in everything." '[15]

Possibly because Day's connections with the cult of Keats
became relatively well-known, his obsession with Balzac has
remained almost entirely unexplored. His interests were divided between the two authors in a way that would have ex-
hausted a less energetic young man. Balzac is not as familiar as
Keats, and it is popularly assumed that the two writers represent the antipodes of romanticism and realism. On the contrary;
Baudelaire recognized Balzac as having all the qualities of a
visionary, a writer of fictions as highly colored as the wildest
romantic dreams. Much more important to an understanding of
Day's compulsive pursuit of Balzac's relics and haunts are the
parallels between aspects of Balzac's character, habits, and
career with those of F. Holland Day.

Keats may have been a sensualist, but Balzac was an open
admirer of male beauty. Moreover, he shared a fascination with
hermaphrodites with his close friend, Théophile Gautier, whose
Mademoiselle de Maupin had not only shocked readers with
the explicit lesbian adventure between two of its main characters, but had established Gautier as one of the first prophets of
the aesthetic doctrine that art was beyond morality. Balzac's
own *Girl with the Golden Eyes* presented a heroine equally in

love with a man and a woman who happened to be half-brother
and sister. The model for the heroine's bisexuality may have
been Balzac's good friend, George Sand, whose overt relationship with a Parisian actress made her even more scandalous
than her novels.

Fred Day was also fascinated by Balzac's notions of purity,
devotion, and unselfishness. As his biographers have observed,
Balzac not only placed supreme value on attachments between
men but dreamed of heroic, devoted friendships purified by
total chastity. Théophile Gautier, in fact, quoted Balzac to the
effect that 'real chastity developed to the highest degree the
powers of the mind and gave to those who practiced it mysterious faculties.'[16] It was the perfect ideology for a young man
like Fred Day who was confused about his own sexuality and
suffered the puritanical repressions of New England.

Day may have been encouraged to pursue publishing by
the example of Balzac, who worked as both printer and publisher for three years, and who contributed, as Day would, to
literary journals of a stalwartly noncommercial nature. Balzac
was certainly a model for eccentric dress: he had made himself
famous by his poverty-inspired addiction to wearing white
monk's robes. Day's eccentricities in the sartorial line ran to
full-length homespun robes of Turkish or Arabic origin, which
he wore both for lounging in his library and as his official garb
in his Boston photographic studios.

Even if Day's idol, Oscar Wilde, had not eulogized Balzac
as an exemplar of vivid imaginative writing, it was probably inevitable that Balzac's theatricality, psychological insights, prodigious love of books, mysticism, as well as his theories on the
influence of the mind over the body, would all become grist
for Day's burgeoning philosophies. Even more appealing to a
young man in search of meaning and direction were Balzac's
monumental ego, his sense of destiny, and his desire for *la gloire*.
One suspects that Day adored Keats but wanted to *be* Balzac.
In 1890, when he finally came to travel Balzac's 'cobbled ways'
as correspondent for the *Boston Evening Transcript*, he wrote
ecstatically to Gertrude Savage: 'Three times already I have
walked through the Rue Balzac and viewed the things the great
one saw. A photo shall be mine ere long.'[17]

Whether Fred Day would have ever taken up photography if the small, hand-held camera and gelatin dry plates had
not been invented is open to conjecture. As it was, the 'detective' and 'hawk-eye' cameras, and later the Kodak, came along

Honoré de Balzac by Aubrey
Beardsley, an illustration for
Scenes of Parisian Life.

just in time to suit his burgeoning interests. What, precisely, was his first camera is not known, although he left some confusing notes about it. It is certain that he rented or used the kind of camera which contained roll film or plates to be sent back to the manufacturer for developing and printing. A possible supplier, Perry Mason & Company, publishers of the *Youth's Companion,* in Boston, offered inexpensive outfits costing no more than $1.75 as an incentive for subscriptions. But even the better outfits, costing as much as $55.00 for 'camera, instantaneous lens, one double dry-plate holder 3¼ × 4¼'[18] would hardly have been beyond Fred Day's purchasing power. At the time the detective camera became popular, in 1886, he was already boasting of having spent one thousand dollars on an edition of John Keats.

We do know what his first subjects were: the literary haunts and houses of local authors, which Massachusetts offered in abundance. He then took pictures of statues and copied painted portraits of the great. Within a few weeks, he began experimenting with portraits of friends. He was somewhat secretive and coy about his new interest, writing to his Aunt Liddy, 'During the last summer I have been into amateur photography — but not a word about it.'[19] In September 1886, he wrote to Gertrude Savage, 'Tomorrow I start out . . . to take some more pictures and expect to do well and if I succeed as well as last time will have an instrument of my own next season.'[20] The following week he complained to Gertrude, 'Sundays [sic] pictures were good – but Friday tried another 'group,' but Grace, as usual, spoiled the plate. My machine has 'gone back' but I shall have a better one of my own next summer.'[21]

The next day, he summoned up the courage to write to a notable of the neighboring town of Dedham.

> *My dear Sir, being much interested [sic] in local historic matters of our 'mother town' I write to inquire whether you know of any objection that might be raised should I attempt to take a few photographs of the Procession, Dinner Tent, Decorations, etc. on Thursday next. . . . Perhaps my being a descendant of one Ralph Day of old Dedham (1660?) gives the additional impetus to such concerns.*[22]

Well might he request permission to take pictures. He would soon discover what bureaucratic torments awaited the unwary

photographer visiting historic sites in Europe. And well might
he mention his presumed ancestor, Ralph Day, for at about this
time Fred vowed some day to write the history of his family
and of the town. He had already inquired of his Connecticut
cousins if they knew of their family crest; no doubt he was disappointed to learn he came from modest farmer stock. It is not
surprising, then, that when he gave up photography in 1917,
he turned immediately to genealogy and town history.

Day's preoccupation with photography demanded a new
persona. To a favorite aunt, he revealed his new enthusiasm:

> *So you think I look like a German artist or pianist or
> 'literateur' with my embrionic mustache! . . . Once
> more I shall start out [photographing] with some hope
> for a better outcome. . . . Just at present I am 'grave-
> yarding' for historical matter.*[23]

Self-portrait by F. Holland Day
in the garden at Norwood, 1887.

When the Athenes Therapes came out for a Sunday jaunt in
the Norwood countryside, in late June 1887, he boasted: 'They
all said it was a good time and I guess it was. I took a picture or
two one of which I will send you.'[24] As time passed, and the
various members of the group complained that he had not been
seeing very much of them, Fred rushed off a series of letters,
simultaneously dramatic, jocular, and boyishly proud. All of
them were teasing explanations which bore the key phrase, 'I
may say I have been married – to Photography, all summer, and
have done some good work.'[25] Or this variant: 'I won't begin
by making a list of excuses only saying I have been married ——
no nothing serious only Photography . . . and a good better half
I find her (for it is a science) you must know.'[26]

Two weeks later, to his friend Ada he reported:

> *How am I? As well as weather will permit. And How
> have I spent my Summer? —— Well you must know
> that I was very much infatuated last season, and this
> Summer I have been married —— now, don't open
> your eyes —— only to my camera – and have become
> a full-fledged amateur in the art of photography, and
> a most delicious time I've had of it, too . . .*[27]

He was pursuing photography largely on his own, and he was
undaunted by difficult assignments. In a letter dated December
16, 1887, he teases another friend to whom he was sending
proofs recently taken. 'I know you will like the one made by
gaslight best for in that you kept much more still than in any of

F. Holland Day's first gaslight photograph, 1887, of friends in one of his literary groups.

the other pictures.'[28] He signed this proudly, 'The Boy who made your picture.'

The fact that he was attempting pictures by gaslight, and continued to experiment despite technical difficulties and the long and tiring poses demanded by slow emulsions and light-poor lenses, indicates his deep fascination with the new medium. Although 'electric light, oxy-hydrogen lime light, magnesium wire, and the light of kerosene,'[29] were all available to him, none of these was entirely satisfactory; besides, few homes were equipped with electricity in 1887. Much later, when Day was a recognized master of artistic photography, he mentioned these early experiments under gaslight to Alfred Stieglitz, but received no credit for them. Perhaps with good reason: young

Stieglitz had already been experimenting with artificial light, dim lights, and almost no light at all, in order to demonstrate that – given a long enough exposure – you could take pictures almost anywhere. Yet Day's early artistry with gaslight and other controlled lighting cannot be denied.

Fred soon discovered that the camera provided both delight and access to admired authors as well. Now he need not ask for photographs by commercial houses; he could send the aging Reverend Edward Everett Hale some pictures he himself had taken of the old Everett House. 'Old dwellings have a great charm for my photographic eye and I am never so happy as when making pictures of them.'[30] One of the pleasures must have been the assurance of greater success in bright sunlight. Soon he was ingratiating himself with his friends at the Club of Odd Volumes by presenting them with photographs of the local treasures like the Longfellow Cottage.

It is an interesting coincidence that Fred Day took up photography in 1886, the year in which the Boston Society of Amateur Photographers reorganized under the name of the Boston Camera Club. For the first time, they were admitting professional studio photographers, and were looking for ways to secure better relations with similar societies which were cropping up all over America and Europe. The following year saw the establishment of the influential annual Joint Salons, 'held by mutual agreement between the Photographic Society of Philadelphia, the Society of Amateur Photographers of New York, and the Boston Camera Club.'[31] These societies created national, rather than local, competitions and exhibitions, 'open to all photographers, American or Foreign, amateur or professional . . .'[32]

News of the Boston Camera Club's activities and its own annual exhibitions of photographs and equipment now appeared regularly in the pages of *Anthony's Photographic Bulletin* as well as in England's *The Amateur Photographer*. The apparent competition between Boston and London was not entirely imaginary. The London journal gave enthusiastic coverage to 'The Largest Negative in the World,' produced by Allen & Rowell of Boston, measuring three by five feet, and weighing over eighty pounds of half-inch-thick glass.[33] European technical achievements were as heartily reported in *Anthony's*. And both journals offered descriptions by which the photographer of today would have no difficulty recognizing the methods used by exhibitors to sell their new equipment:

*A charmingly and handsomely attired Boston lady
was present in the capacity of a model. . . . As a picturesque addition to the exhibit, the model was a decided success, and we have no doubt many of the
photographers present learned much in the line of
graceful and artistic posing.*[34]

Despite such low enticements, which he despised as vulgar and unfeeling, Fred Day did join the Boston Camera Club,
in 1889, and undoubtedly visited both its annual print exhibitions and its equipment shows. What must have interested him
especially were the new Dallmeyer lenses and the progress
made toward more reliable papers and plates. The inexpensive
platinum papers later became fundamental to his style and his
artistic ideology.

But progress toward aesthetic goals, rather than purely
technical goals, was slow, as Joseph T. Keiley observed when
he came to write his brief history of the Joint Salons.

*In America, while every obstacle imaginable seemed
to be thrown in the path of the onward march of this
new medium for giving expression to the individual
artistic feeling, towards that realm which was pecu-
liarly its own – photography was by no means at a
standstill. Good, and even great, work was constantly
being done. Here one could be found devoting his
spare moments to the study of this art and its possibilities and making comparative studies of the world's
masterpieces in painting, etching, and engraving, in
order to bring that knowledge to bear on his photographic pursuits. Often he was unknown, except to
his small circle of friends, whom by his work he both
educated and influenced. There another might be met,
a lover of Balzac, Thackeray or Poe, who attempted
to perpetuate the types that surrounded him – tried
with his sun-magic to catch a bit of the soul of the
sitter . . .*[35]

How very much like Day all of this sounds! The as yet unknown lover of Balzac was already looking to 'Art' as the source
of his inspiration. He may have had his best early practice in
capturing the soul of the sitter with one of his closest and most
important friends, Louise Imogen Guiney.

Louise Imogen Guiney and
F. Holland Day, shelling beans
on her porch, about 1889.

Enter Louise Guiney and Fanny Brawne

3

Sometime early in May 1886, at a time when Fred Day was boasting that "portraits are my hobby now and a very delightful hobby I find it too,'[1] an old friend from Chauncy Hall brought along a 'Miss Guiney' to call on the Day family in Norwood. She was a handsome, charming woman of twenty-five. Fred, who was twenty-two, was impressed: 'She is now quite a poetess – not a few of her lines having come out in Scribners, Harper and the Atlantic.'[2] Their acquaintance at first, however, was casual. She asked him for some verses from his extensive personal library of poetry. With apologies for his habitual tardiness, he eventually sent them along to her home in Auburndale.

It was not until the following year that any genuine connection began, a connection which her various biographers have interpreted to be a stormy, unrequited passion on her part. Paradoxically, Fred is supposed to have loved her so deeply that his will stipulated his ashes be scattered over that part of the Maine coast where they had vacationed together. When she was in financial difficulties during the early 1900s, he purchased her Maine property and erected a chalet on the very spot her modest cabin had occupied. They traveled together, worshipped Keats together, argued about literature and religion together, and remained lifelong allies and friends. He published her books; she introduced him to Boston society and British poets. She posed for his camera, always discreetly dressed, and often with her two Saint Bernard dogs. For seven or eight years, they were incessantly in each other's company, at the opera, the theatre, in the secret meetings of arcane literary societies, and at brilliant dinner parties. In the course of her lifetime, she wrote him nearly seven hundred letters. All of these he meticulously saved.

For biographers who have read only her letters, it has seemed undeniable that Louise Imogen Guiney – poet, critic, journalist, and darling of Boston literary circles – was *the* woman in F. Holland Day's life. He obviously adored her. Yet the character of that adoration has remained a mystery, largely because Day's letters to Guiney were burned by her friend, the writer Alice Brown, who believed them too indiscreet for public scrutiny. Some writers have assumed that the only obstacle to the consummation of Guiney's passion must have been Fred's impotence. But copies of his letters, which he kept in sturdy black ledgers at Norwood, cast a more peculiar light on the romance that haunted Day for decades.

In fact, Louise was related to the Days through a distant cousin named Carter. No doubt this attenuated kinship made her seem more approachable to Fred, who, despite his new mustache and scruffy short beard, was still very much a boy. She had a formidable reputation: Oliver Wendell Holmes had called her his golden guinea. Her poetry was said to ring of individuality tempered with a scholarly reserve. Despite mischievous eyes and an irrepressible sense of humor, she was imbued with a devout, saintly Boston-Irish Catholicism, a solace to her but certainly at odds with Fred's New England Unitarianism. Four years older than Fred, Louise was burdened by a grim poverty that kept her habits unfashionably simple. And she was doubly burdened by intermittent deafness and ear pains, which increased in severity as she grew older. It was an agony she bore with astonishing fortitude, but no poet in love with the sound of words and the music of the world can willingly relinquish the sense of hearing. Not until she was in her fifties did an English doctor finally discover that she had an inoperable vascular lesion near the brain.

When she met Fred Day, Louise Guiney was established. Fred was still floundering, although his camera seemed about to provide a true center to his life. Louise did the sensible thing: she encouraged him in his photography. When the editors of *American Magazine* accepted some of her verses, they also requested her picture. Would the aspiring portraitist care to try her as a subject? Fred bridled. He felt unskilled and clumsy. Nevertheless, she must have persuaded him. On November 12, 1887, she received a typical amateur photographer's confession.

> *Alas My Poor 'Subject' – Alack-a-day! Behold the 'proofs' of mortal vanity (on the part of the Artist – ? – not the sitter). Two plates were utterly gone . . . but try again is as good a motto for big folks as for little ones. . . . And now comes a most miserable confession – a thing I never did but once before – expose twice on the same plate.*[3]

Apparently, neither of them gave up easily. In less than a week, he wrote to her again: 'O Thou Personification of Patience! – with this most trying photographic process. . . . Indeed it is nothing short of angelic of you to make a martyr of yourself.'[4] Again, on Thanksgiving eve, he both thanked her and chastised her in one letter. She had moved in her pose at her windowseat, and spoiled an otherwise excellent plate. Back again he went, and the little notes sped back and forth by that nineteenth-century miracle, a twice-a-day post delivered by railway.

By Christmas of 1887, Fred had relaxed enough to call her 'My dear Lou Guiney,' and was writing letters full of literary bravado which he admitted were 'à la E. E. Saltus,' a popular iconoclast. Early in January 1888, Louise introduced him to her godmother, Louise Chandler Moulton, one of the grande dames of Boston and London literary society. She was an imposing woman who could boast of being able to invite to dinner celebrities such as Alphonse Daudet, George Moore, and James McNeill Whistler. Mrs. Moulton greeted Fred effusively, saying, 'Now Mr. Day I shall expect you to take the place left vacant here by My Own "B.B." '[5] Fred responded modestly that no one could take the place of her most trusted 'guard,' Bernard Berenson. 'B.B.' was in Paris, where, among other things, he was supplying Fred with photographs of favorite authors.

By now, 'Miss Guiney' had become 'Ma bonne Sœur Lou!,' and she continued to be Fred's 'good sister' through the

Louise Guiney as 'The Muse of Poetry'; wood engraving by Timothy Cole, 1921, from Day's photograph of 1888.

early part of 1888. When his portrait of her appeared in *American Magazine,* he was wonderfully pleased and proud. Eventually, another of his portraits of Louise, posed with a wreath of laurel leaves crowning her hair, inspired a wood-engraving of Louise as the Muse of Poetry by the then well-known artist, Timothy Cole.

The friendship between Fred and Louise quickened with the discovery, sometime in 1888, that they shared an obsessive fondness for the poet John Keats. With daffodils, incense, laurel leaves, and other poetic paraphernalia, they initiated the first of their annual celebrations of their idol's birth. No doubt they indulged in private readings, and lamented together

Keats's sad destiny. Louise had already dedicated her first volume of verse, *White Sails,* to their 'Johnny.' When one of her many artist friends, the sculptor Anne Whitney, carved a singularly uninspired bust of Keats, Fred was dispatched to take its picture.

The relationship seemed to be warming considerably. A letter Day wrote to Louise on December 21, 1888, begins, 'Ah, My Dear Lou! What Sweetheart was ever so good to her love-lorn youth as you? Nay, not even my most glowing imagination can make one to match. You may be sure you shall have the very first proof from the plate of the Keats bust . . .'[6] As a Christmas present, he sent her a plaster copy of the famous Haydon death mask of Keats (the unfortunate source of inspiration for Miss Whitney's pallid bust). But he sent the mask anonymously. When Louise returned not one speculation about the identity of its donor, he wrote to her on December 29: 'Dear Lou! Ah! by his lovin-fool-ship! But you haven't one half so much of that most womanly virtue – Curiousity . . .'[7]

This 'lovin-fool-ship' and 'My Dear Lou!' have sounded temptingly like romance to biographers. The amusing truth is that on the same day he used exactly the same phrases in a letter to Louise Moulton, Guiney's godmother. He had sent her a copy of the Keats likeness—also in plaster, and also anonymously![8] Typically, he had discovered a gallant conceit which pleased him. It was habitual with him to indulge in exaggerated courtly gestures. What seems odd is that Louise Chandler Moulton and Louise Imogen Guiney never compared letters or commented on the kind, and common, donor of the Keats mask and many other gifts.

When Guiney had first written to Moulton about her new photographer friend, it was in these terms: 'You will find my little Fred Day . . . a gentleman *au fond* and a fellow deserving of your open door.'[9] She happened to enclose a copy of a newly written sentimental love lyric with this letter. One hardly introduces a lover or a sweetheart as 'my little Fred Day,' or copies out a love poem to him for the edification of a godmother.

THE LILAC
Above the wall that's broken
And from the coppice thinned
So sacred and so sweet

The Lilac in the wind!
And every night the May wind blows
The lilac-blooms apart,
The memory of my first love
Is shaken on my heart . . .

One could expect an outpouring of such tenderness to be directed at Fred Day himself, if, indeed, he *was* the recipient of Louise's affections. It is curious that she seems never to have copied out any of *her* love lyrics for *him,* except those about to be published by Copeland and Day, the firm he established in 1893. Generally, her voluminous correspondence was characterized by gallantries, witticisms, flattering epigrams, and enthusiasm. She shared her brighter side with all her friends, including her 'little Fred Day.'

In writing to Louise, Fred attempted maladroitly the light, teasing, flirtatious manner in which she excelled. Enjoying their game, he seized every opportunity to let her think they had a special relationship bordering on infatuation. Typically, when he consulted the popular astrologer-medium, Mrs. Piper, he made sure to report that she had asked, 'And who is Imogen?'[10] Louise responded haughtily: 'Your Imogen affair is perfectly funny – You know I am horribly skeptical on spirits and mind-readings and occult powers in general and see nothing but the risibilities of them.'[11]

Such vehemence on her part did little to diminish his increasing reliance upon spirit readings. After all, not only was William James studying Mrs. Piper's spirit voices, thought transference, extrasensory perception, and the supernatural world in general, but the American Society for Psychical Research was devoting considerable attention to Piper's phenomena. Fred, in fact, had been corresponding with the Society since 1884, and its secretary cited Day and Mrs. Piper as being good 'friends.'[12]

Mrs. Piper was more than a friend; she was Day's oracle. On April 2, 1889, Fred wrote to Louise Chandler Moulton of a tremendous decision he had just made. Mrs. Piper had foretold he would make an advantageous change in business. Inspired, he promptly sent in his resignation to Barnes & Company, and decided to tour Europe in the company of Louise Guiney.

Lou takes her tricycle with her and I shall lug along
my camera for use on poor Keats grave . . . and many

other spots to delight my heart and hers and there
may be something I can do for yourself in the photo-
graphic line? [13]

At this point, the Day–Guiney relationship took a bizarre
turn. On April 1, he wrote Louise an enthusiastic note beginning, 'My Dear Mother!,' [14] and announcing that the *Pavonia*
was to be his ship to Europe. He intended to take along a
bushel of baked beans, the Boston favorite. 'My Dear Mother!'
is certainly a startling, and revealing, nickname for a sweetheart, one which Louise's biographers have either ignored or
overlooked. In writing to him about arrangements for the proposed tour, Louise responded, 'Now that I am going to be your
mother . . .' [15] A few days later, he once again gushed, 'Instead
of going to Church this best of Good Fridays as all good Chris-
tians should be I am here at 5 PM writing to my companion in
arms and my adopted mater!!' [16]

Since so many of her letters from now on would address
him as 'Sonny,' or 'Sonnikins,' or 'Sonny dear,' the etiology of
this unexpected nickname becomes absolutely clear. Louise
Guiney had an active maternal need, one she persistently foisted
off on cats, dogs, and physically unthreatening young men, especially poets and the artistically inclined. Toward Lionel
Johnson, a delicate but brilliant poet who became one of William Butler Yeats's best friends and an intimate of Oscar Wilde,
she felt admiringly maternal. How she and Fred actually accomplished the psychic adoption is not documented. Perhaps
Louise suggested that he was very much in need of being cared
for, and that she would be happy to do so while they were
abroad. A typical letter to her during their travels in 1890 was
addressed, 'My Precious Mater!,' and signed, 'Your Sonny – till
you have a better.' [17]

What is so remarkable about this pseudo-maternal relationship was that it had a clear precedent in the famous depen-
dency of Honoré de Balzac on his private muse, Madame de
Berny. Not only did Balzac call the older woman 'Mamma,' but
he several times commented that 'She was a mother, a woman
friend, a family, a man friend, an adviser . . .' [18] Louise Guiney
was all of these to Fred Day, and there is no reason to doubt
that Day was inspired by his knowledge of Balzac's intimate
but pure relationship with Madame de Berny. That he knew
they would be chaste with each other must have made the

flirting with Louise all the more attractive, because it was so free of consequences.

Perhaps, too, Louise had confessed to some sorrow about not having had children. Unmarried at twenty-eight, she was what the Victorians called a spinster, but she hardly fit the conventional notion. Louise had warmth, even love, to spare. At this point, too, Fred displayed an openly affectionate disposition. Each of them had been an only child. She was older and appeared wiser. More importantly, while her flirtatious personality seemed to beckon young men, she seems to have been psychologically overwhelmed by the early loss of her adored father, who had been a general in the Civil War. Her colleague, co-author, friend, and earliest biographer, Alice Brown, observed that no man could ever have lived up to the romantic image of Louise's soldier–father.[19] It seems only fair to remark that she may have been playing at love with Fred as much as he was acting out his needs with her.

There are other sides to the story. Louise was a free spirit, an early advocate and practitioner of women's rights, a young tomboy who had loved climbing and hiking. Every portrait of Louise reveals her as vulnerable, yet strong. As for Fred, in many ways he resembles the charitable, well-meaning hero of George Santayana's *The Last Puritan* – always giving, asking nothing in return, but incapable of true love or real passion for a woman. It seems paradoxical, therefore, that so many of his earliest camera subjects *were* women, posed magnificently and sensuously in exotic costumes. Day purchased many of these costumes during the European tours of 1889 and 1890, when he and Louise seemed determined to shock their Boston relatives with the apparent intensity of their unmarried relationship.

A letter of April 5, 1889, begins, 'My Good Mother!' Once again, this not to Anna Day but to Louise Guiney.

> *What a fraud you are, yes a fraud to come in and see my prima mater and go out without seeing myself, and most especially when the long-looked-for lodgings are secured. Of course I want to know where they are. My Mme Day couldn't remember so you see it isn't safe to leave any important word with her. But I am glad though there are those rooms for your humble [servant] is somewhat subject to headaches where solitude is quite necessary*

*for his comfort, and to the comfort of others as well
for that matter.*[20]

This is the first indication that Fred Day suffered from
migraine. It must have been severe enough to make him wonder if he could ever live with anybody, and these torturous
headaches remained with him until he died. Certainly they
help to explain his deep and frequently expressed empathy
with Louise's physical ailments.

How Fred came to have sufficient personal funds to take
off for Europe at this time is uncertain, although he may have
inherited an aunt's small fortune. His parents acquiesced to his
abandonment of his Barnes & Company career, because he simply lied to them about how long he intended to be gone. He
also convinced them to let him purchase European furnishings
and fabrics for the proposed redecoration of their Norwood
mansion.

Louise preceded Fred to London in May, accompanied by
her aging, ill mother. On June 1, 1889, in the company of
Louise Chandler Moulton and other notable Bostonians, Fred
sailed for England. His passport, issued on May 31, describes
him as age twenty-four years, ten months; five feet nine inches,
with a medium forehead, gray eyes, prominent nose, small
mouth, pointed chin, light brown hair, and full face. No mention was made of the large ears; he was disguising them by
letting his hair grow longer. A trifle handsomer now, in his
own way, no doubt he pleased Louise as her escort to the London literary haunts. The fact that her mother was along could
not have done much to further their intimacy. And, of course,
Fred's own mother was to meddle in the tour before very long.

Louise must have believed that the trip was undertaken
primarily for Keats. Their mutual friend 'B.B.' – Berenson –
was now in Rome, and presumably could be counted on to lead
them to Keats's grave in that city. Yet despite her talk about
visiting Rome, Louise never ventured out of England. Fred was
to take pictures of all the places that Keats had inhabited or
visited during his life. In England, at least, it was to be a pil-
grimage, with John Keats the focus of their worship. They
were by no means alone in this fancy. In bookish Victorian society, the worship of Keats had been progressing rapidly since
the Pre-Raphælites had discovered and illustrated his medieval
epics. But it was Oscar Wilde, perhaps more than any other,

Miniature portrait of John Keats
in profile, about 1819.

Portrait sketches of Keats by
Benjamin Robert Haydon, about
1818.

who had deified Keats as 'a Priest of Beauty slain before his
time.'[21]

It was as a 'Priest of Beauty' that Keats attracted Fred Day.
For Louise, the agony and brevity of the poet's life could be
understood and accepted in Christian terms. The fact was,
however, that Keats had explicitly rejected Louise's crucified
Christ as an emblem of pain, sin, and torture. He had turned
instead to the sunlit joys of Apollo, the God of Poetry. For
Fred, now more occultist than Unitarian, there still remained a
choice between the martyrdom of the crucifixion and the revels
of pagan Hellenism. It was the most conspicuous conflict of the
artistic and intellectual elites of the 1890s and of the Decadence. Keats had set in motion the Cult of Beauty, it was true,
and Day came to believe in this with all his heart. No one
could have foreseen the extremes to which that cult would be
carried by the androgynous æsthetes of the fin de siècle.

Fred was still innocent of these extremes. He had not yet
been exposed to Paris sufficiently to absorb the direct teachings
of the Decadent poets, nor had he yet encountered the chic
homosexuality, publicly flaunted, of so many of the English
æsthetes. The tour began crystallizing his own proclivities, both
sexual and æsthetic. He landed in London open to all new impressions, eager for contact with the ghost of Keats, and immediately set about making glass negatives of Hampstead. Louise
was frankly more interested in Oxford, the former seat of Car-
dinal Newman, and the center of æsthetic Catholicism, where
Walter Pater reigned supreme. But Keats came first. She urged
Fred to pursue all possible memorabilia. 'Perhaps we shall find,
too, some portrait of Mrs. Lindon!'[22]

Mrs. Lindon was Fanny Brawne, the pretty young object
of Keats's passion, who had been scorned by his biographers as
vain and shallow. Louise had a practical reason to be interested
in Mrs. Lindon. She had just contracted to write a magazine
article about her and had unexpectedly learned of some unpublished Fanny Brawne letters which might illuminate her relationship with Keats. Having discovered that the poet's sister,
Fanny Keats y de Llanos, was (rather incredibly) still alive in
Madrid, Louise urged Fred Day to contact the aged woman
with all possible haste. And it was here that the Day–Guiney
relationship suffered its first strain.

According to Guiney's partisan biographers, Fred behaved
in a manner both feckless and unpredictable. Louise simply

Miniature portrait of Fanny
Brawne, 1818.

could not get him to Madrid. 'But when he shook himself free
of Hampstead and London and crossed the Channel to Paris,
he abruptly turned north for a holiday in Brussels!'[23] Fred is
supposed to have contacted Fanny Keats half-heartedly by post,
and then cavalierly ignored her response. 'Whereupon, with
characteristic unpredictability, notwithstanding Louise's plead-
ing attacks to follow up his strike, he sailed for Boston in November [1889].'[24] The reader will have anticipated that eighty-
six-year-old Fanny Keats died almost immediately thereafter.

What a comedy of misinterpretations! Because of the
Fanny Keats incident, a long-lasting and totally unfounded impression was established indicting Fred Holland Day as unre-
liable, lackadaisical, and dilatory. In fact, Fred showed an admirable consistency over the years, and generally had good reasons for his actions.

The reality concerning these visits to Paris and Brussels
during the Fanny Keats negotiations is easy to ascertain. Louise
Guiney was not the only traveler who had contracted to do
some writing. 'F. H. Day' had already signed with the *Boston
Evening Transcript* to serve as literary and cultural correspondent during the summer and fall of 1889. He was to provide
news of the literary and artistic events of the season. To Paris
he went, therefore, to report (as the headline later read) on
'THE GREAT BALZAC'S RELICS,'[25] new materials which had
been recently uncovered. He continued to Brussels to attend a
large sale of Balzac memorabilia. And Day had been corresponding with the Vicomte de Lovenjoul, a Belgian aristocrat
and Europe's foremost Balzac expert, who had important news
indeed. He had purchased 'a veritable relic of Balzac, an album
which the great man had constantly with him and in which he
scribbled . . .'[26] Day was to be permitted access to this significant find. All of these activities were reported in both the *Boston Evening Transcript* and *The Critic*. Fred's only delay during this period was in sending the Vicomte some photographs
he had taken of the Balzac house in Paris.

Fred and Louise were obviously competitors in the literary
trade, but perhaps could not confess this to each other. She
wanted him to pursue the Fanny Keats story; he had his own
Balzac leads to follow, his own fame to enlarge. Louise was
completely aware of Fred's intentions of traveling to Brussels.
She had, in fact, helped to translate his letters to the Vicomte
de Lovenjoul, an obsessive and wealthy bibliophile and collector

F. Holland Day at twenty-six, probably taken in London, 1890.

Carte-de-visite portrait of Day in Paris, 1889.

of Balzac memorabilia. As far as Fred knew, the Fanny Keats lead to Fanny Brawne might prove fruitless. It was ungracious of Louise to become irritated with him when she was simply too poor and too held down by her mother to pursue her own interests to Madrid. This would not be the last time she was furious with him for being able to indulge in activities that her own resources did not permit.

It does seem peculiar that Fred Day should interrupt an important European tour to dash home for six months, only to return again the following June. But he had pressing reasons. His parents, having lost patience with his long absence, were now pressuring him to come home. In October 1889, he wrote to Gertrude Savage that his mother was pestering him about wanting to do some traveling of her own, with him as escort. 'My father wants her to go away and she I think is more than willing in which case I shall probably reach Boston sometime before the middle of December.'[27] By November, he admitted:

> Every letter I get from the Day mansion in Norwood, which by the way are all from my mother, have a word about California. You know she is greatly distressed about my clothes, on all occasions, and now she says I must come well stacked with them as she will want me to look well 'this winter in California.' Still these remarks seem like 'springs to catch woodcocks with' for she hasn't once said she would go.[28]

The Days had already begun remodeling their Victorian mansard-roof house as a half-timbered Tudor equipped with electricity and other modern conveniences. Understandably, Mrs. Day wished to flee all the confusion, an escape that would be facilitated if Fred came home to either suffer with her or help her avoid the noisy upheaval. Convinced he was about to be forced to accompany his mother west (as when they had gone to Denver together), he interrupted his own pursuits. In December, the *Boston Advertiser and Review* carried the following social note.

> Mr. Fred H. Day arrived from Europe on Sunday over the Cunard line. . . . The Saturday before he was present at a banquet given by the Lord Mayor of London to about two hundred of the nobility. Mr. Day and P. T. Barnum were the only Americans present.[29]

Fred Day's 'prima mater,' about 1890.

P. T. Barnum was famous for having originated the maxim, 'There's a sucker born every minute.' Quite possibly, Fred felt the sting of that phrase when he arrived home to discover that his 'prima mater' had no intention of fleeing to California. Meanwhile, Louise was hardly hiding her frustration with him. A letter to her godmother reveals a touch of acerbity.

> *Not a soul have I seen lately, save Mr. Frederic. Fred sailed yesterday, in a huge ulster and a close-reefed cap, accompanied by trunks many and heavy enough to make the air blue with profanities wherever he goes. He will tell you, with flourishes, how he lunched with Sir Charles Dilke, and dined with that excellent 'Ebrew Jew,' Lord Mayor Isaacs, in Stationer's Hall. He has not left me in an orphaned state, for I have so many of his commissions to attend to, that I cannot well forget him up to New Years.*[30]

Shortly afterward, she wrote to inform Fred that Fanny Keats had died in Madrid. He was disconsolate. 'I shall never forgive myself for not going to Spain this summer,' he assured Louise, although he had little choice because of his commitment to the newspapers. She persuaded him that the family in Madrid would still welcome his visit, and that it was now certain they did possess several Fanny Brawne letters which could possibly revolutionize public opinion about her.

On Sunday morning, June 15, 1890, the *Boston Courier* offered:

> *Mr. Fred Holland Day, of Dartmouth Street, and now at his house in Norwood, will sail again for Europe Saturday, to be absent until December, perhaps longer. He will remain in London only a few days before going to Oberammergau, after which he will visit London, Paris, and other cities, and will probably go to Spain.*[31]

The *Boston Herald* had already apprised the literary set of Day's imminent departure in pursuit of Keats and Balzac. Neither paper found it necessary to explain the attraction of Oberammergau, as it was one of the most talked about and fashionable pilgrimages of that year. A tiny Bavarian hamlet, Oberammergau was hosting its famous Passion Play, an event offered only once a decade. It featured dramatic tableaux and

Above: detail from a wood engraving depicting the Oberammergau Passion Play of 1890;
below: Rosa Llanos y Keats and
her husband, Juan, taken by
Fred Day in Madrid, 1891.

presentations on every aspect of the passion of Christ. Pictures of the actors, photographs of the tableaux, poems written on the occasion, names of the socially prominent who would attend were featured in mass-circulation journals like *Harper's Weekly* and *Scribner's*. As a mass-media event of the 1890 season, its only competition was the Wagner festival at Bayreuth.

The fact that 'Sonny' Day was to visit Oberammergau before pursuing the Fanny Brawne letters in Spain was clearly driving Louise Guiney wild with impatience. Neither of them could have envisioned, of course, that both the Brawne letters and the Oberammergau experiences would bring excesses of fame and notoriety to Fred Day. It was at Oberammergau that Day conceived the idea which led eventually to his ambitious and controversial sacred subjects of the 1898–1900 years. It was in Madrid that he made one of the greatest literary finds of the century, the letters of Fanny Brawne to Fanny Keats.

Meeting with the Llanos family, Day photographed them all. He had difficulty with his exposures. 'It was not his fault,' Rosa Llanos y Keats, Fanny Keats' daughter, wrote to him

Pages from the letters of Fanny
Brawne to Fanny Keats, bound
in book form at the Keats House,
Hampstead.

afterwards, that except for the portraits the photographs did not
come out well.'[32] As for the letters, Keats scholars have criticized Day's handling of the transactions. There seems to be
considerable question whether the letters were on permanent
loan or an outright gift, or merely temporarily lent for purposes
of publication. In any event, Day came away from Madrid in
possession of the priceless Brawne letters. And from London,
he wrote pleadingly to Herbert V. Lindon, the son of Keats's
sweetheart.

> *My dear Sir: –*
> *Last year I gave myself the pleasure of writing to you*
> *regarding one or two subjects connected with your*
> *mother, which you very kindly answered, though not*
> *seeing fit to give me the information I desired. I fully*
> *appreciate your emotions and respect them. Since that*

time much information has fallen into my hands
which I hope will help to restore in the public mind
a better estimate of Mrs. Lindon.[33]

Lindon refused to respond. His mother had been damned
as a coquette who had broken the heart of one of England's
greatest poets. As Fred offered him no access to the letters, Lindon clearly decided to protect his own privacy and refused to
grant permission to publish the letters. Day was dumbfounded.
He would later be accused of taking the letters home to hoard
them bitterly and vengefully for 'forty-three sterile years.'[34]
Actually, he made many efforts to have them published, but
Lindon's refusal was adamant. If Fred had any hope of gaining
fame by publishing a new and illuminating book about Keats
and his beloved, it was as effectively crushed as if the letters
had never existed.

Curiously, he never showed the originals of the Brawne
letters to his dear Louise Guiney, either in 1890 or afterward,
although he did show her some penciled copies. She pretended
to be understanding, but she was genuinely furious. Her article
about Fanny Brawne had gone to press bearing the old clichés.
Was Day simply selfish? Or was he legitimately concerned
about being sued by Lindon for revealing material then under
the tightest copyright protection? Louise did receive a lock of
Keats's hair, fashioned in the shape of a lyre, which the Llanos
family had generously given to Fred. And he and Louise did
campaign together for the memorial to Keats in Hampstead
where, in 1894, they erected a copy of the Anne Whitney
marble bust. But the fact that he continued to withhold the
precious letters from Guiney, as dear to him as she was, seems
yet another demonstration of their lack of fundamental commitment to each other.

Despite the psychic adoption, his real mother, Anna Day,
remained the dragon of the fortress. Louise was his dear friend,
his confidante, an eager procurer of interesting models for his
camera, a companion in literature, one of the best known of his
published authors, and an object of compassion in all her in-
firmities. Gertrude Savage, with whom he always seemed to be
at ease, escaped him to marry another; they remained the best of
friends. His suggestion, made half in jest, that he had 'married'
photography, and had 'wedded' the camera, turned out to be
prophetic.

Lyre-shaped brooch with strands
of Keats's hair, given to Fred
Day by Rosa Llanos y Keats in
1891.

4

Visionists, Cultists, Decadents All

F. Holland Day returned from Europe completely transformed. Louise had teased him about the stupefying numbers of trunks he took home with him; these, however, were merely filled with decorations for the renovation of the house, and worked no change on his identity. But the Louvre, the Prado, the British Museum had precipitated his radical metamorphosis from bibliophile to passionate æsthete. He had an immensity of visual impressions to sort out, absorb, and essay in his own work. Aware of what had happened, he wrote to Gertrude Savage: 'I didn't know I was so much a lover of the beautiful till this trip. It has blossomed out in my crop to a great extent.'[1] He was now a dandy in the Whistler style, complete with dashing cravats, top hat, cane, white gloves, and a radiant self-confidence.

Freed from his bookish job, he had at last been able to indulge his interests in the arts and in psychic research. He had haunted the Society for Psychical Research in London. Mrs. Piper herself was in England for a series of experiments that year. He had been delighted to discover that England harbored innumerable spiritualists and arcane societies committed to magical practices under the guise of neo-Christianity. It was inevitable that, on his return to Boston, he would become involved with an eccentric and sometimes notorious group of young poets and artists who combined worship of the occult and the supernatural with æstheticism, ritual, and drugs.

One of this closely knit group was Herbert Copeland, a young man who became Fred's partner in Copeland and Day, the publishing firm which would be the first expression of his æsthetic ideals. In Gertrude Savage's lively exchange of letters with him during the summer of 1889, she mentioned one of her brother's friends and seemed eager to arrange a meeting between them. Day was intrigued.

> *Indeed I should be much pleased to meet Mr. Cope-*
> *land. I have often heard you speak of him, and I think*
> *I've heard you say he was something like me, which*
> *if he is will give me a double interest, for one always*
> *likes to see oneself as others see them.*[2]

A few weeks later, Gertrude sent him a sample of Copeland's handwriting, and Day observed, 'Mr. Copeland's "hand" is surely much like mine in some ways very markedly – I should take it to a graphologist & see if [he] finds like inclinations.'[3]

Gertrude's brother, Philip Henry Savage, had been a Harvard friend of Herbert Copeland. But it was doubtful that Philip was pushing this proposed meeting with an enthusiasm equal to his sister's. A few years younger than Day, but already making a reputation for himself as a poet and classics scholar, Philip seemed eager to gain Fred's attentions for himself. One oddly erotic letter of Philip's contained a fantasy about Fred's probable flirtations with 'witching French maidens'[4] and a surprisingly explicit description of his own naked body, the excuse being that wearing summer bathing trunks had quite marred the consistency of his skin color. This exhibitionistic exercise did not arouse the response that Philip may have desired, for the following year he wrote Fred Day a most poignant letter bemoaning his unsuccessful search for friendship. Unfortunately for Philip, Fred seemed much more interested in pursuing Herbert Copeland. He wrote urgently for Copeland's address, which Philip supplied before turning his attentions elsewhere.

It is a pity that no record remains of the first meeting between Herbert Copeland and Fred Holland Day. All we know is that Day followed a familiar routine: he captivated Herbert's mother with boxes of fresh strawberries and sweets. He enticed her to pose for his camera, and one of Herbert's first letters to him formally requests some prints from this rare photography session with his mother. Did Fred find Herbert very like himself, as Gertrude had suggested? It could have been simply that Herbert was well-connected and experienced in the literary world, because he was employed by one of Boston's most successful magazines, *Youth's Companion*.

A camera portrait of Copeland taken by Day, possibly late in 1892, reveals the young Harvard graduate, class of '91, to be slight of build, somewhat monkish of face – like a gaunt Zurburán, only blond – mustached and bearded, with an air of languid sensitivity. Mutual acquaintances disagreed: some found him nervously unhealthy, somewhat of a fop (or 'dude,' as the slang had it then), or wittily enthusiastic; others thought he was dissipated and dry.[5] Dissipation had as yet left no mark on his face. He appeared to be a well-educated, debonair, sophisticated young bachelor with literary ambitions. Fred may well have been deeply flattered to resemble such a man, although he was already far outdoing Herbert in the bohemian style. With his hair longer than ever before (and certainly longer than was the acceptable fashion), wearing his full Van Dyke beard now sharply pointed, a pince-nez snapped on his nose, and sporting brocaded vests and dark, elegant suits, Fred had a reputation for eye-catching costume. He now began to sign his correspondence 'F. H. Day,' or 'F. H. D.,' often using the Latin for Day – *Dies* – by which he became known among his intimates. As *Dies,* he became secretary to one of Boston's most exclusive societies, the Visionists, a group including Copeland and Philip Savage, and led by Ralph Adams Cram, who later described it as 'made up of the madder and more fantastic members of the Pewter Mugs.'[6]

In the Visionist group were the poet Bliss Carman, the designer–architect Bertram Goodhue, the painter Tom Meteyard, the typographic genius Bruce Rogers, the printer Daniel Berkeley Updike, the poet Richard Hovey, and the publisher Herbert Small, who had been Copeland's roommate at Harvard. Most of what we know about the Visionists comes to us from Ralph Adams Cram, a genuine eccentric who eventually became a highly successful Gothic Revival architect. It is somewhat startling to read Cram's description of the Visionist's little hideaway in Province Court, in the heart of Boston's business district.

Portrait of Herbert Copeland by F. Holland Day, about 1892, when they were planning their publishing partnership.

On the walls, the painter-members had wrought
strange and wonderful things: the Lady Isis in her
Egyptian glory, symbolic devices of various sorts,
mostly Oriental and exotic. In some indefinable way,
its place had a mildly profligate connotation, which
misrepresented it utterly.[7]

Although Cram's memoirs testify that nothing stronger than
beer and tobacco were consumed, the police did look in at the
late-night meetings with suspicion. Nevertheless, Cram insisted
that the Visionist headquarters were utterly 'innocent of any
aroma other than that of pipes and cigarettes, or, on occasion,
the lingering perfume of incense when Herbert Copeland officiated as Exarch and High Priest of Isis, clothed garishly in
some plunder from Jack Abbot's trunk of theatrical costumes.'[8]
Cram revealed much more about the peculiarities of the group,
hinting about Fred Day's activities especially, when he came to
write his bizarre little book, *The Decadent,* the first publication
of Copeland and Day.

Only two women were permitted to join in the heady literary, mystical, and occult games played at Province Court:
Louise Imogen Guiney and Alice Brown. Cram thought Louise
the most delightful creature alive, a fanciful Irish sprite, a comrade in arms against bourgeois mediocrity, materialist crassness,
and the ignorance of the lowly masses. Nowhere does he indicate whether Louise was actually permitted to share in the
Visionist rituals of initiation or celebration. In fact, nowhere
does Cram specify these rituals. Why Herbert Copeland was
masquerading as 'Exarch and High Priest of Isis,' rather than,
say, court jester, and why the walls of the Visionist hideaway
were decorated with Egyptian symbols, can be discovered only
by studying the cults of the 1890s.

One major clue comes from Fred's relationship with
William Butler Yeats. It had been Louise Guiney who had introduced Day to the English equivalents (and originals) of the
Boston bohemians. A recognized poet with Irish connections,
and well-liked by Yeats, Guiney was able to bring Fred along
to Yeats's newly formed Rhymers' Club in London, where they
met Richard LeGallienne, Ernest Rhys, John Lane, and a frequent guest, Oscar Wilde, whose wife was a confirmed mystic.
Yeats, of course, was known to Bostonians, as he wrote regularly for the Irish–American newspaper, *The Boston Pilot.* In

Several of the Visionists on the porch of the renovated Day mansion, 1892: Copeland, Guiney, Tom Meteyard (in hammock), Ralph Adams Cram (standing), and Alice Brown; Day's parents are at rear.

his columns, he frequently expounded Pre-Raphælite ideals. Yeats was especially appealing to Fred Day because the poet had long espoused the doctrines of Dante Gabriel Rossetti, who envisioned the artist as 'priest of the imagination.'[9] This became a slogan for the nineties, and it was certainly Day's.

Yeats was searching for any dogma which could counter scientific materialism. At first, he found Theosophy attractive, and idolized the colorful Madame Helena Blavatsky, who had founded the movement in 1875. The publication in 1877 of Blavatsky's enormously popular book, *Isis Unveiled,* had precipitated a surge of pseudo-Oriental and Egypt-worshipping societies throughout America and much of the world. Garbed as High Priest of Isis, Herbert Copeland may have been simply enacting some watered-down Theosophist ritual. But if neither Copeland nor Cram took Theosophy too seriously, the occult movement in general had made a permanent impact on Fred Day's inner spirit.

When Fred met Yeats in 1890, the fiery young poet had already broken with Theosophy over its ambivalent attitude toward magic; Yeats wanted the movement to accept all forms of magic, so long as these were used to benefit mankind. He had already been initiated into a much more cabalistic society called The Order of the Hermetic Students of the Golden Dawn. Resembling the Rosicrucian groups which were then burgeoning throughout western Europe, its fanatical Christian mysticism offered its members a presumed link with the wisdom of all ages and all religions. The specific symbols and ritual of the

Wood engraving of William
Butler Yeats by Robert Bryden,
from William Archer's *Poets of
the Younger Generation,* 1902.

Golden Dawn may have been a direct, and therefore crucial,
influence upon Day's ensuing obsession with the sacred subjects as well as other Symbolist images.

There was nothing frivolous about the Golden Dawn.
When Yeats underwent his initiation at the Isis-Urania Temple
No. 3, in the spring of 1890, he had already accepted the doctrine that proclaimed, 'The Symbol of Suffering is the Symbol
of Strength.'[10] Moreover, he had to accept 'the Bonds of Suffering and Self-Sacrifice.'[11] It was not an idle vow. The initiate
actually underwent a symbolic crucifixion in which he was
bound by ropes to the 'Cross of Suffering.' With the ropes literally cutting into his flesh, Yeats – and all would-be members –
had to repeat a long lesson in cabalistic theology.

That ritual suffering linked to Christ seized on the minds
of poets and artists is undeniable. Oscar Wilde's wife – although
not he – became an initiate into the Golden Dawn. The more
hedonistic the decade became, the more contrition and remorse
acted as a counter-balance. The more scientists insisted that nature was the ultimate reality, the more artists championed nature
as symbol of a Swedenborgian other-world. The paradox of re-
garding perceptible, material phenomena as symbols of a spirit
world existing parallel to the natural world apparently posed no
difficulties for fin-de-siècle neo-Platonists.

Yeats was under secret vows, and whether he confided the
details of his ritual crucifixion to Fred Day can only be conjectured. They did openly discuss Theosophy and spiritualism,
and held a vital and intense discourse about the supernatural.
We cannot know whether Yeats's ritual crucifixion precipitated
in Day's mind the psychological decisions that led to his most
famous series of photographs, *The Seven Last Words of Christ.*
Yet Fred Day revealed to Herbert Copeland how seriously he
admired the concept of suffering as a redemptive experience
which brought both maturity and contact with the spiritual
world. Yeats and the Rhymers' Club mystics helped to crystal-
ize Day's intuitive leanings. When F. Holland Day climbed
onto his own cross to pose as Christ in 1898, he was acting out
one of the major preoccupations of the 1890s, an obsession not
only of artists in the *Rose et Croix* group but also of Paul
Gauguin and his Nabis colleagues.

Yeats was then just beginning his monumental *Works of
William Blake,* issued by Quaritch in 1893. Day supplied him
with Blakeiana from his own library, and in sharing thoughts

about the mystic poet, Day and Yeats argued about the propriety of experimenting with black magic. When Madame Blavatsky died in 1891, Day mocked his Irish friend: 'Your poor Mme Blavatsky is gone to the eternal shades! And are you now reinstated in your old theosophical position from which the heresy of *black magic* drove you?'[12] Blavatsky had left no fewer than one hundred thousand mourning devotees all over the world, although most serious scholars of psychic phenomena in her lifetime discredited her completely. Yeats, in his utterly sincere way, had been duped into posing for 'spirit' photos, one of which showed him seated with an ectoplasmic head rising out of his own. Day was never seduced by such nonsense, possibly saved by his convictions about of what photography could, and could not, do. Nevertheless, his own picture *The Lacquer Box* (plate 15) is an attempt to record a spiritualistic experience of a kind which the English, including American expatriates like Whistler, had made fashionable. The trick was to rub a Japanese lacquer box until its special emanations made it possible to communicate directly with the spirit world.

Day's dramatic *The Vigil* (plate 13) is another document of some undisclosed ritual connected with one of the mystic cults. It is probable that the symbolism of this picture was directly derived from Golden Dawn ritual, in which the sword was the symbol of human reason and the power of critical analysis, to be used against the demons of doubt. The special robe, so elegantly arranged by Day, represented silence and secrecy.[13]

The Visionists had been entertaining notions of establishing an avant-garde publishing house, and formed the nucleus of a literary group which founded two little magazines. The first of these was *The Mahogany Tree,* a weekly journal devoted to literature and the fine arts, supported only by subscription. Among its contributors were the young Willa Cather, Herbert Bates, Louise Guiney, Ralph Adams Cram, and Fred Day himself. In his premature excitement over *The Mahogany Tree,* Fred rushed off its first issue to Yeats, and soon regretted it.

> *I am in no way connected with the 'M.T.' except as the designer of the cover and occasionally supplying a book note when copy fails them. I asked that it be sent to you before I knew ought of its character and*

Above: *The Lacquer Box;* below: *The Vigil,* both by F. Holland Day, about 1899.

Visionists and 'Knights Errant':
Cram, Copeland, and Goodhue,
probably by Day in 1892.

*now I am half sorry for fostering on you a thing so
amateurish, Savage's verse being practically the only
decent thing in it . . .*[14]

Day may have contributed to the magazine only as a favor to
his new friends. A note from Copeland on February 8, 1892,
indicates that 'Most of the number, except the signed articles
and your own, was the product of my aching hand.'[15] The same
note advised Fred that Herbert would be 'glad to go to Norwood with Gertrude and Philip any time. . . . Have wanted to
meet Mr. Cram for some time.'[16]

Ralph Adams Cram was a strong-jawed fellow with a
somewhat mincing pencil-line mustache and black-circled
pince-nez. He favored long clay pipes and a distinctly aristocratic attitude toward American democracy. Cram was the
force behind the group's next journalistic venture, *The
Knight Errant,* which became one of the most influential bibe-
lots of its era. A quarterly, it was the joint production of Cram,
the designer Bertram Goodhue, F. Holland Day, Herbert Copeland, and the printer of the Elzevir Press, Francis Watts Lee, a
friend of Day's who was also beginning to dabble in art photography. Lee, who was invited to join the group in November
1892, remarked in confusion: 'They tell me I am visionary in
some ways but I do not know that I am therefore a Visionist.
May I seek light from Dies?'[17]

Dies – Day – was happy to oblige. *The Knight Errant,* a
Visionist enterprise, was intended as competition for the English journal *The Hobby Horse.* On its cover rode a knight in

Left: portrait of Ralph Adams Cram by F. Holland Day, about 1892; right: cover for *The Knight Errant,* designed by Bertram Goodhue, 1892.

full armor, ready for a holy war against mob democracy and machine-made artifacts.

> *Men against an epoch; is it not that after all? One by one in this last night, the beautiful things have disappeared, until at last, in a world grown old and ugly, men, forced to find some excuse for the peculiarity of their environment, have discredited even beauty itself, finding it childish, unworthy, and — unscientific: not only beauty in Art, but beauty in thought and motive, beauty in life and death, until the word had become but a memory and a reproach. This is the condition that demands the new chivalry.*[18]

This was the governing ideology of the *Knight*'s editors, derived directly from William Morris, one of the prime movers

in Pre-Raphælite medievalism. Morris inspired Bertram Goodhue's pronouncement: 'This age is not one in which any true
art may flourish fairly. The parching simoon of commercialism
and the bleak frosts of ignorance and apathy are the very attributes we have left of those once pleasantly-changing seasons
of the golden ages of art.'[19]

Although Ralph Adams Cram, himself a gothicizer of
buildings, was an admirer of William Morris, it was undoubtedly Fred Day who introduced the direct influence of Morris's
decorative work. He had met Morris in the summer of 1890,
when Morris was setting up the Kelmscott Press, his outstanding contribution to the art of printing. Fred's enthusiasm may
have persuaded Morris to invite him to share in some of the
early productions, as a partner in the press. It was an extraordinary opportunity. For some reason, perhaps financial, perhaps
that season's involvement with the Fanny Brawne letters, Day
hesitated. Morris went on without him to create some of the
most enduring masterpieces of printing, including the so-called
Kelmscott Chaucer.

Fred Day was not ashamed to serve as book reviewer and
page designer for *The Knight Errant,* as he had been for *The
Mahogany Tree.* In it he and his Visionist cohorts fought many
good battles against the philistines – against the despiritualizing
aspects of modern life and the heartless factualism of the Émile
Zola brand of realism. They championed beauty, *japonisme,*
William Morris, hand-craftsmanship, æstheticism, literature,
and great painting, but the venture lasted only four issues.
They were important issues nevertheless, in which the idea of
the Decadence signified youthful rebellion and progress, not
the slow death or viciousness we ascribe to it today.

Defeated or not, the Visionists were as lively as ever. On
August 14, 1892, the *Boston Courier* announced that the editors
of *The Mahogany Tree* and of *The Knight Errant* 'gave a very
delightful entertainment at their summer home in Norwood.
Three of these young writers are keeping bachelor's hall there,
cooking and doing all the household work themselves.'[20] The
dinner, supervised by Cram, was 'delicious and daintily
served.'[21] Some snapshots of them at their culinary duties leave
no doubt as to the exuberant nature of their relationship, as
well as the continuing difficulty Day was having with indoor
exposures not controlled by studio conditions. When not serving as gourmet, Cram was propagandizing his Order of the

'Bachelor's quarters': Cram, Copeland, and Goodhue in Norwood, probably taken by Day in 1892.

A medieval dinner party at the Day mansion, with Visionists and members of literary societies, about 1893. Day presides at rear, Louise Guiney is at left front with Ralph Adams Cram.

White Rose, a fervently monarchistic society which already included Louise Guiney, Day, Copeland, and other æsthetes.

The newly renovated and refurbished Day mansion was the setting for various theatrical rites, revels, and pageants of the Visionists and the White Rose. There is no more vivid example of Day's aristocratic leanings than the decorations he

Detail of the ivory miniatures of
the Parthenon frieze that em-
bellished Day's library walls.

purchased for his house. During his European travels, he had
been inspired by various castles; in one letter to his mother, he
sketched the bedroom of the château of Louis XI, with all the
bed draperies and brocades. This bedroom he replicated for
himself, down to the last tassle and the wall fabric, a bold design in crimson and black. His friends called it 'the devil's room.'

The new library was even more elaborate, his most prized
and inventive creation. The Boston papers felt called upon to
report these dazzling renovations.

> *The library in Mr. Day's house, with its rare editions
> and its tasteful decorations, would drive an envious
> mind mad. A reproduction of the frieze of the Par-
> thenon surrounds it, and it is full of queer and cosy
> recesses, unexpected stairs running up to bookcases,
> odd retreats where a reader may sit in comforts that
> beget pleasures.*[22]

The library would be the source of many unpleasant rumors.
Day was, understandably, reticent about the workings of the
library, especially the hidden panels in which he secreted his
most precious editions, the letters of Fanny Brawne, pencils
and notes touched by Oscar Wilde and other idols, and similar
treasures. The miniature ivory frieze of the Parthenon was
shipped from London by Messrs. Brucciani, who also supplied
the large casts of Della Robbia choirboys which hung over the
mansion's main entrance fireplace, and a curiously maimed version of the Laocoön which leaned over a doorway.

Each room in the house bore F. Holland Day's distinctive
imprint: the Burne-Jones effects in a bedroom, the stained-glass
windows in the dining room, the rosewood- and mahogany-
paneled walls. William Morris would have approved the manner
in which Day was carrying out the Pre-Raphælite ideal of
beautifying and ennobling one's surroundings.

Sometime late in 1892, Herbert Copeland and F. Holland

'The devil's room – Day's bedroom at Norwood, reproducing French chateau furnishings.

Corner and upstairs alcove of Day's renovated library, about 1893.

Day came to an understanding about the establishment of a publishing house to rival the Kelmscott Press. Given their Pre-Raphælite loyalties, it is not surprising that the first book they hoped to publish was Dante Gabriel Rossetti's *The House of Life*. What actually saw print first was a book which Ralph Adams Cram later characterized as a youthful indiscretion. In November 1893, the twenty-nine-year-old Day notified a friend that 'Copeland and Day' was truly established.

The Keats corner in Day's library. Sarony's portrait of Oscar Wilde is at the left; Haydon's death mask of Keats is left of the central column; about 1894.

I think I didn't tell you that we are to print for Cram a book called The Decadent. *We act only as his agents He paying all bills. He has tried so very hard to 'do the Oscar' but failed so ignominiously that he will probably not put his name to it, but no persuasion of Herbert's or mine has had the least effect to leave it in M.S. It will appear most 'queer' before Christmas.*[23]

Most 'queer,' indeed. The frontispiece to this fascinating indiscretion, published – as predicted – anonymously, and subtitled 'The Gospel of Inaction,' was a red outline drawing of a geisha girl catering to two young men, one bearded, the other limply 'Greek,' smoking from a narghile. Fred Day was much given to this type of smoke. In reading Cram's description of the sup-

THE DECADENT: BEING THE GOS-
PEL OF INACTION: WHEREIN ARE
SET FORTH IN ROMANCE FORM
CERTAIN REFLECTIONS TOUCHING
THE CURIOUS CHARACTERISTICS
OF THESE ULTIMATE YEARS, AND
THE DIVERS CAUSES THEREOF.

PRIVATELY PRINTED FOR
THE AUTHOR MDCCCXCIII

The Decadent by Ralph Adams Cram, Copeland and Day's first publication, 1893. The frontispiece was designed by Bertram Goodhue.

posedly fictitious library in which the action – or rather, the inaction – takes place, one can only wonder how much of *The Decadent* was modeled after F. Holland Day and others of the Visionists. The tone of the book must be read to be believed:

The room was vast and dim . . . a mysterious wilderness of rugs and divans, Indian chairs and hammocks, where silent figures lay darkly, each a primal cause of one of the many thin streams of smoke that curled heavily upward; smoke from strange and curious pipes from Lahore and Gualior; small sensitive pipes from Japan, here and there the short thick stems of opium pipes, and by the motionless Mexican hammock a splendid and wonderful hookah with writhing stem. . . . And everywhere a heavy atmosphere that lay on the chest like a strange yet desirable dream; the warm, sick odour of tobacco and opium, strong with the perfume of sandalwood, and of roses that drooped and fluttered in pieces in the hot air.

Around a brazier of green bronze, on the floor,

before the fire, lay the three men who were gently breathing in the bland opium, their dark figures radiating from the queer brazier wrought of two ugly dragons chasing each other around a great globe of Japanese crystal . . .[24]

This was not so much 'doing the Oscar,' for Oscar Wilde had copied this same lapidary style for his *Picture of Dorian Gray* from J. K. Huysmans's *À Rebours,* one of the most influential books of the Decadence. Huysmans had based much of this hermetically sealed world, strangely burdened with anti-realist, antihuman fantasies, on the real life of one of the most notorious dandies and homosexuals of the age, Robert de Montesquiou, who was Marcel Proust's patron. Cram was not nearly as successful as Huysmans or Wilde, undoubtedly because he chose to use this opium-laden and smothering scene as an excuse for heavy-handed political pamphleteering. The last paragraphs of *The Decadent* epitomize the escapism which Cram believed had infected the age.

> *'Malcolm,' said Aurelian, 'beyond these fortress walls lies the world – the nineteenth century, seething with impotent tumult – festering towns of shoe factories and cotton mills, lying tradesmen and legalized piracy; pork-packing, stock-brokers, quarreling and snarling sectarians, and railroads, politicians, mammonism, realism, and newspapers. Within my walls . . . is the world of the past and of the future, of the fifteenth century and of the twentieth century. Here have I gathered all my treasures of art and letters; here may those I love find rest and refreshment when worn out with hopeless fighting. Suffer me to live here and forget, or live in a living dream of dreamless life . . .*[25]

I have inflicted this much of Cram's *The Decadent* on the reader because it is appallingly prophetic of Day's ultimate retreat from the world. It was only partly a facsimile of his lifestyle in the 1890s; more accurately, it was a facsimile of what the Boston public *imagined* his lifestyle to be. However scandalous this first publication from Copeland and Day may have been, it was not on a scale with their heretical importation of the English Decadents.

5

Publishers and Poets

American book publishing in the 1880s was a piratical, dog-eat-dog enterprise manifesting some of the virtues and all of the vices of the Industrial Revolution. Thanks to the recent invention of the Linotype machine and high-speed presses, books were inexpensive and abundant but they were also shoddy. Cut-throat competition and thoughtless mechanization had encouraged haphazard typography, cramped page layouts, and the use of eclectic illustration lifted from the popular magazines. Foreign authors, unprotected by copyright, were denied their royalties. In general, the publishing industry reflected perfectly the tasteless commercialism which was anathema not only to the William Morris coterie in England but also to their American disciples.

Some signs of rebellion were apparent in the founding of the Grolier Club of New York in 1884, a prestigious society devoted to the study and promotion of book arts. In 1887 F. Holland Day helped to establish Boston's Club of Odd Volumes for the same purpose. In 1890 Day had been the first of the Visionists to have personal contact with William Morris at the very moment that the influential Kelmscott Press was founded. But perhaps 1891 was even more important to the Boston group:

Portrait of F. Holland Day, publisher, about 1893.

Portrait of Bertram Grosvenor
Goodhue, designer, by F. Holland Day, about 1893.

the passage of the International Copyright Act secured trans-
Atlantic cooperation and ended the American piracy of English
authors; Walter Crane, one of the Kelmscott Press artists and a
well-established book illustrator, visited Boston and gave praise
and encouragement to the *Knight Errant;* and the firm of
Roberts Brothers in Boston published a photographic facsimile
edition of Morris's *The Story of the Glittering Plain,* which
had an immediate impact on the design ideas of Bertram Grosvenor Goodhue.

Goodhue had been trained as an architect and therefore
attracted Ralph Adams Cram, but he was so interested in typographic design that he toyed with the notion of joining Copeland and Day as a full partner. Enormously talented, he decided to freelance for the surprising number of excellent small
publishing firms which sprang up in Boston in the early 1890s.
His work graced Daniel Berkeley Updike's Merrymount Press,
Stone and Kimball – better known, perhaps for Will Bradley's
striking designs for their publication, *The Chap-Book* – and,
later on, Small, Maynard & Company. While F. Holland Day
had a well-developed sense of page layout and good typographic
design, without Bertram Goodhue the high reputation of the
firm of Copeland and Day would be considerably diminished.
With his sparkling designs and his mischievous disposition,
Goodhue was undoubtedly the most imaginative of the book
designers until Bruce Rogers moved East and joined the Visionist group in 1895.

Publishing houses may spring up as a late-night whim to
serve the cause of literature or fine design, but they die unless
they have regular infusions of two commodities: money and
talent. Lewis Day supplied the money, liberally bolstered with
sound business advice. Herbert Copeland, however, had no in-
vestment capital to speak of; his editorial position at the *Youth's
Companion,* which he maintained for several years, was expected to serve as a conduit for potential authors. Fortunately,
Fred Day had not only met William Morris in that crucial
summer of 1890, he had also met the avant-garde publisher,
John Lane, whose Bodley Head imprint was already established. As soon as the international copyright was secured, Day
and Lane agreed that they would each make a fundamental
commitment to publishing poetry. Without Lane's list of excit-
ing British authors such as Oscar Wilde, Francis Thompson,
Richard LeGallienne, John Davidson, and Lionel Johnson, it is
conceivable that Fred Day could never have considered starting

Portrait of Herbert Copeland, partner, by Day, about 1893.

his own firm. Lane, moreover, offered connections with illustrators and designers of the caliber – and notoriety – of Aubrey Beardsley and Walter Crane.

Another source of contacts and talent was Louise Guiney, who was put on the Copeland and Day payroll within a year of their establishment, at the munificent wage of fifty cents an hour (about five dollars per hour today). Her main tasks as a reader for the firm were to encourage young poets and propose new manuscripts. It was Louise who brought a significant number of Catholic poets into the firm, although Herbert claimed Father John Tabb, one of Copeland and Day's greatest successes. As usual, Louise had conflicting emotions about the new firm. To Bertram Goodhue she wrote enthusiastically: 'I am "tickled" beyond measure with the prospective shingle at 69 Cornhill and am ready to dance every time I think of it. . . . It's orful jolly, the whole thing.'[1] But she could not resist taking a backhanded dig at her precious 'Sonny' when she wrote to Richard Garnet, Keeper of Books at the British Museum.

> *Mr. Day, in a small way, and chiefly to amuse himself, I fear, and to indulge his really exquisite tastes in the technique of bookmaking, has gone into the publishing trade for himself, and has a cosy office on our Cornhill, which is a hive of bookstalls and whose houses all date back to 1711.*[2]

These deprecating remarks referred in part to the fact that Fred was continuing to experiment with photography. Louise, who knew nothing of the visual arts and even less of the new art of photography, considered his involvement with the camera to be a species of play. Some of her irritation was undoubtedly caused by Day's having financial freedom, while she was forced to accept hackwork to support herself and her mother. She understood little of what an æsthetic revolutionary her 'Sonnikins' had become. For Day was about to make his first major impact on the American scene, through his championing of the design ideals of William Morris.

Day was such a devotee of the Kelmscott Press that he owned both a copy of the expensive Chaucer and an even rarer copy (one of seven printed on vellum) of the Kelmscott Keats. It is not surprising that the first book bearing the Copeland and Day colophon and imprint was modeled after William Morris. This was Dante Gabriel Rossetti's sonnet sequence, *The House of Life,* which appeared in 1894. The paper was handmade,

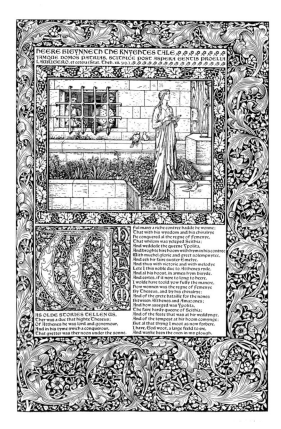

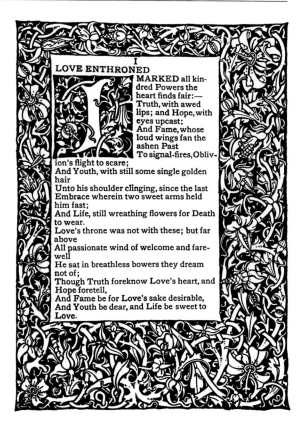

The medieval look: left, the
Kelmscott *Chaucer*, 1896, designed by William Morris and
Edward Burne-Jones; right, Rossetti's *The House of Life*, Copeland and Day, 1894, designed
by Bertram Goodhue.

the initials were designed by Goodhue, and the book fit well
into the hand. But it was much more than the ideal of medievalism that Day espoused. He wanted to revive the art of read-
able, interesting typography and simple page design – small
and comfortable books uncomplicated by hectic Victorian layouts. He had, of course, a fierce love for poetry, and he wanted
to give full support to the new 'singers of songs,' as the 1890s
public liked to call them.

If any volume of poetry was a popular success, Copeland
and Day's first book of American authorship was certainly that.
Songs from Vagabondia, by Bliss Carman and Richard Hovey,
had such vitality that it became a collegiate cult item. Their
macho gaiety, their Whitmanesque delight in freedom, and
their simplicity of rhythms made Carman and Hovey the most
popular of all the Copeland and Day authors. Their appeal was
direct:

> *Midnights of revel*
> *And noondays of song!*
> *Is it so wrong?*
> *Go to the Devil!*[3]

End papers designed by Tom Meteyard for *Songs from Vagabondia,* 1894.

HAVE LITTLE —— CARE THAT
LIFE IS —— BRIEF.
AND LESS TH—— AT ART IS LONG.
SUCCESS IS IN —— THE SILENCES
THOUGH FAME —— IS IN THE SONG.

When *More Songs from Vagabondia* appeared in 1896, it was another critical success. Edward Arlington Robinson wrote that Copeland and Day had produced books that 'first gave American readers reason to suspect that we might after all have a contemporary American poetry.'[4] Carman and Hovey were preachers of the heartiest male comradeship:

> *The words that pass from lip to lip*
> *For souls still out of reach!*
> *A friend for that companionship*
> *That's deeper than all speech!*[5]

They unabashedly saw sexual analogies in the violence of war:

> *Three of us in love with life,*
> *Roaming like wild cattle,*
> *With the stinging air a-reel*
> *As a warrior might feel*
> *The swift orgasm of the knife*
> *Slay him in mid-battle.*[6]

Both Carman and Hovey had been roistering members of the Visionists, the Pewter Mugs, and the more obscure Procrastinatorium, and had therefore been closely associated with both Copeland and Day. But undoubtedly the old Harvard tie was proving to be Copeland's invaluable contribution, for Carman and Hovey had been his schoolmates.

· BLISS · CARMAN ·   · RICHARD · LE · GALLIENNE ·   · FRANCIS · THOMPSON ·

Above: wood engravings of three Copeland and Day authors by Robert Bryden; below, title page designed by Will Bradley, with typical Copeland and Day's printer's mark, 1895.

Father John Tabb's small book of poems was their next American success, and it was duly exported to the Bodley Head, where John Lane still had Elkin Matthews as partner. Tabb made an astonishing impact: 'Mr. Wilson, of the University Press, tells Mr. Day that no other *first* book of American poetry has gone through so many editions as mine, with the exception of Miss Dickinson.'[7] Meanwhile, the *English Poems* of Richard LeGallienne and Francis Thompson's *Poems* were imported from the Bodley Head. LeGallienne was not quite so well received by American critics, but he was at the center of the British Decadent group and the reporter of much of its gossip. William Archer decided that 'there is such a thing as looking a part too well; and Mr. LeGallienne's eminently poetical exterior, taken along with his liquid and exotic name, have done some injustice to his real talent. Such a name and such a physiognomy are hard to live up to.'[8]

LeGallienne's *Robert Louis Stevenson: An Elegy and Other Poems,* published in 1895, bore a striking title page designed by Will Bradley. He was one of a distinguished series of artists for Copeland and Day who included John Sloan, Maxfield Parrish, Tom Meteyard, Charles Ricketts, and Ethel Reed. Reed was not only a talented designer but one of Fred Holland Day's best models for the camera. With his instinct for the dramatic, he framed her dark good looks in flamboyant plumed hats. 'Ethel Reed in the grand feathered hat' and *The Gainsborough Hat* (plates 1 and 5) were two outstanding early achievements. Ethel Reed devised the delightful posters and

Day's portrait of Ethel Reed in
The Gainsborough Hat, 1895,
and her poster for *Arabella and
Araminta.*

covers for several books in Copeland and Day's 'Yellow Hair'
children's series – Gertrude Smith's *Arabella and Araminta* and
Louise Chandler Moulton's *In Childhood's Country.*

The Moulton book quickly died, but *Arabella and Araminta* was a huge success, despite the fact that Ethel Reed was
much criticized for her unconventional decorations. *The Book
Buyer's* critic predicted that when Aubrey Beardsley saw *Arabella,* he would 'shed tears of great joy . . . and the children
will go to bed and dream about little girls who look like glori-
fied queens of spades.'[9] Apparently, American critics were not
prepared for Beardsley's influence on what came to be known
as Art Nouveau. Will Bradley, who produced the first poster in
that style as a cover for *The Chap-Book,* had already provoked
savage parody,[10] and it was he who had inspired Ethel Reed.

The Moulton disaster had been published over the objections of Louise Guiney, who gave an honest opinion of her godmother's work. 'I do not think for a moment Mrs. Moulton's
verses for children will be of the slightest value.'[11] Unfortunately, this was not the only time that Day ignored Louise's
literary advice. He and Herbert pressured her into publishing a
poor collection of her own stories, under a title she detested:
Lovers' Saint Ruth's and Three Other Tales. Brought out in
1895 at Christmastime, the book revealed what she herself acknowledged: fiction would never be her forte. It was dreadfully
clichéd and artificial: ' "Miss Carter!" His heart-thuds made it
hard for him to be punctilious. "Are you hurt? Idiots that we
were to chose this place! We might have known . . ." ' and 'As
they descended the rough foot-path, the Sargeant longed to
offer his arm; but he knew her stoicism, her natural physical
savoir-faire, and he chivalrously refrained.' Louise should have
refrained. Furious with herself, she wrote to a friend, 'I ought
to have stood fast.'[12] As they were hardly short of talent for the
season, it is a mystery why Copeland and Day cast aside their
own high standards for literature and forced a poet into an in-
compatible form. Perhaps Day was trying to be charitable.

Oscar Wilde's *Salomé* and *The Sphinx,* and John Lane's
The Yellow Book were all doing well in 1895, despite the
Wilde court case and the scandals. This was the year that
Copeland and Day brought out the first in the Oaten Stop series
of poets, Richard Burton's collection, *Dumb in June.* Described
as a 'demure little book clad soberly in Quaker garb,'[13] it offered the homely virtues and quiet aspirations of the *Hartford*

Courant's gentleman editor. These verses were the antithesis of Copeland and Day's most sensational offering of 1895, the first book of poems by the radical realist, Stephen Crane.

If Copeland and Day had published nothing else, history would offer them a niche with *The Black Riders and Other Lines.* Crane had already published *Maggie: A Girl of the Streets* in 1893, and *The Red Badge of Courage* had appeared in 1894 in an abridged newspaper version. Copeland and Day may have believed they were prepared for everything unconventional, but the unrhymed, arrhythmic verses of the twenty-three-year-old Crane were so defiant and outspoken that the publishers struggled to cut some of them from the final publication. John Barry of *The Forum* had sent Crane's manuscript to Copeland and Day as the most avant-garde publishers of poetry in America, and Crane was angered by their unexpected caution.

> *We disagree on a multitude of points. In the first place, I absolutely refuse to have my poems printed without many of those which you just as absolutely mark 'No.' It seems to me that you cut all the ethical sense out of the book. All the anarchy, perhaps. It is the anarchy which I particularly insist upon.*[14]

It was the vehement, atheistic anarchy which gave the Boston firm second thoughts about public reaction. Eventually, Crane's strong will won out. In a cover which flaunted a bold Art Nouveau orchid, designed by Fred Gordon to suggest that Crane's work was strange and exotic, *Black Riders* immediately won vast critical attention. Crane was hailed as 'the Aubrey Beardsley of poetry.'[15] The design of the cover, as well as the odd spacing of the text, elicited from the haughty Amy Lowell the comment, 'No method more certain to obscure the sincerity of the work could well have been devised.'[16]

The year 1895 was not simply a major publishing year for Fred Day. He was elected unanimously to the newly formed London society for art photography, the Linked Ring Brotherhood, and this honor signaled the beginning of his gradually diminishing dedication to literature. For two years he had been amassing a striking series of portraits of women. Much of the business of publishing had been left to Herbert while Day and Louise Guiney traveled to England for the Keats memorial ceremonies at Hampstead in 1894. But while

Art Nouveau orchids for the cover of Stephen Crane's *Black Riders,* Copeland and Day, 1895.

he was pursuing both Oscar Wilde and Aubrey Beardsley, Day had made certain that the firm was publishing solidly Catholic poets like Francis Thompson and Lionel Johnson. Thompson's *Sister-Songs* appeared in this most productive year of 1895, along with Walter Pater's *The Child in the House: An Imaginary Portrait* and William Butler Yeats's *Poems,* jointly published with T. Fisher Unwin of London. All three writers were burdened by the general aura of the Decadence, which American readers distrusted, but there was no denying the genius of Thompson, the scholarship and brilliant prose of Pater, the Celtic imagination of Yeats.

The American audience admired Thompson's fervor, and welcomed his Christian mysticism as a counterbalance to the atheistic Crane, but they found Yeats's storytelling more to their liking. The first version of 'The Wanderings of Usheen,' later called 'Oisin,' carried the pleasing description of a lovely and romantic maiden. She was like a figure out of the medieval fantasies of Howard Pyle, an artist much admired by Day.

> *His mistress was more mild and fair*
> *Than doves that moaned round Eman's hall*
> *Among the leaves of the laurel wall,*
> *And feared always the bowstring's twanging.*
> *Her eyes were soft as dew drops hanging*
> *Upon the grass-blade's bending tips,*
> *And like a sunset were her lips,*
> *A stormy sunset o'er doomed ships.*[17]

Left: Louise Guiney and Alice Brown in walking costume for their 1895 tour of England; right, portrait of Alice Brown, possibly taken by F. Holland Day.

Louise Guiney was well pleased with this very Catholic and Celtic list of poets. She and Alice Brown had collaborated on one of the three commemorations to Robert Louis Stevenson which Copeland and Day had seen fit to publish. In 1895, she and Alice took a walking tour of England to write a travelogue for a women's group. When they returned to Boston, they were greeted by a delightful absurdity: there was Fred, their enthusiastic publisher, standing on a barrel at the pier with the green and gold poster for Alice's novel, *Meadow-Grass,* pinned to his chest. Day had good reason to feel playful: *Meadow-Grass* was the most successful fiction the firm would publish. It sold what was then the impressive figure of nine thousand copies in all editions. Alice had already completed a collection of verse; *The Road to Castaly* was rushed into publication the following year to take advantage of the novel's reputation. 'Candlemas,' from that collection, won her high praise: 'The song is an inspiration that ought to take its place in every "Golden Treasury" of English lyrics.'[18] One stanza, the last, may suffice to convey its qualities:

> *My birds, come back! the hollow sky*
> > *Is weary for your note.*
> *(Sweet throat, come back! O liquid mellow throat!)*
> *Ere May's soft minions hereward fly.*
> *Shame on ye, laggards, to deny*
> *The brooding breast, the sun-bright eye,*
> > *The tawny shining coat.*[19]

This kind of pleasant, sunny, uncomplicated verse was

Louise Guiney's *Nine Sonnets at Oxford,* Copeland and Day, 1895, designed by Goodhue.

well within the range of Louise Guiney's talent as well, but she had become melancholy since the loss of Stevenson in 1894. 'Stevenson was my Only. I feel as if I can never write again with any faith in myself or what I am doing.'[20] It must have been a relief when Day commissioned her somber *Nine Sonnets Written at Oxford*. Designed and decorated by Bertram Goodhue, *Nine Sonnets* was a return to the medievalism of William Morris's Chaucer. Privately issued by Copeland and Day as a Christmas offering to their many friends, the book spawned several unconfirmed rumors. The first was Day's boast that he had presented the book to William Morris, who took it to his wife and asked what she thought of it. 'This is the best you have ever done,' she is supposed to have replied.[21] There seems to be even less support for the tale that the Bodleian Library paid highly for the book at auction, in the mistaken belief that *Nine Sonnets* was a William Morris production. After all, the colophon plainly identified the work. Still, at first glance, the Goodhue designs are so overwhelmingly Gothic that the uninitiated might have been fooled.

Day often seemed envious of the close friendship between Alice Brown and Louise Guiney. When he found some excuse to criticize his most popular author, Louise defended her teasingly by commenting that Alice was an excellent companion, a caring person, and every bit as much a bohemian as Fred himself.

The style of the Copeland and Day books was unpredictable. When Fred himself designed the title page for Charles Knowles Bolton's *On the Wooing of Martha Pitkin,* he skillfully imitated the typography of the eighteenth century. *Martha Pitkin* was a verse narrative of colonial New England, a surprising little success, with three limited printings in one year. Bolton, like Philip Henry Savage, was a Harvard graduate who had gone into the gentlemanly profession of librarianship. Savage's *First Poems and Fragments* came out in 1895; a modest and unadorned volume, it had a sequel three years later, only a year before his early death from pneumonia. Both Bolton and Savage apparently encouraged Herbert Copeland to publish Charles Macomb Flandreau's *Harvard Episodes.* An inconsequential work of pseudorealism in which the undergraduates spouted slang, it eventually became Copeland and Day's second-largest seller.

Like the owners of most small publishing houses, Copeland and Day were beset with practical problems. The firm never made any money to speak of, and the losses were borne by Fred Day and his father. Herbert borrowed increasingly as time went on. Even the author of the top seller *Arabella and Araminta* had to plead for her royalties; she complained that she had not understood her contract.[22] As Day began to concentrate on photography, Herbert Copeland must have felt abandoned. Fortunately for him, in 1899 when the firm finally had to fold, an old Harvard roommate who was also in the publishing business came to their rescue. Herbert Small and his partner, Laurens Maynard, undoubtedly had been encouraged by the example of Copeland and Day when they began their publishing venture in 1897. When they purchased the remainders of some sixty titles from Copeland and Day, they doubled their own list and reissued some of the originals. But Small, Maynard & Company never enjoyed the aesthetic influence of their predecessors, and, like Copeland and Day, they went down under the onslaught of the ever-expanding large publishing houses.

In six short years, Herbert Copeland and F. Holland Day had achieved a permanent place in the history of American publishing, bringing out a total of ninety-eight titles of belles-lettres and two journals. They had managed to introduce many of the great British poets to their first American audiences. They had published the outrageous Oscar Wilde and the anarchistic Stephen Crane. Thanks to John Lane's assistance and Day's profound commitment, poets on both sides of the Atlantic found strong support for their work. Day even published a work he knew would make no profit: *Songs from the Ghetto,* a translation from the Yiddish of Morris Rosenfeld. Through his charity, Day brought Rosenfeld to national attention, and permitted him to write full time. Copeland and Day were among the few publishers in America to whom anyone would have considered sending *Black Riders* or any other unconventional verse. And, of course, Day was instrumental in bringing to America not only William Morris's medievalism, but also his craftsmanly ideals. These ideals were reflected with equal vigor in the modern designs flavored with Art Nouveau, and in their pseudo-colonial publications. All their books manifested an integrity of design and a handsome utilitarianism which rarely have been matched.

Copeland and Day encouraged Canadian poets as well; Duncan Campbell Scott was one of their best authors. While they published many classics (the sonnets of Shakespeare and of Elizabeth Barrett Browning), they also introduced unknowns such as Isabel Whiteley, Hannah Parker Kimball, Kate Whiting Patch, and Josephine Preston Peabody. If occasionally they published indifferent poems or obscure prose, on the whole they managed rather well. Compared with their competitors, they evinced a greater willingness to experiment and to brave Boston's potential wrath with controversial works. What made them notorious in their own time, of course, was Day's unswerving support for the most outrageous figures of the nineties. Yet no one who knew F. Holland Day well would have been surprised by his allegiances. He was not only a man of the nineties, but an artist of the nineties. For the best reasons and the worst, he was intent upon identifying himself with the most unregenerate and fantastic aspects of the Decadence.

Several of the many variations on the Copeland and Day printer's mark: *Sicut lilium inter spinas.*

Oscar Wilde in 'aesthetic dress,'
1882, by Napoleon Sarony.
Day's favorite portrait of his idol.

Oscar and Aubrey, Sun-Gods and Wraiths

6

There was a time in American letters when an author would do anything to have his book 'banned in Boston.' That imprimatur guaranteed that the general public would believe his work to be prurient, titillating, and forbidden. For Copeland and Day, however, being banned in Boston was no joking matter. It was something of a miracle that their press survived the censure that the Decadents and the modernists aroused.

Day used Louise Guiney as a barometer of what Catholic opinion might tolerate, and she never minced words with him. He was mistaken in believing her to be an enlightened progressive, as her fundamental literary insights were attuned more to the seventeenth century than to the revolutionary nineties. A typical conflict between Fred and Louise concerned George Moore. Fred was most partial to Moore's aestheticism, but Louise wrote:

> *Why, O why must you say that little Moore is 'virile'? He is active, daring, wilful, perverse, stuck-up, posing analytic morbid, independent, silly, vehement, insistent, stubborn, smart, unspiritual.*[1]

One can only wonder what adjectives she would have added if

she – or Day, for that matter – had known that Moore, priding
himself on his resemblance to the Parisian diabolists, 'kept a pet
python and cultivated paganness by watching it devour rabbits
alive.'[2]

If George Moore irritated Louise, she drew the line at
Oscar Wilde. In 1891 Wilde had published *Intentions,* a volume of essays in which his philosophy of inaction – a type of
passivity implying acceptance of whatever happens – had
stirred Ralph Adams Cram's contempt and wrath. Wilde had
insisted that all art was amoral, to be judged only on its own
internal merits. As a believer in the Keatsian ideal of beauty,
Fred Day had no difficulty accepting Oscar Wilde's aphorisms.
But when he persuaded Louise to read *Intentions,* she replied
with her usual frankness.

> *Of course I have been through Oscar's book. (Essays
> don't stick long in this gullet.) I think it immensely
> amusing: the reader gets almost as much fun out of it
> as the author. The paradoxes are the most brilliant,
> inveterate, conscious go-to-I-will-be-'sassy'-clever things
> in the world. . . . Some of his originalities are in Mon-
> taigne, some in Thoreau; one famous one in Anatole
> France. . . . The book hasn't the slightest serious value.*[3]

Such candor could have hardly endeared her further to
Fred, who had long worshipped Oscar Wilde. As all his intimates knew, he kept a large sepia portrait of Wilde in his most
precious library alcove, the corner devoted to Keats. Wilde, in
fact, had done more than any other single writer to propagan-
dize Keats, and it was through his influence that Keats became
the most popular model for poets of the 1890s.

The photograph of Oscar Wilde owned by Day had been
taken by the well-known New York studio operator, Napoleon
Sarony, in 1882. Wilde had been on his first American tour, a
spectacular and often ludicrous jaunt organized by Richard
d'Oyly Carte to publicize his production of the Gilbert and
Sullivan operetta *Patience.* This satire mocked the English æsthetes so severely that it was a wonder that Wilde and Whistler
did not sue. Instead, Wilde came willingly, under contract to
appear in 'æsthetic dress,' to pose for Sarony as genius incar-
nate. He dressed flamboyantly in velvet knee breeches, formal
evening jacket, Tyrolean cape, and other romantic costumes. It
was easy to imagine him walking 'down Piccadilly with a tulip
or a lily.'[4] When he came to Boston, the Harvard students

Oscar Wilde in a smoking jacket, 1882, by Sarony, taken during Wilde's New York trip.

threatened to attend his lecture in 'dress coats, knee breeches, and silk stockings, with lilies in their buttonholes.'[5] On January 31, 1882, Wilde lectured a boisterous Boston audience on the significance of the Pre-Raphælites and William Morris's revival of craftsmanship. They were agreeably surprised by his seriousness.

Fred Day was still a student at Chauncy Hall at this time, and he was greatly astonished to encounter his idol at South Station one afternoon. Ten years later, he described this encounter for *The Mahogany Tree*, employing the indirect method – 'my friend the Bibliophile' – which Victorian literary proprieties demanded.

> . . . *he approached the Unapproachable, and in the sweetest tones his changing voice could assume requested of the Sun's God his autograph. The Great One looked down upon the youth with that sunny smile so often and cruelly maligned as 'incubating,' and taking the pencil, slowly traced his name in calligraphy rather more curious than his appearance. The gates swung open and the throng passed through. For years this slip of paper and the pencil tied with yellow ribbon hung on the wall of my friend's library, who still keeps them though far from the gaze of the commoner.*[6]

At the moment of this first meeting, in 1882, Wilde was untainted by scandal. He was known primarily as James Whistler's friendly rival for the leadership of the æsthetic movement. Ten

'Just like a lily among thorns' –
the Copeland and Day printer's
mark.

years older than Day, Wilde was the perfect adolescent hero: tall, handsome, already world famous, fearlessly defying convention. They shared many things: a passion for Keats, Balzac, and Oriental vases, a domination by over-protective mothers. They both adopted languid airs, and preached the cult of the beautiful. By 1894, however, when Copeland and Day imported Wilde's *Salomé* with Beardsley's provocative drawings, the public's attitude toward Wilde had changed from amusement to suspicion. *The Picture of Dorian Gray,* despite Wilde's protestations of its profound morality, had alerted the Puritans to the Sun God's symptoms of decadence.

Wilde's *Salomé* was among the first publications John Lane sent to Copeland and Day. Appealing to some of the undercurrents of Byzantine perversity present even in Boston, it was a *succés de scandale*. It spoke of cruelty mingled with beauty, kisses dripping with blood, and women as castrating fiends like those recently portrayed in paintings by Moreau and Khnopff. It had the kind of satanic sensualism calculated to make Louise Guiney's nerve ends jangle. She praised the superior qualities of Lionel Johnson, a brilliant Oxford graduate whose verses surpassed even her own in their religious fervor. 'A calm, virgilian young man, small and silent, with a knowing side-long smile,' [7] Johnson became one of Yeats's best friends. Yet he was also a very close friend of Oscar Wilde. One can only wonder if Louise knew this, or knew that Lionel Johnson had introduced the young Lord Alfred Douglas – Bosie – to the author of *Dorian Gray* in 1891. Swiftly becoming infatuated with each other, Bosie and Oscar shut poor Lionel out of their friendship.

For Copeland and Day, 1894 saw the publication of *Salomé* and Wilde's relatively unknown longer poem, *The Sphinx,* to which Charles Ricketts gave a most eccentric design. But the genuine sensation was their importation of *The Yellow Book,* a journal that left its mark upon the entire decade. *The Critic* called the first number of *The Yellow Book* 'the Oscar Wilde of periodicals.' Wilde had rapidly become the symbol of everything sensational, æsthetic, perverse, exotic, affected, intellectual, and showy. It was assumed – incorrectly – that he went about bearing a limp lily in his hands. As Oscar became the symbol of æstheticism, so his favorite flower, the lily, became the symbol of the æsthetes themselves, and the printer's mark of Copeland and Day. 'A rose garland encircling a stem

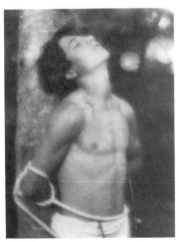

Above: the tomb of Keats in Rome; below: one of two versions of St. Sebastian by F. Holland Day, 1906.

with three lilies spouting from the top,'[8] this motif was adapted to different styles according to its use – for the English Love Sonnet series, for example, or for children's books. The motto of the firm was *Sicut lilium inter spinas*: 'Just like a lily among thorns.'[9]

Day was so preoccupied with publishing, and with his campaign to raise funds for the proposed memorial to Keats, that it is difficult to understand how he found time for photography. Yet no sooner had he returned from Hampstead, late in 1894, than he opened his first photographic studio in Boston. It was located on Pinckney Street on fashionable Beacon Hill, a few doors from Alice Brown's apartments and in the thick of artistic and literary society. The impetus for this move was undoubtedly his first encounters with the Linked Ring photographers in London, whose approval of his work kept him from giving exclusive attention to the Keats affair.

Fred claimed that he was inspired to create a memorial to Keats in England when visiting Westminster Chapel with Louise. That may be true, but he certainly must have known of Oscar Wilde's efforts along these lines, and he would have read Wilde's threnody on the tomb of Keats in Rome. For Wilde's motifs appear in Day's own camera work, and represent the typical interweaving of morbid sensuality and bathos, the essence of the Keatsian appeal.

> *As I stood beside the mean grave of this divine boy, I thought of him as of a Priest of Beauty slain before his time; and the vision of Guido's St. Sebastian came before my eyes as I saw him at Genoa, a lovely brown boy, with crisp clustering hair and red lips, bound by his evil enemies to a tree, and, though pierced with arrows, raising his eyes with divine impassioned gaze towards the Eternal Beauty of the opening heavens.*[10]

Day produced only two St. Sebastians, rather late in life, but the masochistic passivity and transcendent suffering of this saint had a peculiar and widespread appeal in the nineties. The 'Guido' of Wilde's prose was, of course, Guido Reni, whose paintings of the crucified Christ had a crucial effect on Day's series of work on sacred themes. We have already seen how important Yeats's experiences with suffering were to Day, as they exemplified the unity of suffering, beauty, and salvation. Suffering demanded recognition.

F. Holland Day and Louise Guiney presiding at the dedication of the John Keats memorial at Hampstead, 1894.

For two years, Fred and Louise had been establishing Friends of Keats groups, and cajoling funds for the memorial. The patrons of this movement included half the intelligentsia of London and Boston. The invitations to the ceremony were printed at the Kelmscott Press. On July 16, 1894, a thousand persons attended the commemoration, including the gaunt Aubrey Beardsley, whose erotic drawings for *Salomé* were creating even more of a scandal than Wilde's play. Day wanted Bret Harte to make the presentation, but could not find him in time for the ceremony, and so was persuaded to do the job himself. The Keats expert Sidney Colvin officiated, Sir Edmund Gosse gave the acceptance speech, and a letter by Swinburne was presented; Day, much too modest to acknowledge his right to preside, disappeared quickly into the throng before he could hear encomiums on his accomplishment.

He may even have gone off with Beardsley, for by this time they had become acquainted through the kind offices of Frederick Evans, a London bookseller who later became one of the greatest architectural photographers. It was Evans who had taken the famous portrait of Beardsley that Oscar Wilde detested. He was not overly fond of Beardsley in any event: 'He

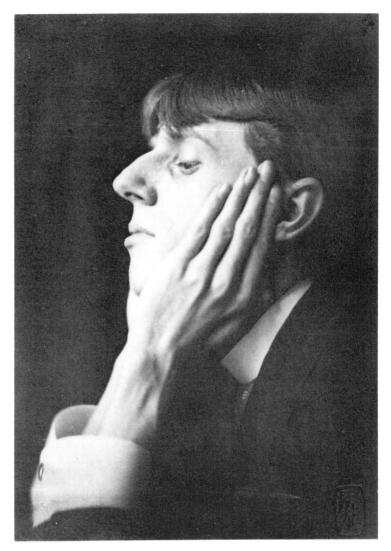

Portrait of Aubrey Beardsley by Frederick Evans, about 1893 – 'a face like a silver hatchet.'

has a face like a silver hatchet adorned with grass green hair.'[11] When James Whistler met Beardsley, he commented, 'Look at him! – he's just like his drawings – he's all hairs and peacock plumes.'[12] The consumptive young genius had his revenge on both of them, by caricaturing Wilde in the illustrations for his own *Salomé,* and mocking Whistler as a monocled Great God Pan, cloven hoofs and all.

Wilde and Whistler had become so used to outraging bourgeois sensibilities that they must have been surprised to discover a skinny, mortally ill youth was putting them to the ultimate test. If anyone epitomized a fin-de-siècle mood, an egomaniacal dandyism, a bizarre exoticism like that in Japanese drawings and prints, and an absolute rejection of realism, representationalism, impressionism, and naturalism, it was Aubrey

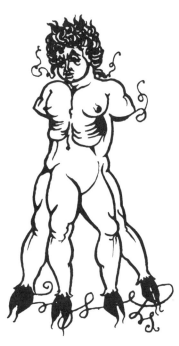

Above: hermaphrodite by
Beardsley for *Le Morte d'Arthur*,
1892; below: one of Beardsley's
grotesques for the *Bon-Mots*
series.

Beardsley. For Beardsley, beauty was intimately connected with
whips, grotesqueries, shadows in which strange vices were
committed. He was known to draw only by the light of thirteen
candles, a practice which Fred Day either copied or adopted
from the same cabalistic doctrines.

Max Beerbohm mocked Beardsley as a 'dyahbolist' – a
diabolist, that is, in the upper-class pronunciation. There were
rumors about Beardsley's transvestism. *Punch* articles dubbed
him 'Weirdsley Daubery,' 'Awfully Weirdly,' and 'Daubaway
Weirdsley.' Masturbatory fantasies obsessed him. Frequent
themes included young boys offering fruits to the ithyphallic
Herms of Pan, a motif which Day pursued in the 1900s. His
emblem, the penetration of a crevice between two lines by a
third line ejaculating three drops, spoke of an obsession with
sex. He took the repressed lusts of the Victorians and spewed
them across paper with a mastery of form which may outlast
both Wilde and Whistler.

When he first saw Beardsley's drawings, Fred Day was
smitten at once. On May 20, 1893, he wrote to J. M. Dent, the
British publisher who gave Beardsley his start in illustrating a
new edition of Malory's *Le Morte d'Arthur*.[13]

> *My dear Mr. Dent! . . . the more I look at Beardsley's
> work the more it astonishes me and the more I desire
> to meet him, and know him, which I hope I may have
> the pleasure of accomplishing in the fall when I ex-
> pect to be in London.*[14]

Back from Dent's famous Aldine House came some Beardsley
publications and drawings, for which Day thanked Dent pro-
fusely.

> *Your 'Bon Mots' with Mr. Beardsley's astonishing
> grotesques has arrived. The drawings have quite
> shocked us out of all consciousness here for the time
> being. . . . I have the 'Merlin taketh the shield . . .'
> framed and hung over my desk above the full page
> which appeared in the Pall Mall magazine. Could
> you, I wonder, get for me a proof of the drawing for
> Oscar Wilde's* Salomé? *– I wish to add it to my copy
> of the book. And by the way we expect to bring out
> the American edition of Mr. Wilde's forthcoming
> story – Kindly remember me as always at your service.*[15]

Beardsley's portrait of himself tied to a Herm of Pan, prisoner to a phallic symbol.

The arrival of the drawings not only 'shocked us out of all consciousness' but precipitated a serious quarrel between Day and Bertram Goodhue, who was so eager to see them that he stole a key to the publisher's offices to give himself and Daniel Berkeley Updike first crack at them. Updike, after all, was Day's competitor at the Merrymount Press, and the incident strained his relationship with Goodhue almost to the breaking point. Curiously enough, it was Day who apologized first for losing his temper.

It is a good indication of Day's attraction to the outrageous and original, and his flirtation with scandal, that he was attracted to Beardsley. The young artist's intellectual sensuality had much in common with Day's nature. Even Louise found

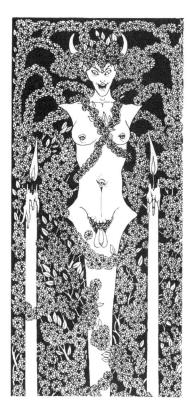

Detail of the unexpurgated title page by Beardsley for Wilde's *Salomé,* as it appeared in London.

Beardsley quite marvelous. But Herbert Copeland behaved the cautious Puritan at this juncture. He had already irritated Fred when, commenting on a character in a book they were considering for publication, he concluded, 'Her beautiful soul did her no good.'[16] Day exploded.

> *I believe there never existed the smallest particle of real beauty that did not perform its mission of good. Beauty does not work for compensation and is, therefore, so much surer of its reward. The greatest compensation I know for beauty or anything else is in our inner consciousness. Beauty cannot beget foulness upon this soil, nor foulness beauty.*[17]

Whatever their ideological disagreements, poor Herbert was left in Boston coping with the repercussions of Day's æsthetic choices. In that summer of 1894, as we know, Fred went off to England to meet Beardsley, to pursue Wilde at dinner parties, and to become the closest of friends with Frederick Evans, who shared books and photography with him. He attended meetings of the Society for Psychical Research, and negotiated with John Lane for *Salomé* and *The Yellow Book. The Yellow Book,* a journal in book form, had been Aubrey Beardsley's idea. He and his friend Henry Harland had put John Lane up to bringing out 'the most interesting, unusual, and important publication ever undertaken. It will be charming, it will be daring, it will be distinguished.'[18] And it was, with writers like Henry James and artists like Walter Sickert contributing. In reality, its reputation was far more daring than its actual contents, with the possible exception of some of Beardsley's wilder drawings.

By the following May, *Salomé* and *The Yellow Book* had been published on both sides of the Atlantic. The only accommodation to Boston's sensibilities was the modest expunging, on the title page, of the Herm of Pan's penis. Despite this precaution, the general response in Boston was complete shock. Copeland hastened to inform his partner about the uproar.

> *The Critic gave a very bad notice of Salome, and a dangerous one in a way – for it hints that the book is both blasphemous and nasty as to pictures. I hope no one will pick us up. . . . Nothing very exciting has happened but I feel all the time as if something were going to happen usually that I shall be in jail for 'Salome' or that we smash all up. Probably this comes*

'The Climax' – Beardsley's illustration of Wilde's quintessential castrating female, Salomé, 1893.

from the unaccustomed sense of responsibility and as regards 'Salome,' a guilty conscience.[19]

Even the Boston Public Library instantly secreted the horrifying *Salomé*.

Lee tells me they have put Salome under lock and key in the 'Inferno' – terrible thought! I don't see much excuse for that action, but the more I see of the book the filthier I think it is —— [20]

Herbert also reported, with mixed feelings, that *The Yellow Book* was enjoying huge sales, and that he had been forced to order additional copies. 'I'm sure that when Beardsley disclaims any evil intentions in "Salome," ' wrote Herbert de-

Two pages from Beardsley's *Le Morte d'Arthur* revealing the strong influence of Japanese prints.

spondently, 'he adds lying to his other bad manners. If no more proof than the face of things is necessary, it seems to me we have it in the Marquis de Sade, Zola, etc. I'm sure he is a low-minded person.'[21] Copeland could hardly contain himself. He rushed off letter after letter to London by steamship.

> *. . . Beardsley himself I'm convinced is a low unspeakable person – the most excuseless thing of filth yet discovered is in the beautiful photogravure frontispiece to the Mort D'Arthur' – a thing about which there is no possibility of mistake or dispute. I wish we had never had anything of him. I'm seriously afraid that it will compromise all our future books for some time – he and the 'Yellow Abomination' combined. Don't on your life get him to do anything for it.*[22]

Day, who was busy reviewing the London Salon Exhibition of Photography, and enlarging his acquaintance with the English photographers as well as the publishing crowd, paid little heed.

Considering that within ten years of this episode Herbert Copeland became an overt homosexual, it is touching to read his pleas to Day to maintain distance from the Decadents. Fred was actually contemplating sitting for a Beardsley portrait.

> *Don't let Beardsley draw you. I think it would be
> compromising now to have him see one and Heaven
> only knows what he might do in a sketch—even if
> not in the one he sold you – he might make another
> . . . which you would not see – It is with fear and
> trembling that I await the Yellow Book with its this
> time 24 pictures and fifty more pages – I hope in so
> public a thing AB will be decent but I fear.*[23]

Copeland also tried to persuade Day to reject further Decadent
literature, especially after the response to Wilde's eccentric
poem, *The Sphinx,* a luxurious item printed in red, green, and
black.

> *Don't think we'd better take Wilde's 'Ingenious His-
> tory of Mr. W.H.' unless we can first see the proofs.
> I'm really afraid we have a bad reputation as I find
> some people take the Decadent wrong and everyone
> naturally takes 'Salome' wrong and if we have to
> keep 'The Sphinx' that is not pretty – I guess we'd
> better cut out Oscar and Aubrey – they're a rotten
> pair . . .*[24]

One can only wonder what Herbert meant by taking *Salomé* or
Cram's *The Decadent* 'wrong.' What was involved in taking
them 'right'? Perhaps Copeland was more sensitive – or perhaps
Day could more easily accept a new style of art. As a disciple of
Wilde, he truly believed that the enjoyment of art lay beyond
morality. Certainly he had a better sense of posterity, for among
Copeland and Day's writers and illustrators, few are more
highly regarded today than Beardsley, or more famous than
Oscar Wilde.

There was more justice in Louise Guiney's intense dislike
of Wilde. She found him not only sassy and pretentious, but
violently anti-woman. What she saw in Beardsley despite his
horrifying females is beyond conjecture, unless it was his illness
and helplessness. But several critics of the nineties suggest there
was a serious split in the psyche of that decade, especially in
the symbolist art which had so wide an influence.

> *At one extreme we find woman as the embodiment of
> purity (in the virgin) or of selfless maternity. At the
> other she appears as the lustful destroyer, as Eve the
> temptress, as Salomé, as a sphinx, a harpy, a siren
> and a vampire.*[25]

Several explanations for this violent antithesis may shed some light on Fred Day's psychological development. The increasing freedom of women, the pressure for the vote, the refusal of wives to remain in the role of dependent chattel, the example of femmes fatales like Sarah Bernhardt who mocked Victorian conventions – all these were disruptive to the stable, severely repressive patriarchal society. It is Fraser Harrison's notion that the formerly confident upper-class Victorian male began to falter in the nineties:

> *The threats and demands represented by the ever ac-*
> *celerating movement toward female emancipation on*
> *all fronts seems to have unnerved and unbalanced*
> *this group of men and driven them to seek comfort*
> *and oblivion in homosexuality, prostitution, addiction*
> *to alcohol and opiates, sterile relationships with chil-*
> *dren, and, in some cases, forlorn celibacy.*[26]

Undoubtedly one way to revenge one's trembling ego would be to turn to love of other men. But it seems psychologically simplistic to try to explain away the paradoxical misogyny of writers like Wilde, whose doting mother had dressed him, in typical Victorian manner, as a girl, and whose many female friends adored him, not only as a famous writer but as a trusted confidant.

Given his inclination to idolize Wilde and admire Beardsley, it is perhaps surprising that Fred Holland Day was not a misogynist. Many of his first successes as a photographer depended on his empathy with women, as well as his ability to enhance their idiosyncrasies. He had no simpering, shallow ideal of womankind; rather, his women subjects were revealed as strong and unique. Many times he sought out Near Eastern and Mediterranean types, whom he dressed in Algerian, Moroccan, and Turkish costumes, or draped in stunning white fabrics whose folds were sculptural affirmations of the female form (plates 1, 2, 3, 4). He had a fine eye for the way light blazes through yellow hair, or the way a leopard skin contrasts richly with diaphanous veils (plate 6). And it was a portrait of a woman that won him the attention of the Linked Ring. Unfortunately, there were still such strict prohibitions against photographing the female nude in America that Day attempted very few.

Day's sympathy with women was evident not only in his early photography but in his publishing, and his courtesy to older

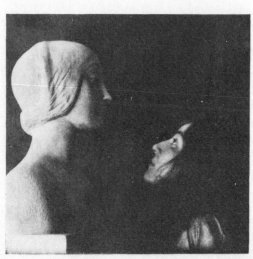

The Question.

A Study.

Melancholia.

Three portraits of the same model, sometimes called 'Pepita,' by F. Holland Day, published in *Godey's Magazine* in 1898.

women. This makes it perhaps more difficult to assess Day's regard for Oscar Wilde, who, like J. K. Huysmans, had sworn to rid fiction of all women and mawkish love stories. It makes it even harder to assess his increasing fascination with homosexuality.

Wilde's own love story was proceeding quickly. By 1894 he no longer hid his infatuation for Lord Douglas, who, in fact, offered a volume of his own poems to Copeland and Day. Thanking Bosie for the pleasures of having dined with him and Wilde in Soho that summer, Day wrote the young aristocrat a carefully worded rejection. Wilde, meanwhile, was writing passionate letters that found their way into the hands of blackmailers. The unhappy affair was brought into court in 1895,

Cover of the first issue of *The Yellow Book,* published jointly by John Lane and Copeland and Day, 1894.

when Wilde sued Lord Queensberry, Bosie's father, for libel over an accusation of sodomy. When Wilde, in an astonishingly self-destructive act, permitted himself to be arrested, he was seen being carried off to the police station with a large volume bound in yellow under one arm. The press reported this fact, and John Lane's publishing offices were stoned. Wilde had not been carrying Beardsley's *The Yellow Book,* but a copy of Pierre Louys's *Aphrodite,* bound, like most French novels, in brilliant yellow. But the damage had been done.

'It killed the Yellow Book . . . and it nearly killed me,' John Lane later observed.[27] Copeland and Day were fortunate to be in America, but even there the repercussions were enormous. When Wilde was sentenced to two years in prison, the precious boys and youths like hyacinths (as he liked to call them) dove for cover, grew mustaches, and were seen playing rugged sports.[28] Several of the English aristocracy actually left for the safety of France. The downfall of Wilde was an international scandal of such proportions that it shattered the Decadent movement. The cry for Beardsley's skin went up immediately. Many authors who had promised to contribute to *The Yellow Book* announced that it was either them or Beardsley. John Lane was forced to sack Beardsley, who went off to begin the last phase of his short life seriously impoverished.

The impact on Copeland and Day was considerable. John Lane established a New York office in 1896. *The Yellow Book* died of attrition – and for want of the excitement of Beardsley's drawings – in April 1897. By then, Beardsley was terminally ill, and was being courted openly by a famous and wealthy homosexual, Marc-André Raffalovich, who had recently converted to Catholicism. He persuaded Beardsley, too, to convert, promising him financial support if he did. One year later, on March 16, 1898 (a few months short of his twenty-sixth birthday), the astonishing and provocative genius of Beardsley was gone.

Fred Holland Day was in Boston when news of Beardsley's death was published. Shocked and grieved, he and Louise Guiney decided to commemorate his death. Day favored a solemn high mass in his honor. Louise had been loyal to Beardsley, convinced that he had been maligned by false rumors. Yet she knew Boston, and she knew the Catholic community. Some of the Catholic laity were already opposed to any mass at all for such a heretic, and Louise had to exercise great tact in moderating Day's demands. She even sought aid from her good friend

Portrait of Lionel Johnson in his Oxford University gown, before 1890.

Oscar Wilde in evening dress, by Napoleon Sarony, 1882.

Lionel Johnson, who 'loved Beardsley. Knew him well, and will be able, as a fellow-convert, to tell what made the latter come into the Church. I hope we shall get something truly interesting, as well as authentic.'[29] Louise obviously was unfamiliar with the details of Beardsley's conversion, and was, as usual, being amazingly naive about Lionel Johnson.

Day had always relied upon Louise's knowledge of Catholic ritual to guide him into correct procedures. She advised him copiously. Seeing how melancholy he had become over Beardsley's death, she offered him books like Saint Francis's *Little Flowers*. Finally, Fred accepted the idea of a 'low' requiem mass, and it was duly celebrated on April 23, 1898. The invitations caused such an uproar that Louise became seriously frightened and dismayed. Day insisted that Beardsley had lived a life of vice only in his imagination (as perhaps he himself had been indulging), and Louise promised to write an exculpatory article. The article was never written, but the episode made a vivid impact on Fred Day. A few months later he committed himself to his sacred subjects, after a period of fasting and complete isolation.

As for Oscar Wilde, the former Sun God dabbled briefly in photography himself, after his imprisonment. In his usual paradoxical way, he noted, 'Cows are very fond of being photographed, and, unlike architecture, don't move.'[30] He visited for a time with the Baron von Glœdon, a photographer of 'Sicilian youths "noble and nude and antique." '[31] Incorrigible to the end, apparently: von Glœdon's pictures catered to pederastic tastes, although they had been reproduced, in all innocence, by several American photographic and literary journals.

When Oscar Wilde died on November 30, 1900, F. Holland Day was in London. He had become one of the most famous photographers in the Western world. It was ironic that conservatives and adherents of 'naturalistic photography' labeled Day 'the leader of the Oscar Wilde School.'[32] It was meant as an insult, to damn him with affectation and intellectuality, not necessarily to calumniate him as homosexual. It was purely an æsthetic condemnation. What his sex life was, nobody could tell, for he had never flirted with making public his preferences in the manner of Oscar Wilde. But Day would not have denied the influence. He had learned from Wilde and the æsthetes to believe in Art and Beauty, Imagination and Artifice, ideals not yet accepted by many critics of photography.

Portrait of Alfred Stieglitz by
Gertrude Käsebier, 1902.

7

Mr. Stieglitz Takes Notice

The æsthetic ideologies to which F. Holland Day gave his complete loyalty in the 1890s were in direct conflict with the notions that had governed photography for five decades. He came to photography at the historic moment when it was attempting to become 'Art,' and he was destined to become one of the most controversial proponents of this recurring idea.

Previously, there had been somewhat abortive attempts to place photography securely within the hierarchy of the fine arts; these attempts included the 'blur beautiful' of Julia Margaret Cameron, who had persuaded all manner of famous writers to pose for her in sheets, gauzes, and other mock-Arthurian garb. There had been the ambitious tableaux, composites of tasteful nudes and moralizing elders, of Oscar Rejlander. And, of course, there had been hordes of genre scenes characterized by teary sentiment, farmer's daughter suggestiveness, and rollicking peasantry. The problem was that no one was quite sure what might elevate photography from merely a recording medium to the level of imagination that presumably marked easel painting. An equally fundamental difficulty was that painting had degenerated into academic exercises featuring pseudoclassical gods and goddesses (tantalizingly nude behind diaphonous

veils), bathetic Bible motifs, or homely cottage scenes where
pale waifs endured the scrutiny of the village doctor.

Photographs imitated the subject matter of the Pre-
Raphælites, with unwittingly hilarious effects like Henry Peach
Robinson's turgid *Lady of Shalott* of 1861. But as the Barbizon
painters, and then the Impressionists, began to influence ideas
of both style and subject matter, a considerable improvement in
photographic ideals occurred, at least in the area of landscape
photography. In 1889, taking his cue from the Impressionists,
Peter Henry Emerson offered the following dictum in his influential book, *Naturalistic Photography:* 'Wherever the artist has
been true to nature, art has been good; wherever the artist has
neglected nature and followed his imagination there has resulted bad art. Nature, then, should be the artist's standard.'[1]

Since Oscar Wilde had stated categorically that nature
imitated art – thus making him one of the first philosophers to
recognize selective perception – it was inevitable that there
would be a serious split between the two major camps of photography. The æsthetes were together (more or less) on one
side; the factualists and documentarians were on the other.

To the traditionalists, a beautiful print was one that possessed good technical quality, edge-to-edge sharpness, and subject matter understandable by any viewer. To Emerson, a beautiful photograph imitated the diffusiveness of natural vision,
avoiding the harsh contours of the daguerreotype. To Henry
Peach Robinson, a beautiful photograph had sentiment and
painterly composition. To Alfred Stieglitz in the 1880s, a beautiful photograph imitated the compositional effects, peasant
subjects, and genre scenes of German Barbizon painters like
Max Liebermann. In the 1890s, he shifted his ground to the
Impressionists, creating some of his first masterpieces, including
Paula, The Terminal, and *Wet Day on the Boulevards;* at the
same time, he clung to the homely glimpses of mothers and
children so dear to his German masters. In the twentieth century, Stieglitz once again learned from what was happening in
painting and followed the Modernist, Cubist, Abstractionist
lines, greatly to his and photography's benefit.

But to F. Holland Day, none of these proved to be useful
models. Never a landscapist, he could not follow Emerson. No
matter how he admired Robinson, that master's posed bucolic
tableaux and soap-opera deathbed scenes were inimical to his
sophisticated personality. Stieglitz's handsomely posed, pseudo-

Scurrying Home, by Alfred
Stieglitz, 1894. One of his most
popular pictures of this decade.

spontaneous portraits of mothers and children, or Dutch peas-
ants scurrying along beaches, were respected by Day but not
particularly admired for their æsthetic achievements, although
they were almost always technically daring. Nor could subjects
like Stieglitz's sweated horses steaming in the snow attract Day.
Like Balzac, he cared only for the individual human being.
During the 1890s, Day seemed dominated by three aspects of
photography: the control of dramatic lights and darks, the psychology of an attractive sitter, and a combined mystery and
exoticism bordering on dreamlike states of intensity. Some of
his female subjects were so intensely observed that they resembled captured butterflies fixed on the glass of his lens. He had
gone far beyond the easy sentimentality, absurd posturing, and
quick outdoor impressionism of his own time, back to the man-
nerists, to the baroque painters, and ultimately, to the rational
dramas of the Renaissance. Yet, because he did not dress many
of his models in the costumes of those prior periods, the mixture
of contemporaneity and powerful composition was like nothing
ever before seen in photography. The only photographs that
bore even a remote resemblance were those in the so-called
Rembrandt chiaroscuro. The only paintings that some of his
exotic models resembled were those of the romantic Delacroix.

That is not to say he did not lapse into his own absurdities
from time to time, or border on the obscure as he pursued high
themes from classical antiquity. But nothing Day did, with the
single and major exception of the sacred subjects of 1898, ever
quite equalled the foolishness of, say, Joseph T. Keiley, ad-

Evening, by F. Holland Day,
about 1896, imitating a painting
by Flandrin.

mired by Stieglitz, whose notion of drama in photography was to take pictures of actors dressed in their costumes for plays. On the other hand, Day never achieved the sense of imaginative freedom of textures which Frank Eugene, one of the greatest of the Stieglitz circle, enjoyed in pictures like *The Horse,* where direct manipulation of the negative achieved a bold etching effect.

Day was not only a practitioner in search of high art ideals; he was also a campaigner. If we judge by his articles in *Camera Notes,* he was adroit and direct in his responses to the typical traditionalist belittling of photography. Could photography be considered an art when the camera was merely a mechanical device? Of course: the camera operator had control of light, environment, ambience, and choice of lens. Could a photographer be said to partake of an artistic style? Could a photographer have a unique style? Of course: the photographer used his imagination to preconceive what the final effect of his labors would be. But how could a photographer exercise imagination if the mechanical device simply recorded what was in front of it? Simple: follow three rules.

> *1st, Do not permit the ease with which the thing before you may be reproduced to lead you into reproducing poor things. 2d, Permit yourself to read absolutely nothing relative to the technical production of photographs. By observing this dictum one's mind is kept free from being dogged by the errors of others, and more susceptible to the influences of his own errors and achievements, which are of the greatest value and the only means by which any true knowledge may be obtained regarding the possibilities of the camera. 3d, Become a student and lover of art if you wish to produce it . . .*[2]

The first dictum would have been accepted by anyone. The second was the foulest heresy. The traditionalists, particularly in England, had spent so many years sweating away under the restrictions of limited techniques that it was infuriating even to suspect that their shared experience might count for nothing. The third suggestion seems hardly controversial, yet, as Gertrude Käsebier was to discover, photographers were expected to have technical training, not art-school preparation. Day advocated such preparation in the strongest terms.

*To suppose it is possible with the aid of a camera to
concoct a landscape without previous knowledge of
method and effects of Dürer, Leonardo, Troyon,
Corot and Constable, were on the face of it hopeless;
and on the more difficult and less successful side of
figure work an intimate knowledge of line and composition is even more necessary to the man behind
the camera. And this knowledge cannot be obtained
through attention devoted to the photographic representations so generally circulated, but must be obtained directly from past masters of their craft –
Memling, Rembrandt, del Sarto, Velásquez, Titian,
Rossetti. The list cannot be too large or the knowledge too intimate. By tying one's self down to such a
system, and only by so doing, will the art of the camera ever be justified in the eyes of those whose ap-
plause we care for.*[3]

A Whistleresque portrait by
F. Holland Day, after 1900.

This manifesto would certainly have won the approbation
of Henry Peach Robinson, dean of English art photography,
whose handbooks on art composition for photographers ran into
many editions. Day's approach, when followed too literally, led
to photographs that precisely imitated the subjects, poses, and
light scales of the Dutch and Italian masters, adding nothing at
all of the photographer's own imagination. Yet Day was implying, as had Robinson before him, that the world would discount
the art of photography until it could compete with the grand
effects of painting.

For Day, there seemed little danger in following his own
prescriptions. To study the masters in portraiture simply meant
incorporating their lessons on composition, chiaroscuro, design,
light, background and foreground detail, and the all-important
psychology of the pose. The painters he admired were many,
yet his æsthetic judgment was actually quite slow to appreciate
the decorative moderns epitomized by Whistler. In 1889, for
example, he had written to Gertrude Savage that the titillating
near pornographies of Adolphe William Bouguéreau, a popular
French academician, had much caught his fancy. 'The Love
and Psyche was in the Salon and a most wonderful thing. He
is surely a good head above all other French artists of today and
possibly of any other day.'[4] The following spring, in 1890, during his six-month stay in New York, Day spent a good deal of

time studying the traditional graphic-arts media. Typically, to
Louise he wrote:

> *My Bestest Mater!*
> *There is an exhibition of Whistler's etchings, draw-*
> *ings, and a few paintings now going on at the Grolier*
> *Club – I never could quite appreciate it all by myself*
> *and hardly suppose I ever shall now. I'm too old to*
> *learn new tricks as that. It requires far too much dex-*
> *terity of eye to wander among his 'Harmonies' and*
> *'Nocturnes.'*[5]

He was all of twenty-six, and already finding himself 'too
old'. This letter is especially ironic considering that in a very
few years a critic would write of his work: 'In his bold treatment
of light his work reminds us of Whistler . . . while Chavannes
comes to mind when studying the symbolism of some of Mr.
Day's compositions.'[6]

Artists often reject outright the first glimpse of the art that
causes them to re-evaluate their own æsthetic tastes. Shortly
afterward, as in Hollywood movies, the rejection turns into a
passionate embrace. Day's early pictures were recognized as 'so
utterly different from any other photographer's that we must
turn to the painters for a comparison.'[7] As noted earlier, many
of these portraits were of young women in exotic costumes and
enigmatic poses, in which 'the richness and depth of his shadows, in some cases violently contrasted and in others delicately
modulated, shows him to be a disciple of the Rembrandt school
of chiaroscuro.'[8] There was nothing of the potted palm, baroque half-column, velvet drape, and painted backdrop of the
commercial studios in any of his portraits.

It would be comforting if we could establish a firm chro-
nology of F. Holland Day's early portraits, but he did not begin
to date his pictures with any regularity until about 1898, and
any studio notebooks which he might have kept were lost forever in a catastrophic fire in 1904. If we do not know precisely
the name of his camera, or, indeed, his precise working methods, we do know the name and date of the picture which won
his election to the most distinguished photographic society of
the decade. A critique written in 1898 notes that

> *Mr. Day does not work often in highlights; and yet,*
> *what is certainly one of his finest pictures is very lib-*

Hannah, the portrait that won Day election to the Linked Ring Brotherhood in 1895.

erally illuminated. This is the picture that got him his election to the Linked Ring. The study called 'Hannah' is surely one of the masterpieces of photography. Besides the great technical cleverness shown in the achievement of desired effects, the spirituality of the thing is overwhelming. A whole novel is compressed into that meagre figure and in that face, pallid and lean with asceticism and resignation. The unity of all the details of costume, pose, and lighting, and the simple forcefulness of the pathos of the saintly woman are nothing short of great art.[9]

Fortunately for posterity (for the print is gone), the journal in

Mrs. Potter by F. Holland Day,
1896.

which these praises appeared reproduced a considerable number of Day's pre–1895 pictures. *Hannah* was not in his Rembrandtesque mood, but much more resembled the lighting he
used later for pictures like *The White Cap, 1899.*

Perhaps his best-known and most popular portrait of the
mid years of 1894 to 1896 was *The Gainsborough Hat,* a handsome rendering of his successful poster designer, Ethel Reed,
who also favored him with many other striking poses (plates
1, 5).

He had always loved the theatre, and now he often pursued actresses to serve as models for his camera. As his Boston
reputation grew, they in turn began to pursue him, and his
small, square studio, equipped with both northern and southern
exposures,[10] grew in notoriety. His photographic attentions to
one such actress, Mrs. Potter, in December 1894 or January
1895, brought down Louise Guiney's teasing wrath.

> *Why photograph Mrs. Potter? She's a pretty woman,
> and is clad bewitchin', I know, in that play. But any-
> body can photograph an actress. I want to keep your
> camera 'high and aloof,' sacred to inspired non-
> professionals with unstudied charms.*[11]

Meaning herself, undoubtedly. When *Mrs. Potter* was later
shown in a private exhibition, the *Boston Journal* effused, 'for
exquisite softness and generous grace [it] is like unto a portrait
of a young woman that in the treatment of light and shade suggests a love-illuminated, love-glorified face seen in a strange and
anxious dream.'[12]

Day's interest in the theatrical effect was duly noted, not
always with approval. Sadakichi Hartmann seemed to be of
two minds:

> *There is no photographer who can pose the human
> body better than he, who can make a piece of drapery
> fall more poetically, or arrange flowers in a man or
> woman's hair more artistically. He would have made
> (seriously speaking) an excellent manager of the su-
> pers of a dramatic company like the Saxon-Meininger
> [sic]. . . . There are passages in his portraits which are
> exquisite, but all his representations lack simplicity
> and naturalness. He has set himself to get painter's
> results, and that is from my view-point not legitimate.*

Young woman in Moorish headdress, by F. Holland Day, about
1894.

*He has pushed lyricism in portraiture as far as it can
be without deteriorating into a mannerism; even his
backgrounds speak a language of their own, vibrant
with rhythm and melody; they are aglow in the dark-
est vistas. Day is indisputably the most ambitious and
accomplished of our American portrait photographers.*[13]

As the novelists say, we anticipate; this commentary was not
written until 1899. It indicates the advantages of the painterly
approach and some of the dangers.

Day was fortunate in his models. There was nothing coy
about his young females, either in his pictures or in real life.
They could occasion the strongest responses from viewers: 'one
Italian face explains the origin of mariolatry.'[14] But who the
model was for the much-admired *Hannah,* or how this portrait
came to win him membership in the Linked Ring Brotherhood,
is not entirely clear. We do know for certain that the picture

Tow-headed girl on leopard skin,
by F. Holland Day, about 1895.

was produced in 1894, when Day's work came to the attention
of George Davison, one of the founders of the Brotherhood who
had been much applauded for his impressionistic landscapes.

The Links, as they called themselves, began as a group of
English cameramen, Davison and Henry Peach Robinson
among them. In 1892 they decided to establish a society for the
advancement of photography as art. They had no firmly established dogma about what might constitute 'pictorial' photography, and no restrictions on what printing techniques were
acceptable, but they all adhered to one shibboleth. Ordinary
silver-chloride prints were unsuitable as wall decorations. Anything that could overcome the dual abominations of sharp focus
and shiny paper was welcome.[15] Blurring, differential focus à
la Cameron or Emerson, use of the rich density of photogravure

Portrait of a young woman, by
F. Holland Day, about 1895.

Pepita, second version, by
F. Holland Day, about 1895.

inks, the velvet silvery-grey softness of the new platinum papers, special lenses, printing on coarse-grained papers were all acceptable.

The advent of new technology made the artistic ambitions of the Links more easily attainable. This was the gum-bichromate process, popularized in 1894 by the French photographer Robert Demachy. The gum print required the application of materials by hand, and permitted manipulation in a wide variety of methods from overlaying to scratching, brushing, and masking. If the artist's hand could now be seen as intervening in the photographic process, the last objection to photography's being considered an art was finally overcome, or so it was hoped. Gum printing was widely adopted by the pictorialists, and led to a decade dominated by the direct imitation of the traditional graphic arts.

F. Holland Day did not pursue this sometimes heavy handed manipulation with the same fervor as his colleagues. He began his career with sepia-toned silver prints, progressed to carbon prints for permanency and richer blacks, and came to rely loyally on two processes: the straight platinum print, or Platinotype, and the glycerine-platinum print alternating with the gum-platinum print, a method he helped to advance. Both glycerine- and gum-platinum permitted delicate manipulations. Platinum paper, in fact, became an absolute necessity to many other photographers as well. Its subdued range of tones, its absolute permanence, and its velvet texture resembled muted mezzotints. Like gum bichromate, this paper guaranteed a graphic-arts quality equal to mezzotint, aquatint, and etching. Both gum-bichromate and gum-platinum prints provided an opportunity for considerable autographic directness of creation.

George Bernard Shaw, writing about some gum portraits of himself by Frederick Evans, accurately revealed the impact of these new processes.

> *Compare them with the best work with pencil, crayon, brush or silver-point you can find – with Holbein's finest Tudor drawings, with Rembrandt's 'Saskia,' with Velásquez' 'Admiral,' with anything you like – if you cannot see at a glance that the old game is up, that the camera has hopelessly beaten the pencil and the paintbrush as an instrument of artistic representation, then you will never make a true critic.*[16]

Left: *Study of a Baby* by Alfred
Stieglitz, about 1899; right: his
famous *The Net-Mender* of
1898, both from *Camera Notes*.

But there were others who were not convinced that the
essence of photography should lie in imitation. To Peter Henry
Emerson, the controversial advocate of differential focus, for example, the new, manipulated prints were abominations. A force-
ful prophet of what we now call 'straight' photography, it was
Emerson's example which encouraged Stieglitz, Day's greatest
rival, in the art of a spontaneous response to nature, and the
directness of the snapshot.

One can hardly tell from reading the biographies of Alfred
Stieglitz that he ever had a major rival, or that he several times
dallied with glycerine and gum prints and other manipulated
'abominations.' His deviations from the path of unmanipulated
photography, like other inconvenient facts, have simply disappeared. We know of them primarily through reproductions in
the photographic journals. A concatenation of circumstances,
and probably overt malice, eventually connived to make it appear as if Stieglitz – alone in America – had made the sow's ear
of photography into the silk purse of art.

The Links were in no hurry to accept Stieglitz into their
ranks, despite his enviable international reputation, achieved
by patiently submitting prints to competitions and salons. Indeed, in 1893, George Davison politely suggested that his work
was not quite satisfactory. The following year, however, Stieglitz was elected to membership, with another American of equal
distinction, Rudolf Eickemeyer, and was invited to participate

A Study by F. Holland Day, 1898, from *Camera Notes*.

in the annual Salon for 1894. It chanced that both Stieglitz and F. Holland Day were present in London in the summer of 1894, but they failed to meet, although they were both pursuing various members of the Brotherhood. Stieglitz was on his honeymoon; Day was dedicating the memorial to Keats at Hampstead, and becoming further acquainted with Frederick Evans and Aubrey Beardsley. When Stieglitz hurried back to New York even before the Salon opened to the public, Day was still in London and most certainly stayed to see the new prints and to enlarge his knowledge of the English photographers as a group. It may even have happened that he was carrying a portfolio of prints in his luggage, as we know that Davison saw Day's work. In April 1895, Davison wrote excitedly to Stieglitz, who, as one of the first American Links, had been encouraged to seek out new talent.

I have happened on one excellent artist . . . Mr Day (a publisher of Boston). We are promised a selection of his work this next time, the first show he has participated in. I don't expect he cares much for the ordinary kind of exhibition.[17]

That was certainly true. Although he had joined the Boston Camera Club in 1889, Day avoided the annual local competitions, preferring to have intimate showings of his prints at his own studio or at the homes of friends and would-be patrons. He had professional as well as temperamental reasons. His magnificent decorative prints had no place among the stereotyped scenes of domesticity – pussycats in infants' laps or picturesque country lanes. He was also experimenting with male nudes, and may have recognized that the time had not yet come to show these without shocking Boston beyond endurance.

Stieglitz responded to Davison's note with enthusiasm, seeking out Day almost immediately. They did not meet in person for several years, although Day continually invited Stieglitz to Boston and Norwood, but carried on a friendly correspondence until 1900. At the point of Day's election to the Links, in 1895, Stieglitz saw himself as an elder statesman encouraging the younger generation. But the fact was that both he and Day were born in 1864. One cannot help wondering if Stieglitz, despite his vaunted generosity, was not unnerved by how easily Day leapt from obscurity to prestigious recognition from the Links. Unlike Stieglitz, Day had not strained, politicked, competed, or hurried after fame. And Day was unmistakably an original.

Day was immediately perceived as a genius in the new art of photography. After seeing his work for the first time, Rudolf Eickemeyer came away in a state of shock. He wrote to Stieglitz that Day stood alone and unique among contemporary photographers, that he had 'hewn his way through a virgin forest.'[18] It was as if Day had suddenly crystalized the 'art' of art photography and had synthesized all the ambitions of the would-be pictorialists into one miraculous vision.

That Day did this while disdaining technical matters that had obsessed Stieglitz for a decade was all the more amazing, especially since he had been simultaneously involved with his publishing activities. Becoming the third American member of the Linked Ring Brotherhood only a year after Stieglitz was quite an accomplishment; both Käsebier and Clarence White would wait until 1900 for their election. And that Day's was the first American photography collected by Stieglitz was, at this moment in Day's career, the absolute pinnacle of recognition. Yet his best work lay ahead.

Stieglitz, as the best-known American photographer of the mid-nineties, apparently felt no threat as yet. Day's accomplishments only buttressed his own position as the ultimate American arbiter of what was good and bad in photography. Since Stieglitz had been outspoken in his distaste for most American work, the discovery and publication of Day could only be turned to his credit. Stieglitz had been on the editorial board of the *American Amateur Photographer* since 1893, leaving that position in 1896 when he was chastised for interfering with the way amateur exhibitions had been organized for nearly a decade. Stieglitz was trying to establish high standards amid the general mediocrity of those exhibitions. No sooner had he succeeded in creating the Camera Club of New York from two earlier organizations than he established himself as editor of a new journal, *Camera Notes*. It was a logical move to invite F. Holland Day to become one of the journal's first regular contributors, and it was through the pages of *Camera Notes* that Day's unusual images and revolutionary theories came to the attention of the American public.

8

A Purely Greek Point of View

It may have shocked some of the subscribers to *Camera Notes* to open the October 1897 issue and discover one of the first pictures taken in the United States that ennobled a black American. Here was a vigorous, uncompromising young male, regally draped in a striped North African robe, crowned with a headdress of black pigeon wings. He gripped a staff in one hand and with the other held back the robe to reveal a serene body naked to the navel. It was one of the first photographic embodiments of the idea that 'Black is beautiful.'

The photographer, of course, was F. Holland Day; the model, young Alfred Tanneyhill, Day's chauffeur and servant. *An Ethiopian Chief* (plate 10) was one of the first in a Nubian series that Day produced and Stieglitz acquired for his own collection. Tanneyhill, the model for all of them, had a self-possession which suited Day's decorative objectives perfectly. A few racist comments appeared in the press: 'Mr. Day's Ethiopian studies show how barbarically picturesque a negro model can be made with judicious costuming and careful posing.'[1]

Costuming was certainly one of Day's outstanding talents. One reviewer was fascinated by the mysterious effectiveness of simple props like the pigeon's wings. Equally fascinating was Day's skill with skin tones.

An Ethiopian Chief, the first of
Day's Nubian series, reproduced
in *Camera Notes,* October 1897.

*All these figures are more or less undraped, and not
the least praiseworthy feature of Mr. Day's art is his
refined treatment of the nude. There is not the slightest suggestion of nakedness in any of his numerous
studies in which undraped figures occur, and yet no
photographer has ever given the varying values and
multitudinous gradation of flesh tones with such appreciation, sympathy and truth.*[2]

African Chief (plate 9) was even more daringly undraped
than *An Ethiopian Chief.* There are several versions of this
subject; Tanneyhill was apparently entirely naked, but grace-
fully observed the genital proprieties. His black skin contrasted
magnificently with an elaborate chest-and-navel ornament resembling the cicatrices of body scarring, and his hair was bound
by an Algerian or Moorish silver headpiece. Seated in a chair
covered by a leopard skin, and lighted as if through a low doorway, he is majestic and hieratic.

These ornaments were motifs which Day repeatedly employed, not only in his Nubian series but in a few female
nudes, many portraits of 'exotic' women – culled from the South
End of Boston – and, later, in his pagan idylls in Maine. For
several pictures in the Nubian series, Delacroix may have inspired Day's mood, but the final effect suggested the sculptural
strength of Géricault, particularly in the strong side lighting
and the dramatic depth of shadow. Day was pushing further in
his exploration of what the camera could capture, and what
platinum papers could transmit, of subjects offering extremely
difficult contrasts between white and black, light and shadow,
mass and detail.

That exploration became most evident in pictures like *The
Smoker* (plate 12), where the white homespun Moorish robe
is deliberately contrasted with skin darkened in shadow. But
the masterwork of this series was unquestionably the extraordinary *Ebony and Ivory* (plate 11), which Stieglitz reproduced
in photogravure for *Camera Notes*[3] in July 1898. Here Tanneyhill is naked, seated on a leopard skin placed on the floor,
his right arm and left leg making two apposite V shapes. With
their strong diagonals these support a small plaster statuette of
a Roman god with spear. It was one of the many Brucciani reproductions Day owned. The striking contrast between the brilliant white statuette and the mysterious and evocative darks of
the picture made it a sensation.

Above: *Ebony and Ivory;* below:
The Smoker, by F. Holland Day,
1897.

When Day sent him the print for reproduction, Stieglitz was impressed; Day noted that this print was a gift, and was 'the most beautiful in tone which ever came from the negative.'[4] Although he was said to do almost no darkroom work himself, relying on supervision of commercial houses, Day knew exactly what he expected of print quality. *Ebony and Ivory* was universally admired. Even Joseph Keiley, who would elsewhere show Day no reverence, was much taken with the photograph when he reviewed Day's contributions to the Philadelphia Salon of 1899.

> *Of all the pictures exhibited by Mr. Day, that entitled 'Ebony and Ivory' is the most thoroughly artistic, the most finished piece of work that he has ever done. Its tonal values are exquisitely harmonious, and in its conception it is distinctly Greek; indeed, it has but one fault that I can mention: The little ivory statuette is in too high a key of white for the subdued tones of the balance of the picture and is distinctly disturbing. Nevertheless, this is a minor fault, and the exquisite lines and modeling of the dusky figure, as it half emerges from its nocturnal background, are a source of constant pleasure . . .*[5]

To say that something was Greek in conception was not necessarily a compliment, however much the Victorians admired the ancient sculptures. Some of the first such comments came out of Day's extensive one-man show for the Camera Club of New York in February 1898. Here the reviewer for *Camera Notes* found that 'the highest evidence of his technique is his concealment and suppression of it . . . he has aimed throughout his work to suggest, not the mere beauty that delights the eye, but the grace which moves the intellectual and higher sensibilities as well.'[6] It was this appeal to the intellect which was accounted Greek, and it was not a quality calculated to make Day a crowd-pleaser.

The first one-man show at the Camera Club in New York featured much of Day's prodigious output during 1896 and 1897. The range of subjects was formidable. It included the Nubian series, elegant portraits of Chinese males in full costume and authentic setting, mythological subjects like 'the study entitled 'Hypnos,' in which Sleep is represented by an ephèbe with closed eyes, breathing the soporific odor of a

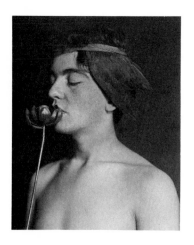

Hypnos, by F. Holland Day,
about 1896.

poppy,'[7] unforgettable portraits of young women in cleverly
arranged white draperies, outdoor studies of a tow-headed girl
in striking back light, and several 'undraped' males hiding their
sexual charms behind bushes and trees. Here for the first time
appeared one of Day's earliest attempts at sacred subjects, his
1896 *Entombment* with himself posed as the dead Christ. The
Savior is lying before his rocky tomb with Mary Magdalen
bowed weeping at his feet. Unusual as it was, it was not this
image of Christ which caught the attention of the critics, but a
pagan theme.

> *Near this remarkable picture [the* Entombment*] is an
> allegorical study, the subject of which is not indi-
> cated. In the absence of any key to the mystery, we
> might suppose the statuesque youthful figure, gazing
> intently from the picture, to symbolize the Genius of
> Greek Art inspired by the forces and phenomena of
> nature as they pass in vision before his eyes, a subject
> involving the ideal embodiment of an abstract
> creation . . .*[8]

We may never discover what prompted Day to combine
these two unrelated pictures, the *Entombment* and this tenta-
tively titled 'Genius of Greek Art,' into a display of a most unusual and controversial kind. When he exhibited these at the
Philadelphia Salon that fall, he had the 'Genius' placed in a
rounded, arched frame decorated with Greek pilasters, and the
Entombment placed below it in a matching frame. The legend
under the 'Genius of Greek Art' now read BEAUTY · IS ·
TRUTH : TRUTH BEAUTY : THAT IS/ALL · YE · KNOW · ON
EARTH · AND · ALL · YE · NEED · TO · KNOW (plate 14).
Among the rarest of Day's prints, the two together were now
making more than the 'ideal embodiment of an abstract crea-
tion'; they were making an ideological statement straight out of
Keats.

The contrast between the serious pagan figure and the
dead Christ is still bewildering and uncannily hypnotic. Was
Day agreeing with Keats that Beauty *was* Beauty because it
must die? Down-to-earth photographers found Day's mythological work unintelligible. In flagellating *Beauty Is Truth,* one
critic took out after the title itself as a starting point.

> *This is very high-sounding and may either be poetry
> or flapdoodle. Let us examine it. Truth is, according*

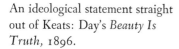

An ideological statement straight out of Keats: Day's *Beauty Is Truth,* 1896.

to modern ideas, what has been proved. On the other hand, beauty is admittedly indefinable.[9]

The editorial then proceeded with a great deal of its own flap-doodle and muddled philosophy.

Keiley, who had so admired *Ebony and Ivory,* was aghast at the pretensions of *Beauty Is Truth.* Almost despite himself, however, he seemed to capture what Day stood for: "the purely pagan idea so admirably illustrated by Petronius . . . that the enjoyment of refined, elegant, sensuous beauty alone was the highest purpose and motive of existence.'[10] He wondered if Day were trying to compare this notion, symbolized by the upper half of the twosome, with the lower, which might have been expressing 'the Christian teaching that man's one object in life was that of attaining spiritual perfection . . . even though he [would] have to face physical death in consequence.'[11]

Left: Day's *In Tanagra,* from *Godey's Magazine;* right: Youth with urn on head, both about 1896.

Keiley could not have known Day's speculations on the Rosicrucian equation of suffering with both beauty *and* spiritual perfection, and so his criticisms were more conventionally Christian in attitude.

> *It struck me as being rather characteristic of Mr. Day's style that the pagan idea was given the first place – for I have long felt that Mr. Day approached all of his subjects, whether representation of 'Christ' or such themes as* Ebony and Ivory, *from a purely Greek point of view [italics added], and that it is on that account that they rarely move the observer to any stronger feeling than that of a cold, intellectual admiration.*[12]

Most of the critics preferred subjects and treatments which elicited 'honest emotion.' Keiley, in particular, liked Gertrude Käsebier's early pictures, like *The Manger,* for perfectly understandable reasons: the subject and mood were both accessible. Some of Day's images, however, seemed as remote as the Hellenic world that had inspired them. His use of the Keats couplet indicates his recognition of the century-old battle between Truth and Beauty. When Peter Henry Emerson had used that couplet on the title page of his *Naturalistic Photography,*[13] it was because he believed that beauty was the result of truthfulness to nature. The Pictorialists, Day among them, were turning away from simplistic verisimilitude and realism to the work of the imagination. Not everyone could follow them there.

The avant-garde Pictorialists and the Links were more in touch with Day's ambitions than were his fellow Americans. They knew he was after a most difficult ideal, one which he could not always achieve. A. Horsley Hinton, a Link and a respected landscapist, compared Robert Demachy's sparkling Parisian joie de vivre with Day's sobriety.

> *Day on the other hand awakens less joyous emotions,*
> *and in his appeal to the sensibilities of his spectators*
> *touches a deeper chord. He makes one feel – Feel*
> *what? Well, I need not attempt to define. Has not*
> *my reader listened to music which has thrilled him*
> *through, and could he not have said that such and*
> *such music made him feel – Feel what? Simply this,*
> *it made him* feel![14]

Of Day's literary colleagues, neither his partner Herbert Copeland nor his 'bestest mater,' Louise, understood what he was doing, although they dutifully applauded his success. Perhaps only Francis Lee of *The Mahogany Tree* and Visionist days joined him in these new adventures, as he was becoming, with Fred Day's help, one of the better Pictorialist photographers. Louise continued to help in any way that she could. She was always on the lookout for suitable models, and during one of her first seasons in Maine, wrote him about the possibilities.

> *I think I have already caught a young model for you:*
> *a ten-year-old with large, rather foreign looking fea-*
> *tures, and first-rate black eyes, with lashes a yard*
> *long. When you see him, if you like him, you can*
> *bribe him to keep his hair uncut.*[15]

That would have been quite an enticement for him. Louise was a generous soul, even if her interests were so literary as to preclude her comprehending the new photography. In May 1898, when Day was preparing for the Philadelphia Salon, she rounded up models and offered herself as a willing stagehand.

> *Sonny dear,*
> *Will next Thurs. or Fri. do for the apple-orchard*
> *photographing? It would suit Janet Grant (I think).*

. . . I'd come to Newtonville station, and help you
carry the camera, properties, etc. It seems rather short
notice, but I have only just realized how far on the
blossoms are. If you can't drum up a model in so short
a time, bring some togs and I'll stand (or hang!) for
you; as I suppose what you're after is landscape and
drapery effects, rather than faces. We'll turn that
away! In the small point of barefootedness, anyhow,
even our lovely Alice P.S. is imperfect! Hostess
(Janet Grant) is a nice old girl but not photograph-
able, according to your point of view.[16]

Models were not that hard to come by, but it was always
pleasant to have one's friends scouting for good ones. Day himself had several sources for models. First, of course, was his established reputation as a publisher and employer of designers
and illustrators. Then, too, some of the Boston matrons knew of
him through his modest society connections. Among these ladies
– one hesitates to use the unVictorian word *women* in this con-
text – was the kind and dedicated Jessie Fremont Beale. Miss
Beale was a social worker devoted to bringing enlightenment
and culture to the poor immigrant children of Boston. She had
already established what were called 'home libraries,' nearly
seventy small collections of books scattered among the poorer
neighborhoods. Prodigies who deserved special attention often
came to her attention, and one day the art teacher of a gifted
thirteen-year-old Syrian boy came to Beale for assistance. Beale
knew she had a patron in Fred Day. He had already contributed a considerable number of handsomely illustrated books to
her home libraries, and had even joined her circle of home visitors who were expected to read aloud to slum children.

November 25, 1896.
My dear Mr. Day:
I am wondering if you may happen to have an artist
friend who would care to become interested in a
little Assyrian boy Kahlil G[ibran]. He is not con-
nected with any society, so any one befriending the
little chap would be entirely free to do with him what
would seem in their judgment wise.[17]

The young boy, Beale suggested, deserved a fate better than
selling matches on a street corner. What the lad needed was
'an artistic education.'

Portrait of Kahlil Gibran with book, by F. Holland Day, about 1897.

Sensitive, brown-eyed, swarthy of skin, black of hair, the young Kahlil Gibran sat for a series of fine portraits over a period of several years. The earliest had him garbed in Syrian folk costume with one of Day's standard exotic props, the leopard skin. Perhaps the best known of these portraits of Gibran showed him in a flattering corduroy suit, either supporting one arm on a large book, or intently reading the same. Solemn as a stick, almost never smiling, and quite as self-possessed as Alfred Tanneyhill, the young Syrian made an ideal model for a photographer who enjoyed meticulous poses and absolutely controlled lighting. They must have made a singular pair: Day in his Turkish robes and turned-up slippers, the boy in whatever variety of costume he owned or could be persuaded to try on, including an Arab burnoose.

Kahlil Gibran in costume, by
F. Holland Day, about 1896.

As soon as Gibran had acquired sufficient English to follow complex thought, Day began to read to him. Among the
many influential works Day introduced to the boy was *The
Treasure of the Humble,* by Maurice Maeterlinck, an author
much admired for his symbolist plays and his spiritualistic messages. Maeterlinck invaded Gibran's soul with talk of 'astral humanity' and other Platonic mysteries, and influenced the im-
pressionable young man to renounce his Catholic upbringing
in favor of a Near Eastern mysticism. Gibran never forgot that
it was Fred Day who had introduced him to this crucial author.
Yet when he came to write his immensely popular *The
Prophet,* there was not one word of gratitude. Louise Guiney
noted this in anger, and wrote to Day, 'Why isn't this book
dedicated to you? (Not that you do good to people for the sake
of being publicly thanked!)'[18]

Day encouraged Gibran to read Richard Hovey's poems,
which he had recently published in *Songs from Vagabondia.*
But his influence was not only literary. He permitted Kahlil to

study and copy his collection of original Beardsley drawings. He introduced Kahlil to the work of William Blake, with such success that the young man soon came to consider himself the master's equal. The drawings for *The Prophet* were so seductive, in fact, that the sculptor Rodin allowed publishers to quote him as saying Gibran was greater than Blake.

That was too much for Louise Guiney. Still a monarchist at heart, she decided that Kahlil's bloated ego was the result of the democratic environment. 'America,' she wrote to Day, 'has a subtle effect on its foreign-born children, on Orientals in particular: they come out of a grave ripened civilization into an air where no values are fixed, and it goes very badly to their heads.'[19]

Day did not share Louise's fierce condemnations, nor some of her prejudices. He assisted Gibran in arranging his own exhibition at Wellesley College, and allowed him to attempt covers for Copeland and Day books. Kahlil even used Day's studio as his own, with all materials furnished. That was unfortunate, for much of Gibran's early work was lost when the studio burned in 1904. After that, they kept in touch for a number of years, but Day never received much gratitude from Kahlil. It is doubtful that he ever expected or wanted it.

Whether or not F. Holland Day became a volunteer settlement-house teacher in order to find picturesque models, he proved himself a responsible member of the Jessie Beale circle. He associated himself particularly with the Parmenter Street House, which in 1894 became a focus for his major activities in 'Christian charity.' Since he gave so much support to this house, he wanted any and all children to have free access to the holiday repasts he helped to provide. He had always been lavishly generous with his friends, and kept Louise Guiney, among others, well supplied with blank notebooks for their writing, pocket and rent money, gifts of fine editions, fruits, candies, and other daily niceties. He was, as Louise put it, 'the bestest of mortals.'[20] During the 1890s, he became a favorite of the children, especially because he arranged frequent outings to the country during summer vacations. He continued this association until 1917.

In March 1898, Day was invited to exhibit at the Boston Camera Club, and brought the three hundred stunning prints that had garnered so much praise in New York. As might have been expected, the Bostonians were shocked, not so much by

Nude shepherd, by F. Holland Day, 1897.

the exotic qualities of *Ebony and Ivory,* nor by the obscurity of his mythological subjects, but by the first frontal nude ever displayed in a photographic exhibit in the city. *Study for the Crucifixion* (plate 16) presented a young man in a posture of writhing *contraposto,* more like one of Michelangelo's slave sculptures than a medieval saint. The Bostonians, used to Day's flamboyant character, acknowledged his debt to Michelangelo, admired his superb platinum prints, and gave him credit for his unique mountings on varicolored tissue papers – a technique later adopted by Stieglitz with good results – but ridiculed his more exotic ethnic subjects, his slant-eyed Madonnas of the street and their brothers with long-lashed dreaming eyes. As

F. Holland Day about 1895, by
Frederick Hollyer, London.

for the nudity, it could have destroyed his career if there had
been any hint of personal scandal.

> *In the extremely difficult problem of finding models*
> *so well proportioned that their naked figures can*
> *stand the test of the camera, Mr. Day has been re-*
> *markably successful. That his nude studies are free*
> *of the look that makes most photographs of this sort*
> *merely indecent, and awkwardly so, is a further proof*
> *of his artistic capabilities.*[21]

That was a most reassuring comment at a time when his work
could have been unjustifiably compared to the flagrant ephèbes
of the Baron von Glœdon. But it was hardly a safe time to
elicit any suggestion of improprieties. During the showing of
his pictures at the Boston Camera Club in 1898, Day's friend
Beardsley had died, with repercussions we have already noted.
There were to be other repercussions.

Day had come to the attention of the public through the
Linked Ring. In 1895, George Davison had praised him highly,
saying that he had at least 'partly succeeded in bending the photographic method to express something of the feeling and character of the work of certain of the Pre-Raphælite painters.'[22] In
the space of three years of prodigious labors, Day succeeded in
mounting an extravagantly praised one-man show containing
three hundred prints of generally high artistic quality, all of
them calculated to encourage the public to recognize photography as a fine art. He had been experimenting with a few
scenes of Christ's passion, for example, the *Entombment* which
was now part of *Beauty Is Truth,* and the sensuous nude study
that had shocked Boston. Now the Beardsley tragedy, so like
the early death of Day's idol Keats, disrupted the steady course
of his images toward the decorative semi-abstractions of Whistler, Puvis de Chavannes, and Beardsley himself. In the summer of 1898, his judgment failed him, and he was about to
bring down upon himself the greatest controversy and condemnation of his career.

One of F. Holland Day's series
of sacred subjects: crucifixion
with Mary, Joseph and saints,
with Day posing as Christ, 1898.

9   A Crown of Thorns

If *Ebony and Ivory* and the sensuous Nubian series had been somewhat of a shock to the public, what F. Holland Day was planning would cause a furor for the next several years. On a hot July day in 1898, what must have looked like a caravan of gypsies set out from Fred Day's Norwood mansion for a hillside not far beyond the town. There, with Day as the leading actor, director, and cameraman, a public Calvary was staged. In the grand manner of a silent film director, Day arranged the supernumeraries (almost all Norwood residents), coached the Boston actors, designed his camera angles, and had himself attached to a large wooden cross imported from Syria.

Not content merely to re-enact the Passion of Christ with himself as the Savior, Day apparently also made his own exposures, using a bulb attached to a long shutter cable. The sky was cloudless, the Norwood natives were restless in the heat, the actors playing Mary and Joseph were suffocating in the authentic costumes obtained from Egypt, and the half-naked Day writhed under his crown of thorns as if in penitence for some grave sin. They all worked one day, rested, returned, regrouped, packed and unpacked their carts and carriages, until some 250 negatives had been taken.

SOME OF MR. DAY'S PHOTOGRAPHIC ART STUDIES.

'Some of Mr. Day's Photographic Art Studies' – caption for a newspaper illustration.

On the surface, this probably seems one of the most bizarre and eccentric acts in the history of photography – but only if we discount the other maudlin Victorian photographic charades. Two other photographers had recently attempted entombments, and even a Rembrandtesque descent from the cross.[1] The difference was that Day himself was posing as Jesus. Although from modesty or prudence he admitted his role only to two friends, Louise Guiney and Frederick Evans, it soon came out that he had starved himself for months and let his hair grow while keeping himself in seclusion at Norwood. When he climbed on the cross, he was an emaciated, tortured symbol of suffering, his ribs protruding like those of a Gothic grotesque.

Day had starved himself not merely for aesthetic effect. He was supported on the cross like the actor playing Christ in the Oberammergau Passion Play, with 'a stout strap beneath the loin cloth, about the bony parts of the hips,'[2] while his arms were held up by fake nails gripping wires which passed around the tightly clenched knuckles. It would not do to be overweight under these circumstances.

Why endure such hardships merely for the sake of a series of photographs? Surely he could have hired some Boston actor to portray Christ. But we have seen some of the psychological genesis of his idea. He had shared Yeats's Rosicrucian ideals. He had defended suffering as an avenue to spiritual progress. As early as 1886, he had identified himself with Keats, and Keats with Christ, finding that Keats's 'wretchedness of spirit'

SACRED ART MODERNIZED

Photograph of the Crucifixion from Living Figures.

Mr. F. H. Day Finds a New and Important Work for the Camera.

The Models for His Group Clothed with Historical Accuracy.

Scene Selected in Norwood Represented as Nearly as Possible Natural Features of Calvary.

Picture Completed Without Marring Either the Meaning or Spirit of the Subject.

Headlines for newspaper article about Day's sacred subjects, 1898.

had become 'almost a crucifixion.'[3] The fin-de-siècle mood identified the artist with the suffering Jesus. And, finally, the death of Beardsley that spring precipitated an emotional crisis which Day could not, perhaps, express in any other fashion.

Day wanted to be the first photographer to prove to a disbelieving world, unconvinced as yet by Stieglitz's Katwyk studies or Emerson's landscapes, that the camera could be the instrument of a true artist. To accomplish this ambition, he seized upon the dominant subject of Western art since the ninth century. It was a subject at once serious, high-minded, significant, compassionate, and entirely suited to the late-Victorian appetite for a faith that materialistic civilization had denied.

Even more important, the subject was relatively new to photography. There was little chance that such a subject would dominate the upcoming Philadelphia Salon. And certainly few photographers could have afforded Day's elaborate staging or purchased all the authentic props from far-off places. The crown of thorns, ordered specifically to his direction, resembled those used by Rubens and Van Dyck in their crucifixions. The wooden nails were carved by a Syrian. The costumes, as Day claimed to the press, were 'such as were used at the time of the actual crucifixion, and procured from designs furnished by archaeological investigation.'[4] Day treated the enormous complexity of the undertaking casually; in a letter to Stieglitz that summer, he referred to the prodigious labor as 'Sacred stuff.'[5]

It is puzzling that he did not admit that he had been pursuing the idea of religious subjects ever since his visit to Oberammergau in 1890. In Madrid, when he was supposed to be concentrating on the Fanny Brawne letters, he instead spent long hours at the Prado. He had written to Louise Guiney on November 29: 'They seem to have the best of Van Dyck's sacred things . . . Rubens religious pieces, too. And Ribera and Murillo and Velásquez til one's eyes watered with admiration.'[6]

In the spring of 1891, he asked of a dealer, 'Could you conveniently jot down the names of any *modern* sacred pieces which you may run across especially in Germany with the name of their artists, you would greatly oblige a caprice of mine which leads me into the collecting of reproductions of such works of this character as are really good.'[7] In 1892, he acquired an extensive catalogue of reproductions of religious art, which he discussed with Louise. She wrote to him,

Do you remember that piece of modern sacred art of which we were speaking not long ago? On the text to the rich young man? 'Sell all thou hast, and give it to the poor'? Well, if you look in Soule's doorway (on the left, just as you step in from the street) you'll find it. Nothing great about it except the thoughtful doubtful Jewish head in profile of said young man: but that, it seems to me, very expressive. The figures in background are bad; and the figure of Our Lord conventional.[8]

Day's copy of the Velásquez *Crucifixion,* one of many art prints he purchased.

Day, of course, had easy access to all the religious subjects he could have desired: several houses in Boston specialized in photographic reproductions of great paintings. Soule, mentioned by Guiney, was one of the most famous, regularly advertising its wares in journals like *Harper's New Monthly Magazine.* For fifteen cents, the reader could obtain a catalogue of 14,000 subjects, all unmounted photographs.[9] The Moulton Photograph Company of Salem advertised 10,000 subjects, as did C. H. Dunton of Boylston Street, Boston, which offered 'Braun's Carbons in great variety.'[10] There was also Franz Haufstaengel's 'Fine Art Publishing' in New York City. But of all the prints that Day must have collected, and the number was surely substantial, only one remains at Norwood: a torn sepia print of the *Crucifixion* by Velásquez. This painting, as well as the many melodramatic Christs by Guido Reni he had seen, must have influenced his photographic series.

By 1893, despite his demanding involvement with publishing, Day was already experimenting with religious subjects, with Louise as his willing model. While their technical quality leaves much to be desired, the two extant prints of Guiney as St. Barbara (and an impressive glass positive of one of the same subject[11]) demonstrate how Day progressed in the posing of subjects and manipulating light. Guiney was delighted with the results, and asked that he make prints of three poses so she could frame them together. She also felt it necessary to 'petition for a halo on each, as no respectable person out of the Roman calendar would be seen without a halo.'[12] Asking his advice on framing, she indicated that she wanted to 'put a thick border of palm-branches and lilies all about the three cards, in true hagiological style.'[13]

It would be amusing to have some comment by Day on what she proceeded to do to the prints. Writing of herself in the Victorian third person, Louise blithely reveals an indiscretion.

> *She hath done away with the evil looks of the neck in No. 2, by a little soft cross-hatching with a sharp pencil, making the shadow fall [vertical] instead of [diagonal]. Try it, for the improvement is vast; and don't grin at her draughtsmanship. That same pencil, discreetly and very lightly deepening shadows and outlines, hath also astonishingly improved No. 1.*[14]

Apparently, Louise did not recognize the general distaste, even in 1893, for the retouched portrait. But her letters are most helpful to us today, for she is one of the few people who recorded Day's early attitudes about print quality. For example, in March she complained that she had asked Fred for three copies of each of the St. Barbara 'look-ups' and 'look-downs' to give away to friends. 'But you and your everlasting high-art ideals have made each and every one unique: and even I rather grudge unique things to my best beloveds, Tom, Dick, and Harry.'[15] This loyalty to the unique print was one of the fundamental tenets of the Pictorialists as a group.

Two versions of Louise Imogen Guiney as St. Barbara, by F. Holland Day, 1893.

Louise was quite useful to Fred on other matters. She informed him about how Christ should be represented in painting and photographic iconographies. When she was on her walking tour of England in 1895, she sent home clippings of interest. Victorian England was beginning to question the historicity of Jesus. A typical question then plaguing artists was 'whether the face they recognized as that of the Christ was the real likeness of a real man. Or, was it only the fanciful creation of an artist's dream?'[16] Should the hair be smoothly divided in an arch over the forehead in Roman fashion, or should a slender lock dangle from the hairline in the style of the Greek church? Day settled for the German look inherited from Oberammergau.

When he sent a description of his 'Sacred stuff' to Louise, who was spending the summer of 1898 in Maine, she wrote back enthusiastically.

> *I can hardly wait to get home to see the 'foties.' It delights me to have you warmed up to New Testament things; for you know I have always wanted you to have a try at them. And I hope you'll go on to that rich and varied field, the Legends of the Saints, bye*

and bye, and turn my publisher into a Modern
Sacred Artist, tooth and Nail.[17]

What a bad influence she could be on him, and yet she did seem
to understand some of the problems of creating art through
photography. She correctly observed, for example, that photographing a physical, real piece of wood carved in the shape of a
nimbus would not do: '. . . the halo is opaque and heavy, and
gives the thing away, inasmuch as it says "camera" unmistakably, rather than brush.'[18] She even corrected Day's form for
the halo. 'That, according to the old painters, is a mere saint's
halo. Our Lord's should always be [and here she inserted a
drawing of a halo with a cross] – Oh, that I could draw!'[19]
Clumsily, she gave him the correct form, 'with a cross-shaped
glory within a full circle, not a rim of light.'[20]

Day apparently sent prints to several friends and acquaintances for their reactions before he submitted his experiments
to the Philadelphia Salon in the fall of 1898. But when he told
Louise he was proposing an exhibition of these new works in
Boston, she wrote, 'The sacred exhibition scheme seems to me
. . . too hazardous. . . . At least, I would not hang these pictures
save in a city where I didn't live!'[21] And she cautioned him not
to send prints to some of her friends in Maine because they
would be shocked.

Day disobeyed Guiney. He had invitations printed to 'a
private view of a small number of photographic studies of
sacred subjects by Mr. F. H. Day to be held at his rooms Number 9 Pinckney Street on Wednesday and Thursday afternoons
November Sixteenth and Seventeenth from four until seven
o'clock.'[22] In small print, the notes explained:

> *Mr. Day is the first to undertake the character of*
> *work represented by these studies, and as some con-*
> *troversy has arisen regarding the legitimate use of the*
> *camera in this field, your opinion for or against ex-*
> *hibition is sought.*[23]

The expected controversy came on several levels. First,
there was the shock of the small, beautifully executed *Study
for the Crucifixion* (plate 16), which had been Boston's first
view of frontal male nudity. Then there was the shock that
photography could presume to be called "Art." Last, there was
the shock of being confronted with the blasphemy, or worse, in
Day's posing for the figure of Jesus.

An early version of *I Thirst* from the *Seven Last Words of Christ* by F. Holland Day, about 1898.

Day was not obviously identifiable in the long shots of Jesus on the cross attended by Roman soldiers or Mary and Joseph. But the series *The Seven Last Words of Christ* (plates 19–25) consisted of close-ups of his face enacting those agonized moments of the Passion. According to Frederick Evans, who reprinted this series in 1912, Day had "a mirror attached to the camera so that he could see his expression at the time of exposure; he made the exposure himself, so the whole effort was a purely personal one. . . . It was a unique effort, inspired by the utmost reverence and carried out with extraordinary success.'[24] Evans was talking about the glycerine prints, sets of which are extant at the Metropolitan Museum, the Royal Photographic Society, and George Eastman House. It is doubtful that Evans, who had the highest technical standards, would have spoken so enthusiastically had he seen the botched progenitor of the series. A grotesquely painted image, *I Thirst* was reproduced to accompany Day's article 'Sacred Art and the Camera,' in *Photogram* for February 1899. Why Day ever lent the journal this coarsely realistic print is beyond conjecture, unless it was proof that he considered all of these pictures experiments. In his article, Day defended the photography of sacred subjects. In an unsigned reply, the editors of *Photogram* decided that 'the living Jesus, with face illuminated by the Divine Inspiration, seems beyond the power of the camera.'[25] A reproduction of one of the later glycerine prints in the April 1899 *Photogram* showed an artistic leap, as if two entirely different photographers were at work.

In his submissions to the Philadelphia Salon of 1898, Day included both *The Seven Last Words of Christ,* in an architectural frame complete with verbal legend, and the *Entombment*. They were accepted by a jury that included Alfred Stieglitz and Robert Redfield. For this, the first juried national show in the United States, the sponsors sought to legitimate photography as art by inviting the eminent painter William Merritt Chase, and two other artists who were not photographers, to join the jury. Its mandate was to select 'only such pictures produced by photography as may give distinct evidence of individual artistic feeling and execution.'[26] One can be sure that Chase, whose paintings had in them something of Whistler, Degas, and John Singer Sargent, would respond favorably to anyone whose photographs resembled his own work.

The Salon, which opened October 24, 1898, was a huge success. It was a genuine revelation of the possibilities of the

F. Holland Day's *The Seven Last Words of Christ,* 1898, in the architectural frame used for exhibitions.

camera. 'For the first time it was realized that a Stieglitz, a Hinton or a Day was as distinctive in style as a Breton, a Corot, or a Verestchagin; that photography is open to broad as well as sharp treatment; that it had its impressionists as well as its realists.' [27] Stieglitz's pictures were praised for their 'quick sympathy' and 'keen eye,' [28] although it was noted, surely to his discomfort, that his prints were not as good as they might have been. Keiley, the main reviewer, suggested that Stieglitz had been too busy politicking to pay much attention to the 'proper interpretation of his negatives.' [29] This was a point, ironically, on which Stieglitz later criticized Day unjustifiably.

Two newcomers to the national scene received considerable attention. Clarence White's *Spring,* an unusual and lyrical triptych, was called 'a poem of true harmonies that stands alone of its kind.' [30] Gertrude Käsebier, a professional in an exhibition supposedly dedicated to the amateur, quickly altered the popular misconception of the studio operator as a hack. Her pictures of mothers and children were considered to be 'distinct artistic creations that are destined to wield a tremendous influence on photographic portraiture in America, and to set a standard for it never before imagined.' [31] It was generally agreed that the First Philadelphia Salon was significant for bringing to the public's attention three photographers whose work had been relatively unknown: Day, Käsebier, and White. For F. Holland Day, the Salon was important primarily because it brought him into a circle with two respected colleagues and friends with whom a friendly competition ensued. He reaped some rewards and some condemnations. *The Seven Last Words* was badly hung, below eye level, making the architectural frame seem disproportionately large. *Ebony and Ivory* was widely praised, as was the *Ethiopian Chief.*

Charles Caffin, one of the most influential American critics, regularly reviewed the Philadelphia Salons for *Harper's Weekly,* a tabloid with cultural aspirations. On November 5,

1898, Caffin remarked that in *Ebony and Ivory* 'the imagination is at once captivated by the sentiment suggested.'[32] But Day's sacred subjects at the First Salon were another matter.

> *The limit of mistake is reached by two exhibits, one of seven heads crowned with thorns, purporting to represent the 'Seven Last Words' from the Cross, and the other, a dead Christ with the Magdalen bathing his feet with her tears. In the latter case a wound has been painted on the side of the model. Surely claptrap and misappreciation of the province and mission of art can go no further.*[33]

As for Day's *Christ on the Cross*, accepted at the Second Philadelphia Salon, Caffin later scoffed that 'such a divagation from good taste is intolerably silly.'[34] At the same time, Caffin damned Stieglitz with faint praise. In his review of November 3, 1900, he remarked that the *Net-Mender* was stiff, and found the most pleasing of Stieglitz's other subjects a rather banal picture of a mother and child, *At the Window*.

Caffin almost always found Day worthy of reproduction in *Harper's Weekly*. And by the time of the Fourth Salon in 1901, Day had the satisfaction of receiving Caffin's unstinting praise.

> *Among these the group by F. Holland Day is unquestionably the most distinguished. All his prints have an unmistakable quality of style, perceptible as well in the conception of the picture as in the tact with which it is realized.*[35]

The American critic Sadakichi Hartmann was as harshly outspoken as Caffin. Yet under a reproduction of *The Seven Last Words* that spanned two pages of *The Photographic Times*, Hartmann called Day's art 'full of delicacy, refinement, and subtlety, an art full of deep thought and charm, full of dreamy fascination.'[36] It was an art which Hartmann believed would appeal primarily to "the intellectual and the refined; to those, in a word, who can understand and can feel.'[37] Day's essential ability was as a psychologist.

> *One feels that in all his works he is master of himself, master of gifts, laboriously developed in a most conscientious study and observation. Only in his*

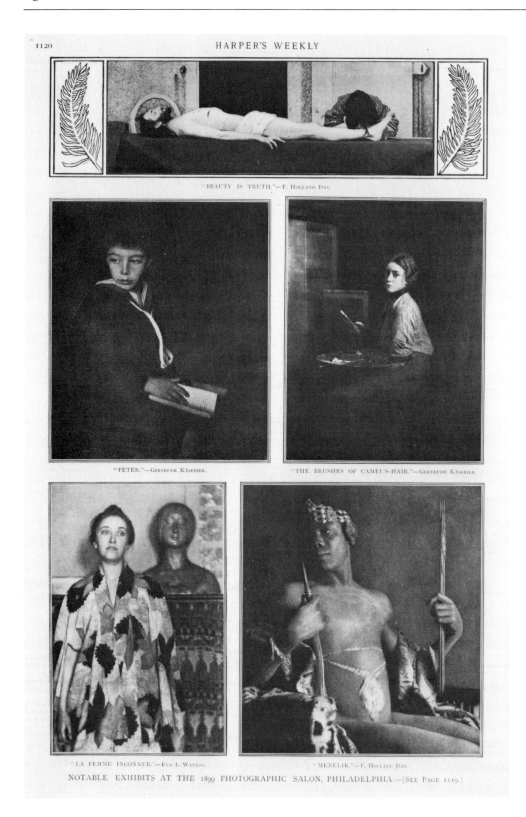

Caffin's reviews, *Harper's Weekly,* 1899 and 1900. Day is represented
at top and bottom right, Käsebier in center.

"Head of Young Girl."—By Eva Lawrence Watson.

"Joseph Jefferson's Son."—By Frank Eugene.

"Zitkala."—By Joseph T. Keiley.

❧ THE ❧ PHILADELPHIA PHOTOGRAPHIC SALON

IT was almost a stroke of genius which three years ago brought about the holding of an annual photographic exhibition in the galleries of the Pennsylvania Academy. The combination of interests is known as the Philadelphia Photographic Salon. The new art thereby gains the prestige of association with such an "ancient and honorable" institution, and the latter, also thereby, maintains its position in the forefront of artistic progress.

In the present exhibition some two hundred prints are displayed; the cream skimmed off an aggregate of nearly twelve hundred submitted to the jury.

Writing for many who will not have the opportunity of seeing the exhibition, I do not propose to discuss it in detail, but to touch upon a few considerations which it suggests as a whole. I spoke of photography, in its latest manifestations, as a "new art," and such indeed it is, for it has reached results that a few years ago one would not have believed possible.

Its newness consists in the discovery of fresh methods of expressing artistic motives; the principles which should regulate the manipulation of the methods are not new. In this respect one notices a clean dividing-line between the various exhibitors. On one side of it are those who have had the discipline of artistic training apart from photography, and on the other those who have not. The former display a sanity of purpose and dignity of method that do not interfere with fancy and inventiveness; while the latter falter and find refuge in muzziness or deliberately strain after originality of treatment.

But the straining after originality is a more serious matter. The term "new art" is much bandied about in Europe just now, and is used to signify a variety of unfledged motives and startling or unusual manners of expression. It uses the human form simply as a decorative motive without any respect for its humanity; rejects its manifestations of healthy beauty for writhings and contortions, seeking a fancied analogy between the movements of limbs and the growth of plants, trying to obtain mystery by muzziness, lighting its subject fantastically and with no reference to the real direction and effects of light, straining to the very limits of morbid imagination so as to surprise, bewilder, and snatch attention.

On the other hand, it is a great pleasure to be able to note the prevalence of a great deal of work honest in sentiment and soundly artistic in method. The Glasgow photographer, J. Craig Annan, maintains his reputation with several fine portraits, frank, earnest work, with much suggestion of each sitter's character and personality; and also with a landscape of mountain scenery, and figures returning home in the evening, in which the lights and shadows are treated in a big manner and convey an impression of vastness and solemnity. Mrs. Gertrude Käsebier shows several handsome portraits, full of character and charm of arrangement, an excellent open-air effect, and a beautiful little play of fancy, called "Andante." For sound and effective management of light and shade special mention should be made of the work by Joseph T. Keiley, Prescott Adamson, Frank Eugene, and the collaborators, Rose Clark and Elizabeth Flint Wade. The first proves what he can do to gain robust effects, and also shows a very satisfactory imaginative study, "The Erlking." Out of a rude scene of railroad cars, sheds, smoke-stacks, and snow Mr. Adamson contrives a handsome picture, vigorous and imaginative, which he entitles "Midst Steam and Smoke." Mr. Eugene's prints are all distinguished by the color quality which he obtains through skilful adjustment of light and dark and attention to the gradations of each. Sometimes his darks are very deep; at other times he prefers a scheme of lights, as in "Mrs. D. and Family." In "Adam and Eve" he shows a really remarkable study of the nude, in which substance, texture, and color are alike suggested. In disagreeable contrast with this sincerity of treatment is a scurry of lines scratched or brushed over the faces, perhaps to hide their identity or else to emphasize the modelling of the figures, but in either case uninventive and unworthy. The joint examples of Miss Clark and her colleague are particularly agreeable in their manner of lighting. The pattern of dark and light is ingenious and effective, and both have a beautiful purity of tone. The "Profile of a Youth," by F. Holland Day, is a very attractive picture in large masses, flatly treated; while his "Portrait of a Man with a Book" exhibits a study of light and shade, full of rich color if a little rigid in arrangement.

Well-chosen scenes, mostly of the sea-shore, animated with figures, are shown by Alfred Stieglitz. One study of a woman mending nets illustrates an interesting point. The camera, instead of catching the right arm at some intermediate stage of its movement, has fixed it when the hand is close up to the shoulder, so that the position is stiff and does not suggest action. Perhaps the most pleasing of all his examples is a picture of a mother and child, "At the Window." Very good landscapes are exhibited by L. L. Peddinghaus, W. B. Post, Edmund J. Steichen, and Amelia Van Buren; moreover, in portraiture there is admirable work by Eva Lawrence Watson, Margaret M. Russell, and Mary Devens. Theodore Hofmeister, of Hamburg, one of the foreigners invited to exhibit, sends examples of colored landscapes, done by the gum-bichromate process. Technically, they will have much interest for photographers, but as pictures they are unsatisfactory, the color being neither true to nature nor agreeable.

CHARLES H. CAFFIN.

"At the Window."—By Alfred Stieglitz.

"Portrait of Mrs. L."—By Gertrude Käsebier.

"Profile of Youth."—By F. Holland Day.

Stieglitz's *At the Window* is at lower left, Käsebier center bottom, and Day's *Profile of Youth* lower right.

> *'Christ Studies' he failed (with the exception of a few plates); the simplicity of 'Open Air' effects proved too strong for him.*[38]

Perhaps Day should have resorted to the cloud and sky negatives which many photographers used to enhance otherwise bland outdoor shots. The 'Open Air' certainly had defeated him. He was a hot-house species that flourished only indoors, in a studio where he could control all details.

Undoubtedly, he was disappointed at the mixed reaction to *The Seven Last Words*, where striking vignetting and texture had compensated for other defects. But he had invested too much emotion to dismiss his hillside extravaganza as a complete failure. In 1899, when he served as juror for the Second Philadelphia Salon, he persisted with his folly, earning Caffin's sharpest criticisms for repeating the dead Christ and weeping Magdalen. That same year, he sent several prints to London, and was greeted with condemnation. But when he once again included a number of the crucifixion scenes in his self-staged exhibition at the Royal Photographic Society in 1900, the outcry was almost unanimous.

Day could never have anticipated the violent reaction to his sacred subjects in England. Outraged letters to the *British Journal of Photography* were so voluminous that the editors felt compelled to publish both sides of the controversy; the battles went on for months:

> *A year or two ago some of Mr. Holland Day's sacred photographs with himself as the central Figure were exhibited and reproduced in this country, and the almost unanimous condemnation with which they were met – clever though they were – should have warned him that a repetition of the offence was not desirable. It is to be regretted that he has ignored English feeling in this matter by showing at Russell Square a number of crucifixion subjects, the crowning objection to which lies in the fact that he himself poses before the camera as representing one whom so many millions of the earth's people revere as the Divine Founder of Christianity! If this were Mr. Day's first offence, it would be open to us to hope that he had acted in ignorance, but as this is not the case, we are constrained to say that it has been reserved for a*

Tableau from the Oberammergau
Passion Play performed in 1900,
illustrated in *Harper's Weekly*.

*photographer from Boston to be guilty of the most
flagrant offence against good taste that has ever come
under our notice.*[39]

This attack on Day's presumption was at least partly motivated
by Sadakichi Hartmann's article, in which he reported some of
Day's renowned eccentricities, such as smoking a water pipe
and wearing Turkish robes. No such eccentric could be allowed
to pose as the Savior.

Day's good friend and colleague, Frederick Evans, the former bookseller who had by this time made an international reputation for his architectural photographs, came to his defense.

> Let me say at the outset that a copy of his picture,
> 'The Seven Last Words' has been in my possession
> for over a twelve-month, and has been shown to very
> many friends and visitors, without at any time elicit-
> ing anything but complete approval. . . . Mr. Day has
> been successful because he has proved so wonderful a
> model, as any dispassionate study of the 'Seven Last
> Words' will at once show; and this brings me to your
> chief point against him, his own posing as the Christ
> model. I would like to ask this question: If Mr. Day
> had taken the Ober-Ammergau actor, Joseph Mayer
> (or his successor) as his model, and used him as he
> had used himself, would your denunciations be as
> fierce or would they even exist? I do not remember
> your ever having fulminated against the photographs
> of the Ober-Ammergau actors in every stage of the
> sacred drama, though they have been published in
> this country. I have now before me a small collection
> of C.D.V. portraits in character of these actors pub-
> lished by Marion and Co. and I would ask where is

*the difference? In both cases a living person is used
as the model because of a supposed suitable personality. . . . Is it possible that what is proper and commendable in a Bavarian is vicious, a 'flagrant offence'
in an American?*[40]

Evans then defended Day as having a 'reverence of motive, an
entire absence of vulgar straining after false effect, a quiet dignity and pathos . . . but how otherwise could it be from an
artist and a gentleman?'[41]

Evans's defense was commendable, but it was hardly in
the interests of pictorial photography to compare representations by actors with an attempt to create high art. There was a
paradox that exposed some of the confusions about the nature of
photography. Several of Day's attackers seemed more aware
of the problem than either Evans or Day himself. The editors
of the *British Journal of Photography* insisted that the most
important issue was the appropriateness of the use of the
camera.

Above: one of several versions of
It Is Finished from Day's *Seven
Last Words;* below: *Resurrection
from the Tomb.*

*The ruthless lens reveals every little trick or artifice
employed in 'faking up' the originals; and we confess
it is with something of a shock that we contemplate
these photographically vamped-up representations.
. . . Mr. Holland Day's photographs [are] repulsive
because we are conscious that the individuality of the
originals has not been, cannot be, so completely
masked or subdued as to destroy the mental persuasion that we are looking at the image of a man made
up to be photographed as the Christian Redeemer,
and not as an artist's reverent and mental conception
of a suffering Christ.*[42]

The ultimate presumption, wrote one irate reader, was to
claim 'that there was as much art in applying chemicals to a
print to bring out a particular tone, as there was in the work of
the artist who applies colours to his canvas through the medium
of a brush!'[43] This letter elicited even more responses. Someone who signed himself 'Tuck' argued: 'Is it true that the lens
and dry plate do not idealize as the painter or draughtsman can
or may? . . . Is Photography so far removed from Art? . . . I think
not! The fault, I feel sure, lies with the artists methods, rather
than with his tools.'[44] Tuck compared the work of Sir Joshua

Reynolds with that of Rembrandt: Reynolds would have failed utterly in any attempt to depict a Descent from the Cross, while Rembrandt, as everyone knew, had created masterworks of such subjects.

The most sophisticated comment came from a Mr. J. J. Vezey:

> *A photograph cannot be good unless it accurately represents the original from which it was taken. Now, as there are no originals left of sacred subjects, it seems to me there is no field for photography in this direction.* In looking at a photograph you cannot forget that it is a representation of something which existed when it was taken[45] [*emphasis added*].

Exactly. This was the dilemma in which photography found itself at the turn of the century. Following Robinson's prescriptions to imitate the composition, design, light, chiaroscuro, and subjects of painting, photographers had thought they would succeed in achieving recognition of the art of photography. They were deluded when they attempted to replicate the exact substance of a Vermeer, a Franz Hals, or a Millet. What became absurd about such charades was that *in looking at a photograph you cannot forget that it is a representation of something that existed when it was taken.*

It must be acknowledged that Day's sacred subjects turned out to be exceedingly bad art and worse photography. With the possible exception of *The Seven Last Words,* they were generally unworthy of an artist who had demonstrated that he knew what to do in the studio. With skies that dropped away pure white, poor lighting effects (except for a few silhouetted crucifixions), and an aura of mediocre stagecraft, the prints were, by and large, abominable. Only the studio-produced, hand-manipulated prints of *The Seven Last Words* can be considered to have achieved any level of feeling or æsthetic effect beyond the imitative.

The furor over Day's attempt at sacred subjects was only a small part of the outrage that greeted his exhibition in London. He was about to be attacked on all sides, and from the rear, by Stieglitz, as well.

A gothic *Crucifixion,* posed by F. Holland Day on the Norwood hills.

The jury for the Second Philadelphia Salon, left to right: Frances Johnston, Clarence White, F. Holland Day, Gertrude Käsebier, and Henry Troth.

10

The New School of American Photography

When F. Holland Day was invited to serve on the jury for the Second Philadelphia Salon in 1899, Alfred Stieglitz sent him a letter marked by an imperious tone:

> *I like you as a Juror – but Miss Johnston! and even Troth. Why not Day to represent the East, Käsebier the Middle States, and White the West? Of course that would leave Phila. out, which would be a good thing for obvious reasons.*[1]

Miss Johnston was interested in posed tableaux. Troth was too deeply entrenched in Philadelphia politics. Stieglitz had decided that Day, Käsebier, and White would be the new photographic triumverate.

Actually, Stieglitz did not need to put this idea into Käsebier's head. She had already written to Day, saying bluntly, 'I hope we three yourself W. and I will be able to swing things on the Jury.'[2] They already believed they were the most talented of the new group, and they shared common aesthetic objectives, sometimes even borrowing motifs and subjects from each other. Congenial to Clarence White was Day's practice of contrasting

Clarence White's *Spring – A Triptych,* 1898, one of several versions.

large masses of black with small, brilliant areas of light, as in White's Day-inspired *Lady in Black with Statuette* of 1899. Day, in turn, found inspiration in White's strikingly painterly triptychs, especially the lovely *Spring,* which Sadakichi Hartmann had already labeled 'one of the masterpieces of American photography.'[3] Each had his own innate Whistlerian *japonisme* encouraged by the others. Käsebier, who was the most outspoken and domineering of the three, never acknowledged that she had learned anything from either of them. At Day's Paris Exhibition of 1901, she would discover to her dismay that F. Holland Day was accounted the aesthetic and political leader. 'My Blessed Art Thou was accused of being an imitation of Day,' she wrote to Stieglitz indignantly. 'They make me sick.'[4]

The critics, of course, delighted in trying to decide which of the triumverate had influenced the other two the most. Hartmann saw Day as belonging to a unique species.

> *Imitators he has in abundance, equals – in his own peculiar line of work – he has none, and he has probably done more to the creating of the 'new school' than any other individual photographer.*[5]

Considering that Hartmann had never before made up his mind whether to mock Day or eulogize him, his comments about the relative merits of Day and Käsebier were probably unexpected. Stieglitz had extended himself in an article for *Camera Notes,* asserting that Käsebier was 'the leading artistic portrait photographer in America.'[6] While acknowledging that such judgments were dependent on taste and individual opinion, Hartmann decided that 'Day strikes me as being far more original than Käsebier by his exquisite imagination, his delightful caprices, his grace and his fancifulness.'[7] Käsebier's art was 'not based on observation'[8]; she seemed unremittingly solemn, and her pictures too closely resembled identifiable paintings by Rembrandt, Holbein, or Cassatt.

Day was much taken by Käsebier, paying her the compliment of imitating her soft effects and mother–child subjects during the next decade, when she was often his guest in Maine. Their friendship commenced in 1899, when they corresponded regularly about the upcoming Salon. Käsebier's portrait studio was in New York City, and despite a very down-to-earth personality, she indulged Day's experiments with long-distance thought transference.

Two of Gertrude Käsebier's most popular subjects: *Blessed Art Thou Among Women,* 1899, and *The Manger,* about 1898.

There is no question but that your thoughts reach me sometimes. You were much in my mind yesterday. Last night my impulse to write to you was so strong that I got out the pen and paper, the same I am using now. This morning comes the package of prints, and all is clear.[9]

Day must have been delighted with this evidence of extra-sensory perception, and equally delighted that his new friend was about to come to Newport, Rhode Island, for the summer, where he could easily visit her by trolley. Since she seemed so cordial, he made the minor tactical error of trying to obtain work for Herbert Copeland through her. The publishing firm of Copeland and Day was folding, and Herbert would be without a job. Unfortunately for 'Partner,' as Louise Guiney called Herbert, Käsebier wrote, 'I am sorry to say I have heard unpleasant things of H. from Canada.'[10] What these unpleasant rumors were she was too much of a lady to say. Day was not considering abandoning Herbert to his alcoholism; they continued to be friends. But Day was going through his own crisis.

The unexpectedly harsh rejection of his sacred subjects by powerful critics like Caffin and Keiley had given him quite a jolt. In confiding this to Käsebier, a motherly figure, he asked if she thought she could ever surpass the magnificent prints she had produced up to that time. She responded brusquely, 'Ask Mr. Stieglitz or I would say Mr. Keiley only that I know you don't value his opinion.'[11] Day held it against Keiley that he was partial to Stieglitz.

Day became so insecure that Käsebier was inspired to write a warm reassurance.

The feeling you expressed about looking at your own prints is a very common one. It often comes to me and I think it does to every serious artist. Such at least has been my observation. Your work is very beautiful and your feeling very true. I know that it is most satisfying to many who do not care for mine at all.[12]

When she went up to Newport to begin preparing new work for the Salon, she invited Day and his friends, Francis Watts Lee and his wife, to stay in what Käsebier regarded as 'a veritable Garden of Eden. I wander about and dream and dream and dream and am unconscious of material conditions.'[13]

As usual, Day charmed the family with gifts of bonbons and fruits, and after he and the Lees had departed, Käsebier wrote a long piece of doggerel to thank them for their company and Day's innumerable small courtesies: 'The birds still twitter, the breezes still blow / Thoughts of you always come and go . . .'[14]

The little idyll continued until September, when Käsebier was notified that the jurors for the Salon were due in Philadelphia on October 5. The marriage of one of her daughters prevented her from traveling down at a leisurely pace with Day, whose company she enjoyed. Stopping off in New York to catch up with Stieglitz and the Camera Club, she noticed that something seemed seriously amiss. Ignorant of the explosive situation which had been developing, Käsebier tried to intervene.

Portrait of F. Holland Day by Gertrude Käsebier, 1899.

> *Stieglitz is delighted with your latest work. Somehow he has an idea you must be vexed with him. I told him I thought not unless it was about the portfolios. He immediately said he would send you one of his own subscription numbers, but I begged him not to until you had met and had a talk. So you see in trying to make peace I have perhaps made mischief.*[15]

The portfolios she mentioned were photogravures of prints reproduced in *Camera Notes* and manufactured by Stieglitz's respected engraving company. It was not the first time that the overburdened Stieglitz would overlook some minor arrangement. But Day could hardly have been chafing over something so petty.

The problems began because, in Day's opinion, Stieglitz was not taking the initiative in organizing the American Pictorialists into a society like the Linked Ring. The Philadelphia Salons, burdened with local photographic politics, had failed to offer an opportunity to unite the practitioners of the 'new school.' Fred Day had suggested to Stieglitz that it was time to move to new centers; he favored Boston. There were many reasons for this choice. Day had met Sarah Sears, an influential society matron and photographer whose exhibition at the Boston Camera Club he helped to arrange. Mrs. Sears not only supported Day whole-heartedly, but had offered to persuade the trustees and directors of the Museum of Fine Arts to make the museum the exhibition center for the Pictorialists. Day hardly concealed his feelings about New York: 'I've never found a place in the world I dislike more – and this too as I have many good friends there . . .'[16] Boston, with its close ties to Europe, its freedom from the commercial pressures of New York, its new talents, and its more dignified atmosphere, was to Day's mind a more suitable place for the new center.

In the summer and fall of 1899, Day continually urged Stieglitz to help him establish an 'American Association of Artistic Photography.'[17] Sarah Sears had convinced the Museum of Fine Arts – if Stieglitz would consent. Could not Stieglitz come to Boston and take charge? Day even offered his own house as lodging for Stieglitz. He made his own position clear: 'I would sooner think of flying than undertake a photographic movement which you would refuse to head in the fullest possible way.'[18]

Portrait of Gertrude Käsebier by F. Holland Day, 1899.

No. Stieglitz could not come to Boston. He was busy with his own exhibition in New York, and he had no intention of assisting Day in establishing a competing center for photography, nor of sharing the reputation of leader with Day. Without Stieglitz's support in America, Day knew he could never establish any American Association of Artistic Photography. Nor could he seize power from Stieglitz, who was firmly entrenched.

Day did the only thing he could have done under the circumstances. He had already acquired a substantial number of prints by major Pictorialists. He could count on his good friends, Käsebier and Clarence White. He had discovered new talents, like Mary Devens. He now wrote to the Linked Ring and asked for permission to mount an historic exhibition of the American Pictorialists at their London hall. It was to be under his aegis and would represent the finest work of the 'new school.' In fact, he intended to call it the New School of American Photography.

Alfred Stieglitz was outraged and refused to cooperate. When A. Horsley Hinton, one of the Links, inquired about Day's intentions, Stieglitz cabled the Linked Ring leaders to warn them that Day had made a poor selection and that the prints were second-rate. Alarmed, and justifiably concerned for their reputation, the Links denied Day access to their exhibition rooms.

That might have daunted a less motivated man, but Day's ambition was whetted by his fury at Stieglitz's deceit. Hardly endearing himself to either the Links or Stieglitz, Day simply went to the rival organization, the Royal Photographic Society, and was granted space at their well-established quarters on Russell Square. It was an audacious move which simultaneously announced that there was, indeed, a New School and that Day was its leader. From that moment, almost everyone in the photographic world was required to take sides.

Since Day sent a circular to his fellow American Pictorialists, it was inevitable that Gertrude Käsebier would discover the major outlines of the trouble. But she still did not seem to grasp that the situation was irrevocable.

> *I am very sorry you did not see Mr. Stieglitz. He*
> *would have been only too pleased to have arranged a*
> *meeting, if he had had any intimation that you were*
> *looking for him. I see very little of him indeed. We*
> *are both too busy, but, I think he is one of the fairest,*
> *broadest, finest men I ever knew.*[19]

It came as a shock to her when, a few years later, she discovered that Stieglitz was unpredictable, undependable, irascible, and imperial. He ended by antagonizing not only Day and Käsebier, but White, Steichen, and many more.

F. Holland Day had been signaling to Stieglitz for a long while that he was giving up publishing; he announced in 1899 he would give all his energies to 'advancing photography.'[20] His many friends in England, including Evans, had been urging him to 'fetch over a small collection of American work and exhibit it in London and Paris.'[21] Then Day had suggested that he might establish a portrait studio in London, and not return. 'Or I may go to Chicago where calls issue from for Exhibitions.'[22] Weak syntax, but unmistakable threat; Day was implying he was fit to arrange exhibitions himself. It must have rattled Stieglitz's composure. In fact, Stieglitz was in poor health and was increasingly fractious in his dealings with the Camera Club of New York as well as with individual photographers.

On April 15, 1900, Fred Holland Day left for London accompanied by his young cousin, Alvin Langdon Coburn, and Coburn's overbearing mother. Alvin was an intelligent, ambitious young man, and Fred had been encouraging him to pursue a photographic career. It was fortunate that he did, for Coburn soon proved to have a remarkable talent for portraiture. Coburn had been invited because the undertaking promised to be strenuous, and Fred needed help. Day was taking with him the enormous number of nearly four hundred original prints,

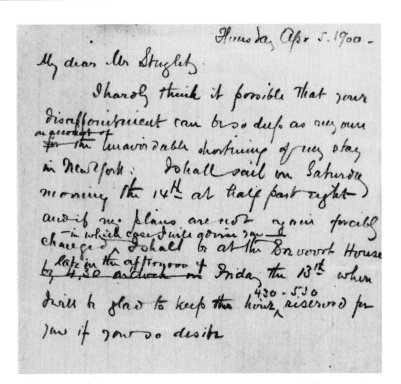

Draft of Day's letter advising Stieglitz that there would be no time for a meeting between them before Day boarded the steamer from New York to London, April 1900.

including works by Käsebier, White, Ben-Yusuf, Alice Austin, Mary Devens, Frank Eugene, Arthur Gleason, C. Yarnall Abbott, Frances Johnston, Joseph Keiley, Francis Watts Lee, Robert Redfield, Sarah Sears, Henry Troth, Mathilde Weil, Eva Lawrence Watson, and other adherents of the new photography. Day also intended to exhibit over one hundred prints of his own, but separate from the main exhibition. Together, they would comprise the largest number of prints by American photographers to be exhibited in London up to that time.

The quality, as well as the quantity, of the show was unexpectedly bolstered by the arrival of twenty-one-year-old Edward Steichen, who was then living in Paris. Day enthusiastically accepted twenty-one prints, and even invited Steichen to join Coburn in hanging the exhibition. Although he early gravitated toward the influential Stieglitz, on whom he would have tremendous effect, Steichen also became a loyal friend to Day.

Fred set up a small but elegant studio on Mortimer Street where, if we are to believe the memoirs of Alvin Langdon Coburn, he was taught by his young cousin to master the darkroom. Day had long scorned the technical aspects of photography, but it is difficult to believe that he had not practiced advanced techniques, for example, in the production of the vignetted glycerine prints of *The Seven Last Words*. We have

Alvin Langdon Coburn at 25
Mortimer Street, London, by
F. Holland Day, 1900.

already noted his reliance upon Boston's commercial printing
houses, but Day had always maintained the highest standards
for his prints, even mounting them himself.

The exhibition of the New School of American Photography opened on October 10, 1900 and as Steichen was to describe it, was 'a bombshell exploding in the photographic world
of London.'[23] The furor was heightened by the fact that the
Linked Ring admitted some seventy American prints to their
annual Salon. It was, in Coburn's words, 'the year of the American invasion.'[24] The editor of the *British Journal of Photography* was disgusted: 'We saw it coming – this Cult of the
Spoilt Print.'[25] For that was how the traditionalists viewed the
mysterious darks, the decorative velvet textures of the subdued
platinum prints, and the generally high æsthetic tone of the

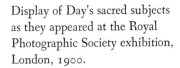

Display of Day's sacred subjects
as they appeared at the Royal
Photographic Society exhibition,
London, 1900.

subjects. The English wanted no part of anything that reminded them of the æstheticism that had led to the Oscar Wilde
scandals. They also saw the New School as an affront to robust,
hearty, realist, masculine England. It was an England that huffily
reminded the world of its invention of paper photography.

> *We live in a free country, and fortunately, or unfor-*
> *tunately, there is no law to forbid people debasing the*
> *powers which sixty years of photographic research*
> *and progress have placed within their grasp; but*
> *when the painful productions of these perverted*
> *users of photography are dragged up from the im-*
> *pregnable security of privacy and held up to public*
> *view, then, in the minds of all sensible photogra-*
> *phers, scorn, disgust, and contempt dispute for pride*
> *of place.*[26]

The target of all the contempt was the overall darkness of
the prints, their generally small size, and the delicacy of their
layered-tissue mounts, which replaced the usually overpowering

'The Cult of the Spoilt Print':
Clarence White's *Lady in Black
with Statuette*, 1898.

carved frames. Especially hated was the array of special effects
originating from the still relatively new use of gum bichromate.

The vituperation was not limited to Day's own work, but
was spread around with an even hand. Steichen's *Nocturne
No. 12, Miss G.* was called a 'young lady who is showing off a
new kind of lattice-work corset, obviously of Yankee origin.'[27]
H. A. Hess's *In Arcadia*, a pleasantly pagan scene of small boys
wreathed and playing on shepherd pipes, was 'mistook at a distance for some bleached earthworms: we presume, however,
that they are ancient Britons.'[28] Gertrude Käsebier's *Boy with
a Hoop* met with derisive laughter.

> *Of course, anyone can see it is a boy with a hoop; it
> certainly isn't a boy with a cow, a horse, or a railway*

Portrait of the critic, Sadakichi Hartmann, by Edward Steichen, 1903.

engine, so that this may be said to be its one good point, but beyond that it is decidedly weak and wishy-washy.[29]

Clarence White received the same mockery that had greeted Whistler long ago.

'Lady in Black,' by Clarence White. This is an excellent title, for there is no mistake about the blackness. At a distance of three feet from the print, it is impossible to distinguish anything but a light muddy patch somewhere toward the top of the print, and this represents all we can see of the face. It may be art, for it is certainly concealed.[30]

The Royal Photographic Society's exhibition of Day's New School proved as much a cause célèbre in the world of photography as the Armory Show of 1913 would be for the astonished American artists. The *British Journal of Photography* warned its readers that the Pictorialists 'will either disappoint, and even shock, their prejudices, or render necessary a total readjustment of their ideas.'[31]

One might have predicted that critics like Sadakichi Hartmann, who had often admired Day, would come forward and attempt to clarify the goals of the New School, so as to render more serious the discussion of the issues. Unfortunately, Day's former champion now turned against him with a petty, inaccu-

'Plastic Psychological Fiddle-sticks': Day's portrait of *Zaïda Ben-Yusuf*, 1898.

rate report. To the English crowd, suspicious of Day's emphasis on the Beautiful, the following story about Day was damning enough.

> *Once a stranger visited him and knocking at the door, heard a most cheerful 'come in,' but entering, found to his great astonishment nobody present. He looked about everywhere, but could find no trace of Mr. Day; then suddenly he heard a clucking sound, looked up and saw Mr. Day sitting on a shelf right under the ceiling, wrapped in an Oriental costume, smoking a water pipe.*[32]

The truth of this ridiculous tale, which prompted cruel speculation on Fred's habits, was that Hartmann had picked up a frequently misquoted piece of newspaper gossip in which a reporter had heard a 'chuckling' sound, not a 'clucking' sound. Day had merely laughed over the reporter's confusion on entering his library at Norwood, where he had built himself a convenient upper reading gallery around two-thirds of the room.

Not only did Hartmann's rumor-mongering provide the English an opportunity to ridicule Day, but one of the critic's phrases of æsthetic criticism became the scapegoat motto for the exhibition. In describing one of Day's portraits of Zaïda Ben-Yusuf, a Philadelphia photographer, Hartmann had been more than usually double-edged.

> *How well he has caught her habit, her ordinary way of being, 'all her little ways.' One feels at once that the artist has photographed her with his heart, if such a thing can be said. The portrait thus conceived becomes a plastic psychological synthesis of the person represented.*[33]

'Plastic psychological synthesis': for most of the English, this was 'Plastic psychological fiddlesticks!'[34] Despite the efforts of two Englishmen, Roger Fry and Clive Bell, to establish a vocabulary in which *plastic* referred to specific characteristics of the visual arts, and despite Hartmann's belated insistence that he had written in a sarcastic tone, the mocking phrase had done its damage. Fiddlesticks it was, and fiddlesticks it would remain. The work of the New School was not only fiddlesticks, but was the bizarre creation of 'Fuzzyographers,' a term the English had been using since Emerson.

Left: Clarence White's *Evening – Interior*; right: Gertrude Käsebier's posterized *Mother and Child*.

Steichen, as amused as he was annoyed by the exchanges in the *British Journal of Photography*, wrote to Day suggesting he laugh it off. 'The poor British J. – and its many letters – what fun – the whole thing in a nutshell – what fools they are.'[35] But for Day it was not easy to laugh about something that meant so much. Unfortunately, the battle was just beginning.

In his opening address to the Royal Photographic Society, Day had made a claim for photography that absolutely infuriated anyone still unconvinced that the camera could produce art. It was not the first time he had made this assertion: photographs should be regarded in the same way as the traditional graphic arts.

> . . . the values of light and shade as produced with the lens run as wide and as truthful as ever were produced by means of slabs of stone or plates of copper. The feeling in textures is presented with as much nicety in a print from a photograph negative as is that from a piece of engraved metal.[36]

This sensible and conservative statement was greeted with even more calumny. The renewed attack advised the readers of the *British Journal of Photography* that 'this so-called new school has been repudiated in the land of its birth.'[37] That was a euphemism for Stieglitz, and it leads one to suspect that the author of the attack was an anonymous member of the Linked Ring who remained loyal to Stieglitz.

Americans, of course, were watching the fracas in London, some with horror and many with glee. The traditionalists, the staid commercial photographers, and the anti-intellectuals all had their say when 'Granpa's Little Talk on Fuzzography' eventually appeared in *Photo Era*. Beside a picture of a drunk in Algerian costume, with the title 'Beauty is Truth – ? With Apologies to F. Holland Day,' it read:

> *A few of these Fuzzyographites have been doing more fighting, and Squabbling, and Calling Names, and making more Protests and Reading More Complaints and doing more Foolish Things than making either Photographs or Fuzzyographs.*[38]

But as the battle spread, involving critics and photographers in England and France, Stieglitz pretended to be removed from it all, as Steichen reported to Day.

> *Have heard from Stieglitz – ahem – his reply to my letters formerly came in several months – to this last one he writes he had just received my letter a few minutes ago – he is all 'blushes and compliments' – so glad to hear direct about the London shows – but does not say* what *he* <u>thinks</u> *of it all.*[39]

The French, on the other hand, were happy to tell Stieglitz and the American public what they thought about Day and the New School. They greeted the Pictorialists enthusiastically when Day brought the exhibition to Paris in 1901. As Demachy stated categorically, 'The French public likes Day!'[40]

> *Mr. Day is what we call in French 'un raffiné,' a man of delicate and subtle taste, who finds particular delight in special color tones and combinations of lines and curves, which either pass unnoticed by the general public or only appeal to their minds after repeated or prolonged study.*[41]

Stieglitz had accepted a long article by Demachy on the

American New School for *Camera Notes*, but when it was published, he apparently felt it necessary to state his own objections.

> *It comprises the work of many photographers of all schools, and is mainly the result of an exchange of prints at Mr. Day's request with the majority of those represented in the collection. Many of these prints were actually unfinished, or what are termed 'seconds,' that is, prints not up to exhibition finish. Hence, much of the unfavorable criticism.*[42]

Both Demachy and Steichen leaped to Day's defense. Demachy declared that no other collection of photographs had given him such a sensation of artistry. Steichen was quite specific:

> *I ultimately became closely acquainted with the work of these photographers, and I never saw better prints from their hands than those exhibited by Day. As far as adequate representation is concerned, I do not think that, except for Stieglitz, any photographer whose work was even moderately known at that time was excluded from Day's exhibition, as his catalogue proves.*[43]

Portrait of Edward Steichen in Paris, by F. Holland Day, 1901.

What was so ironic about Stieglitz's unfounded accusations was the fact that he was in serious difficulties with the Camera Club of New York; they were objecting to his exhibiting prints produced by someone else from his negatives but which he claimed as his own. They *were* his own prints, if you define a photograph as a conception, not an artifact. But Stieglitz had been merciless to everyone whose prints had been produced by commercial houses, Day especially. The details of his confrontation with his accusers were published in *Camera Notes* shortly before his resignation as editor.

That resignation may have given F. Holland Day fleeting pleasure. He had always disapproved of *Camera Notes*, despite his own contributions to it. He had once publicly called it 'a tasteless publication,' and this inevitably implied that Stieglitz was lacking in taste. He would never be able to say that again. In fact, Stieglitz's next publication would inadvertently contribute to Day's own downfall.

The New School of American Photography is today almost completely forgotten, both as a movement and as a per-

Portrait of Stieglitz holding a
copy of *Camera Work,* by Coburn, 1903.

sonal achievement for Day. The reasons for its obscurity are
many and complex: changing tastes, rewritten history, and the
short, ungrateful memories of many who had participated. But
the fundamental reason was one which Day had foreseen – the
immense political power that Stieglitz wielded in the United
States. Quite by accident, in a sense, Day forced Stieglitz's
hand. For Stieglitz now decided to form a group under his own
direction, the Photo-Secession – surely the most documented
photographic movement in the history of photography – and to
articulate his tastes and shifting ideologies in the now historic
publication, *Camera Work.* The first issue of the new journal
was to appear in December 1902, and the measure of Stieglitz's
never-failing nerve was that he wanted to open it with the work
of F. Holland Day. It was an acknowledgement of Day's superior artistry and worldwide reputation.

But what could be more unlikely? Stieglitz had the audac-
ity to ask Day for permission to reproduce his pictures. He intended to use the luxury process of photogravure, assuring
maximum fidelity and permanence. Notwithstanding the se-
duction of photogravure, and not surprisingly, Day refused.
This decision proved to be self-destructive, almost fatally so. By
excluding himself from *Camera Work,* Day inadvertently committed himself to a long and undeserved oblivion.

Many of the Americans may have feared similar fates, and
gave themselves to Stieglitz with hardly a backward glance at
Day. Instead of F. Holland Day, *Camera Work* opened with
Gertrude Käsebier; there was no public announcement to say
she had been second choice, or that the works in this supposedly
revolutionary journal had appeared previously in *Camera
Notes.*[44] The second issue was devoted to the genius of Steichen,
the third to Clarence White, the fourth to Frederick Evans –
Day's friend and champion, who needed American exposure –
the fifth to Robert Demachy, the sixth to Alvin Langdon Coburn, and the ninth and tenth went back to White and Käsebier again. Meanwhile, Day was continuing to show his work
in London, Dresden, Brussels, and Glasgow, and in American
cities as well. He was still a major international figure, probably
more quickly recognized than any other photographer. Nevertheless, in terms of what posterity would reckon, Day could not
be said to exist if he did not make an appearance in *Camera
Work.* Curiously enough, he did, but it was only through
Steichen's portrait of him, a portrait called *Solitude.* It was a
condition in which he would soon discover himself.

11

A Phoenix from the Ashes

It was the first year of the new century: 1901. On January 22, Queen Victoria died. Edward VII assumed the throne of England with the promise of a new spirit of almost libertine permissiveness. A golden age of society balls, breakfast hunts, grand steamship tours, optimism, and frivolity began. If the Decadents had been expecting the new century to revitalize humane ideals, they were gravely disappointed by the unembarrassed cynicism of the profligate rich.

When the Victorian age came to its end, F. Holland Day was in Paris. There he was greeted with adulation, in marked contrast to the snarling London reception. From late February to mid March, the Parisians crowded into the Photo-Club to see the New American School: photographs by Clarence White, Frank Eugene, Eduard J. Steichen (as he then spelled his name), Sarah Sears, Eva Watson, and F. Holland Day. White – whom Day considered a genius – had no fewer than thirty-six prints in the exhibition; the enfant terrible of photography, Steichen, had thirty-four. The favorite of the French, Day himself, had seventy-three, including many of the sacred subjects, the Nubian series, and the female portraits. Coburn had three prints, but Käsebier showed not one print at the Paris exhibition. Had her conscientious loyalty to Stieglitz somehow interfered with her friendship with Day? Perhaps, believing the canards about the quality of the prints, she had told Day that she did not wish to participate. Yet their friendship did not seem impaired by her absence from the exhibition. When she came to London in the summer of 1901, Day gave a grand tea party in her honor, where she met Annan, Hinton, Craigie, Evans, Davison, and others of the Linked Ring. She was the first American woman elected to membership in that still respected society. Clarence White was also fêted that summer.

With the Paris show a huge success, and the prints slated to be sent on to Germany for another showing, Fred Day must have felt he deserved a vacation. He had been busy with affairs other than exhibitions, among these a small favor he had pursued for his old Visionist friend and colleague, Francis Watts Lee. Lee had become interested in a British lens manufactured by the Dallmeyer Company. Since Fred was on his way to England with his exhibition, Lee asked him to collect information about the lens. This simple request led Day into an entirely new experience of photography.

> *The work of this lens was a revelation to myself and some half-dozen American photographers who were in Europe at the time. While the lens was made purely for a portrait lens, I carried it the next Spring to Algiers, and made there what English people told me were the first landscapes attempted with this lens, my experience heretofore being entirely with portrait or figure work. Alvin Coburn procured another, and perhaps Edward Steichen a third.*[1]

According to Day, Francis Watts Lee had been the only one of the 1890s Boston crowd who had 'any knowledge of optics, or much of any relating to technical photography.'[2] He was therefore waiting eagerly to see the new lens when Day returned with Coburn in the summer of 1901.

> *As I was shortly to go into a new studio in Boston, I could not at the moment put my hand on the lens, and enduced [sic] Mr. Coburn to ease Mr. Lee's enthusiasm by loaning him his lens. After some conferences, Mr. Lee loaned the lens to Mr. Smith of Pinkham and Smith, who shared the now growing enthusiasm for a similar lens to be made in America.*[3]

Portrait of F. Holland Day in London, 1901, by Alvin Langdon Coburn.

One of the more fascinating outcomes of Pinkham & Smith's endeavors to duplicate the Dallmeyer lens was that each of the lenses they manufactured was sufficiently different 'that it was quite possible for one interested in the matter to distinguish the author of one print from another provided the ownership of the various lenses put out were known . . .'[4] Day modestly acknowledged that he had a considerable influence in the adoption of this lens by other Pictorialists, but conceded, 'I am sure its work at its best never appealed to anyone more strongly than to me.'[5]

Unfortunately, the landscapes which Day produced on his 1901 visit to Algeria have been lost. But the so-called uncorrected Pinkham & Smith lenses became an intrinsic part of his photographic vision in the next decade. Clarence White, who would shortly join him in Maine, ultimately acquired one of the lenses. Coburn, too, acknowledged his debt, but insisted that he used the lens only as a concession to the soft-focus taste of the times.

Coburn did not acknowledge that another technique he favored was promulgated by Day. This was a mixed process called 'gum-platinum.' The specific look of this process had much to do with Day's new images and with Coburn's successes.

> *In the gum-platinum process the first step was to make a platinum print, which could be either in the normal silver-grey colour, or toned to a rich brown by the addition of mercury to the developer. The finished print was then coated with a thin layer of gum-bichromate containing pigment of the desired colour. I found Vandyke brown especially suitable owing to its transparency, and by having the underlying platinum print in grey, a very pleasant two-color effect was produced. The bichromated print was replaced behind the original negative, great care being taken to get it accurately in register. It was then re-exposed and developed in the usual way.*[6]

Coburn observed that the gum-platinum mixture strengthened the weak shadows of platinum prints: 'The whole process added a lustre to the platinum base comparable to the application of varnish, at the same time preserving the delicacy of the highlights in the platinum print.'[7] It was a process admirably suited to Day's æsthetic, decorative effects.

At the time of the Photo-Club de Paris exhibition, Coburn revered Day. Thanks to Day, Coburn and Steichen became close friends; despite the considerable difference in Day's age, the three of them enjoyed the bohemian and intellectual pleasures of Paris together. Day was drawn to North Africa, whose exotic images and costumes had been attracting him for a decade, and he invited young Coburn along for a tour of Algeria in the late spring of 1901. Fred may have had it in mind to visit André Gide, Oscar Wilde's old acquaintance. But Algeria was in political turmoil, and no sooner had Fred written to Louise Guiney – now nicknamed 'Quinck' – than she pleaded with him to avoid 'the neighborhood of those Arab revolts.'[8] She need not have worried. Day and Coburn romped about in exotic costumes, and, as the story goes, turned up in London com-

Three portraits of Day in Algerian costume by Frederick Evans, London, 1901.

pletely disguised. In Arab burnoose and sunburned faces, they arrived unexpectedly at Frederick Evans's studio. As Coburn remarked later, Evans did the only sensible thing: he photographed them, producing at least three striking portraits of Day.

Day seems to have made an ideal model for his colleagues. Not only Evans and Coburn, but Steichen, Käsebier, White, Hollyer, Keiley, Craigie, and Frank Eugene found his sensitive bearded face and melancholy grey eyes a fascinating subject for the camera. Day had the greatest respect for Evans. He was saddened by how poor the older man had become since giving up the bookshop for architectural photography.

> I sat to Evans again for my portrait yesterday in my
> old studio. He had it fixed up in a most attractive
> way with all his old oak and Japanese things, but its
> a bit thick living and photographing in two rooms —
> and a kitchen.[9]

In this same letter to an old Boston friend, Day remarked, 'Lou [Guiney] has been up from Oxford and I saw her for an hour today. She looks well and hearty, and is so, I judge, not a day older in appearance than when I saw her last.'[10] He also reported, in a paragraph exuding boyish delight, that he had 'put on all my Arab togs the other night and dined with a son of Timothy Cole and his fiance [sic] and called on Miss Devens afterwards.'[11]

No longer one of Day's favorite models, no longer the

focus of attentions which he now lavished on young photographers like Mary Devens, Louise Guiney continued to be blessed by her 'Sonny's' generosity and moral support. She had endured a series of personal disasters since an attack of excruciating deafness in 1897. She was in England now, pursuing research into the lives of seventeenth-century poets at the Bodleian Library, Oxford. It is likely that she had followed Fred Day across the Atlantic when he seemed on the verge of establishing a permanent London residence as a portrait photographer. Traveling with an aged and ill aunt, Louise was descending into a despair which even Day had difficulty ameliorating.

> *This is a pig's letter. I want to have a serious talk*
> *with you before you return, about matters on which*
> *I have spoken to no one, and of which you may have*
> *apprehended something during late years. In plain*
> *truth, I am at bay; absolutely joyless and hopeless,*
> *and done up, so far as anything like original work*
> *goes, for ever.*[12]

Day had just sent her a copy of Maeterlinck's *Treasure of the Humble,* the book which had greatly influenced Kahlil Gibran. Louise thanked him for it, but was too ill to read it just then. Day and Steichen had been off to Paris, where they had both photographed Mæterlinck. Fred's portrait, called *It Is Finished,* caught him smiling faintly over a large transparent bubble of glass, of the sort Clarence White frequently employed. But Mæterlinck was not enough to solace Louise. She urgently needed Fred's financial help. Her father's small pension from the Civil War had run out. She had worked for a time at a frustrating job as postmistress of the Auburndale branch in her home town. Her salary depended on the amount of business she transacted, and the retired Protestant clergymen in her neighborhood had taken exception both to her Saint Bernard dogs and her Catholicism. When they boycotted her, her old champion Ralph Adams Cram persuaded all his friends to do their business with her. Still, the job could not last. She then went to the newly opened Boston Public Library at Copley Square, where her friend Philip Savage had worked until his sudden death from pneumonia in 1899 – all the more tragic because he was newly engaged to be married – and where Francis Watts Lee would be employed for the next decades. Louise had no resources left, nothing but a shack she called 'Shanty Guiney,' on a spit of land on Georgetown Island, Maine. Fred

Day and she had spent summer vacations there since she had purchased it in 1897. Now she asked if Fred would consider renting it or buying it – anything to tide her over the immediate financial emergency.

Of course he would. He lent her money to take care of current problems, and offered to keep the land for her until she chose to return, if ever, to the United States.

> *I can't go home. It gives me the most genuine and involuntary fit of trembling to think of it, much as I long for the faces of my friends. The pace at which everything goes there, the noise, the publicity, the icicles, the mosquitoes, the extreme climatic conditions. I am not equal to facing them now.*[13]

Louise Imogen Guiney at age forty-four, in England

Louise's misfortunes rebounded to Fred's benefit; he would have a new locus for photography, one that was far enough away from noise and publicity, if not mosquitoes. On Five Islands, the location of Shanty Guiney, were pines and boulders, self-contained islands and a surge of open sea, where Greek, Portuguese, and Italian fishermen lived among a few staid Yankee merchants. The community consisted of perhaps a hundred families, spread out among cliffs and inlets noisy only with gulls, cormorants, and lobster boats.

As for Louise, she returned to this haven perhaps only once more, and only a few times to Boston. She spent the next years in cheap lodgings here and there in England while she worked on a volume published posthumously as *Recusant Poets*. Despite physical misfortunes and grim poverty, she was not too poor to be proud or loving. When the sale of the Five Islands property was finally consummated in 1909, it became clear that Louise had intended Shanty Guiney for Fred Day only. She had been offered many times the amount that he ultimately paid for it. It was another demonstration that, no matter how thin the connection from time to time, Fred and Louise cared for each other all of their lives.

At about the time that Alfred Stieglitz was squabbling with the Camera Club of New York, and was on the verge of quitting *Camera Notes,* Day returned to Boston. He was shifting his studio from 9 Pinckney Street on Beacon Hill to No. 29 in the Harcourt Building on Irvington Street. The new studios were twice as large, and permitted him to reserve the old Pinckney Street apartment for social affairs, indigent friends, and visiting photographers. Coburn went on to New York, setting

up a studio within a few blocks of Steichen's new place. While
trying to establish his own business, Coburn worked for Käsebier for a time, so Day always knew what was going on in the
city he detested. In June 1902, Stieglitz formally stepped down
as editor of *Camera Notes.* So little was Fred Day given to har-
boring grudges that he circulated a petition expressing gratitude
to Stieglitz for his contributions to the journal, and wishing
him well in any venture. Only three people could be persuaded
to sign it, among them Francis Watts Lee, and so the petition
died.[14]

Late in 1902, an announcement went out from the new
studio: 'Portraits by a few Leaders in the Newer Photographic
Methods shown during the First Week in December 1902 by
Mr. F. Holland Day at his studio . . .'[15] This was to be a modest
show, primarily of prints which Day had obtained in exchange
for his own, in the custom of the time. The photographers included Mohund Ben Ali of Algiers, Coburn, Demachy, Mary
Devens, Käsebier, Steichen, and Clarence White. Except for
Ben Ali, all of these would soon come into the Stieglitz circle at
Camera Work, and Steichen would become Stieglitz's major
influence toward interest in the avant-garde painters.

Steichen was an ambitious young man. He recognized
Stieglitz as the center of power, yet he did not always like him.
He was particularly horrified, on visiting Stieglitz's home, to
discover reproductions of paintings he found repulsive 'displayed prominently on the walls. They were certainly unlike his
photographs.'[16] They were also as unlike Day's refined taste in
painting as could be conceived.

> There were two very large reproductions of paintings
> by Franz Stuck, the German Secessionist painter.
> One, titled 'Sin,' was of a standing nude. Around her
> coiled a huge snake with threatening eyes. The other
> was the naked torso of a woman emerging from the
> body of a sphinx. Her front claws were dripping
> with blood from the limp body of a man she was
> embracing.[17]

The grossness of these images much offended Steichen, who
shared the common belief that pictures of nudes belonged in
the bedroom, not on public display. But Stuck was merely the
flip side of the æsthetic coin. The tainted lilies of the Wilde
school were only one aspect of the late-Victorian sensibility –
which had also relished spectacles of cruelty. Everyone, includ-

Self-portrait by Edward Steichen, 1902.

ing the Savior and womankind, had been mocked in savage images. In the new, unrepressed Edwardian age, these sadistic icons seemed curiously anachronistic.

Day was trying to secure the position he believed he had earned in the exhibitions of 1900 and 1901. To his dismay, he discovered that Stieglitz was preventing his being invited to direct new exhibitions elsewhere. He found he was once again isolated in Boston, although he certainly retained an international reputation. He still had his allies. In the summer of 1904, while vacationing at Shanty Guiney – now renamed Castle Guiney to honor Louise – he received a note from his brokerage firm.

> *My friend, Mr. T. Curtis Bell, who is cashier at the Lotos Club and I believe well known to you as an amateur photographer, mentioned at the Club the other day that he was very anxious to secure your co-*

operation in some plan for a new society of amateur photographers.[18]

Day had already been approached by Curtis Bell, the self-appointed President of the American Federation of Photographic Societies, with offices at 558 Fifth Avenue, New York. In a letter soliciting Day's cooperation and guidance as the leader of the New School, Bell explained:

> *I also enclose a copy of the Constitution of this Federation just organized and now comprising the Chicago – Boston – Toronto – California – Brooklyn Camera Clubs – the Capitol CC of Washington – the Columbia Society of Philadelphia – Salon Club and Metropolitan CC of NY – and others . . .*[19]

An arch-enemy of Stieglitz, Bell was authorized to appoint four members of the Art Committee, and had selected Day as the first appointment. He also requested that Day choose the others.

> *I also beg to say that, in our opinion, this Federation cannot fail to become a tremendous power in the Advancement of Pictorial Photography,* if rightly used and directed . . .[20]

The implication was clear: Stieglitz was promoting only one kind of photography. Day would be expected to demonstrate more latitude in his tastes and habits.

The American Federation of Photographic Societies was planning an opening exhibition in New York for 1905. But before Day could assume leadership of this group, which promised to restore him to national prominence, he was interrupted by a catastrophe. On the night of November 11, 1904, the Harcourt Building in which his new studio was housed was leveled by a disastrous fire. The clumsy woodcut published in the Boston papers the next day showed the block-long, three-story building engulfed in flames, as firemen vainly hosed down the inferno. Everything was lost. Day's two thousand negatives (the work of more than a decade), his own prints and those of his Pictorialist colleagues, his instruments (including the original Pinkham & Smith and the Dallmeyer uncorrected lenses), his invaluable collection of Aubrey Beardsley drawings, Corot paintings, Japanese prints and artifacts, Chinese vases and porcelains, North African rugs, ivory statuettes, masks, leopard skins, white draperies, Moorish and Turkish costumes, his favorite squat Buddha, his incense burner, and the thirteen candlesticks for which hostile critics had mocked him—everything was gone.

He had only himself, his own genius, some prints sequestered at Norwood, and wealth enough to start again, if he could find heart to do it. Condolences and expressions of horror poured in from around the country. Käsebier and Coburn sent a joint telegram: 'We are too grieved for words.'[21] Käsebier followed with a letter.

> *What a calamity! How did it happen? What a fortunate thing no lives were lost. I have a few of your prints which are at your disposal. Mr. Keiley wishes me to say the same for him. If there are any particulars in the newspapers please send me one and accept my sincerest sympathy.*[22]

Stieglitz summoned up enough graciousness to send a one-sentence telegram expressing sympathy as well. But Clarence White was sincerely overcome with grief.

> *How can I express my feelings, My Dear Mr. Day over the loss we've all suffered. I say all for we have all so enjoyed the studio and the treasures. I will venture no expression, but what can I do or offer? My choicest print is yours as a start on a new collection of photographs and Mrs. White joins in expressions of deepest sympathy. May we hope for encouraging news.*[23]

It was a heart-warming display of affection and support, but no one knew better than Fred Day that he had received a blow almost beyond recovery. Almost all evidence of his accomplishments had disappeared in a single night. He had given prints to Frederick Evans, Robert Demachy, Steichen, Coburn – but not a single glass negative survived.

Not surprisingly, Day communicated to Curtis Bell that he wanted all his prints already submitted to the New York Salon returned at once. Bell attempted to reassure him, but made it clear that Day's work was too important to be omitted from any traveling exhibitions.

> *We feel it our duty to ask that one of them be permitted to go to the other cities as the entire fraternity will wish to admire the remnant of your old work –*

Left: portrait of Gertrude Käsebier by Coburn, 1903; right: portrait of Clarence White by
Edward Steichen, 1903.

*We promise you that it shall be guarded jealously
and returned to you in perfect condition, and your
kindness will give enjoyment to many thousand
admirers.*[24]

Bell also mentioned that the work of George Seeley, one of
Day's protégés, had received the endorsement of the federa-
tion's jury. It may have been small comfort to know he had
supported yet another young Pictorialist. Seeley, a native of
Stockbridge, Massachusetts, eventually would be noticed by
Stieglitz as well.

Curtis Bell was determined that the catastrophic fire not
prevent Day's assumption of the leadership of the new Federation. In May 1905, he wrote to Day: 'We feel that the domi-
nance of your position entitles us to your countenance and direction.'[25] But Day seemed more concerned with recovering his
own capacity to work than in resuming the politics of photography. His relationship with the Federation appears to have
dwindled gradually, and the Federation itself posed no real
threat to Stieglitz's continuing domination. Was Day now re-
senting his friends' success with the Stieglitz faction? Was he
deliberately avoiding them on his rare New York visits? 'Why
did you pass me by?'[26] was the entire content of a note from

The Day house in Norwood, by
Clarence White, 1905.

Gertrude Käsebier dated May 11, 1905. Käsebier was ill with
'mental strain,'[27] and about to go abroad for a specialist's consul-
tation and rest. Although she looked forward to future visits,
she was forced to refuse Day's invitation to spend the summer
with him in Maine.

Instead, Clarence White and his family came to Five Islands for the summer of 1905. Day and the Whites had known
each other since the Philadelphia Salon of 1899, but this was
the real solidification of their friendship. Jane and Clarence
White were both so unassuming and unpretentious that they
had captured Day's affections from the start. Beneath his surface of reserve, Day was a man who longed for the opportunity
to do good, to be helpful, to be appreciated. The Whites provided him with every occasion to exhibit these virtues and became, in fact, a surrogate family for Day.

When Clarence White quit a bookkeeping job with whole-
sale grocers in his hometown of Newark, Ohio, he was determined to support his family as an itinerant worker in both photography and business. Recognizing how poor White would
now become, Day offered him assistance. In return, after the
disaster of the fire, White suggested a change of scene. 'Before
you again busy yourself in the studio, why not come westward.
. . . We Westerners do all the traveling . . .'[28] Perhaps to his
own surprise, Day went out to Ohio and there enjoyed himself
hugely with the White children as well as with White's circle
of friends and colleagues. He became a favorite with his Russian cigarettes and his usual array of gifts and courtesies.

A few months later, when Clarence, Jane, and their two
boys came up to Castle Guiney, Day was already equipped
with a new camera, a new Pinkham & Smith lens, fresh dry
plates, and the spirit to start all over again. While the new beginning would prove slow, it was anything but cautious. Supported by the companionship of the Whites and by his respect
for Clarence's talents, his spirit seemed to rise like a phœnix
from the ashes of the fire. This was to be a phœnix caring
little for the opinions of the world, willing to dare scandals.
He was now a pagan entirely, a Hellene without remorse. He
would seek his pleasures where and when he could find them.

Two heads: boy with Herm of
Pan, by F. Holland Day, 1905.

The Herm of Pan

During the late-Victorian era, pagan themes had served artists as excuses to depict the pleasures of the flesh, but F. Holland Day had been subdued and cautious in his early attempts to poeticize the beauties of the naked male body. His sacred subjects had employed nudity as revelation of spiritual agony. With notable exceptions, his early pagan subjects had been intellectualized, artificial studio portraits: youths with shepherd's crooks, pale adolescents supporting brass urns, or sensitive ephèbes sniffing make-believe tulips.

Occasionally, when Day took his models outdoors, he was able to achieve a somewhat more spontaneous sense of life being lived in true pagan style. Two favorites with the public had been his *Pipes of Pan* and *The Marble Faun,* both of 1897. In the *Kedan,* part of the Armageddon triptych, and in other nudes decorously asleep in forests, he relied upon twilight to supply a sense of mystery. His effects were obviously limited by the technology available in the 1890s.

For a romantic like Day, the new uncorrected Pinkham & Smith lens was the perfect instrument for a new approach to the pagan subjects. From 1905 to 1912, he would use it to create moods of lyrical sensuality in which an undisguised fas-

The Pipes of Pan, above, and
The Marble Faun, below, both
by F. Holland Day, 1897.

cination with the adolescent male form was predominant.
While Baron von Glœdon's naked ephèbes had been delin-
eated with the hard contour of the late-Victorian academic
painters, Day's nudes were magical, with shimmering lights
and shadows. His creations were often veiled in intimations of
mythology rather than blatant homoeroticism. Von Glœdon's
images were secular plebians of the marketplace; Day's were
demigods of the woods and shore. It was a mark of Day's
genius that he could disguise in his models a real-life vulgarity
that we will shortly discover.

The portrayal of demigods and other mythological creatures requires an idyllic setting away from any industrialized
environment. Certainly such themes required privacy. No more
perfect theatre for Day's new photography could have been
found than his new summer home in Maine. Like his idol John
Keats, he might have described it in these terms:

> *I am going among Scenery whence . . . I'll cavern
> you, and grotto you, and waterfall you, and wood
> you, and water you, and immense-rock you, and
> tremendous sound you, and solitude you.*[1]

Keats had written this teasing paragraph foretelling a proposed
trip to Devonshire, England. The coincidence, if such it was, is
that Louise Guiney had purchased her land in Maine precisely
because it had reminded her of Devon. Like their adored poet,
F. Holland Day and Louise Imogen Guiney sought a barbaric,
Gothic inspiration in the boulder-strewn beaches and caverned
cliffs of Georgetown Island. Here at Five Islands, perhaps for
the first time, Day succeeded in creating images that had the
resonance of poetry.[2]

Even Clarence White fell under the spell of Day's classi-
cism that first summer in Maine. White produced some of his
loveliest pictures at Little Good Harbor, including *The Pipes
of Pan,* the *Archer, The Wrestlers,* and *Nude Boy at Bridge*
(not illustrated). The *Archer* was a subject on which both he
and Day worked simultaneously, with delightful results. The
models for these pictures were probably the young White boys.
Day found the two children marvelously photogenic. They
were accustomed to posing for their father and were the most
obedient and pliant of models. Day also made use of the children of local fishermen.

Day had installed a white marble Herm of Pan, a well-

Left: Clarence White's *Archer in Woods,* 1905; right: F. Holland Day's *Archer* of the same summer.

known classical symbol associated with fertility rites, in a wooded grove at Five Islands. It was a most discreet version of a figure known to antiquity as a priapic image: it had the required rectangular pillar as a base, and the armless torso, but lacked the bearded face and conspicuous phallus. In its uncensored original form, it was an image that had obsessed Aubrey Beardsley. He had used it to decorate not only the frontispiece of *Salomé* but many of the initials and chapter headings for *Le Morte d'Arthur.* The statue in Maine was much less malevolent. It had the appearance of a laughing faun, with a charming grin and pointed ears. But Day knew quite well that the Herm of Pan was intended to brood over 'scenes of Bacchanalian revelry and . . . the festivals of Pan and Priapus,'[3] both gods who presided over sexual orgies.

One of the most striking pictures from this summer of 1905 was his 'Two heads: Boy with Herm of Pan' where, once again, Day's delight in strong contrasts between white and dark areas is conspicuous. Clarence White, too, photographed the subject with somewhat more overall darkness.

Another classical motif the two colleagues explored that summer was that of naked boys with shepherd's crooks playing with turtles on the rocks. Day's sunstruck 'Boy with shepherd's

crook and tortoises' (plate 47) was an image he returned to in
later years, always with great subtlety of color and charm (plate
48). The symbolism is complex – linked not only with the
Herm of Pan but with Apollo. Both were depicted as shepherds
with crooks. The tortoise was sacred to Hermes; its shell had
been used to form the sounding box for the lyre, which Hermes
was supposed to have invented. The lyre itself became one of
the major motifs in Day's pictures (perhaps because of its significance to Keats). Hermes was known as a phallic god who
often wore a flat cap with birds' wings on it. The black pigeon's
wings had already been used by Day, and they would find
service here in Maine. They had been kept at Norwood and so
escaped the fire.

Boy offering fruit to a Herm of
Pan, by Aubrey Beardsley.

Day may have attempted many other pagan portraits that
summer. Unfortunately, many of his post–1904 pictures are
undated. It seems likely that he did make at least two portraits
of a nude young man crowned in vine leaves in 1905 before
September's cold arrival forced the group to retreat south
to Norwood. The Whites were Day's guests there before returning to Ohio, and Clarence made a fine impressionistic
portrait of the Norwood mansion.

> *At home we are, My dear Mr. Day and a long jour-*
> *ney we've had. . . . We spent the time in Norwood*
> *very pleasantly and I enjoyed very much the work*
> *I did. . . . Mrs. White and the boys left the city for*
> *Pittsburgh Saturday even and I stayed over until*
> *Monday eve to see Stieglitz.*[4]

On the way home, White had stopped in New York on
business, as he was beginning to think about moving there. He
did move to New York in 1906, bringing himself that much
closer to Day. The Pictorialist Herbert G. French of Cin-
cinnati had written to Day for advice on a project concerning
White: what did Day think about photographic illustrations to
Tennyson's *Idylls of the King?* Day approved enthusiastically,
so White was encouraged to produce a series of books illustrated with his own photographs.

Of course, New York was not only closer to Day; it was
the citadel of Stieglitz's power. In 1905, *Camera Work* had reproduced eight of Clarence White's photographs, including
one of his son clutching an issue of that journal. White undoubtedly believed that Stieglitz would continue to encourage

him. As for the relationship between Stieglitz and Day, there were only further difficulties. Stieglitz had once more solicited Day's prints, this time for an exhibition. The following is from a draft of a letter sent on November 30, 1906:

> *My dear Mr. Stieglitz,*
> *Let me thank you for your kind letter of the 26th inst [sic] proposing my cooperation with the Photo-Secession in forming a collection of my work for exhibition by them in January next. I fear you do not realize how very small is the amount of work I have accomplished during the past two years, nor how small a proportion of what has been done meets sufficiently with my approval for such a purpose. . . . I feel I must once more beg of you a postponement to some future time when I may be better able to submit work more worthy of your acceptance.*
>
> *Regarding an exhibition made up of any possible collection of my prints dating prior to 1900, I can but assure you that it would be wholly and seriously without my approval and contrary to my wishes.*[5]

How well Stieglitz would abide by Day's explicit wishes will be discovered in the next chapter.

It was true that Day had not produced a large number of prints in the two years since the fire, but he had managed to begin the pagan series. Equally important, he had taken a considerable number of portraits of his black servants at Norwood. Produced either in the spring or fall of 1905, these formed a remarkable series of black people as they were, not romantically enhanced by leopard skins and Moorish costumes. In platinum or gum platinum, these strong silhouettes showed once again Day's skillful exploitation of areas of pure white against masses of deep shadow. The titles are descriptive only, as he gave none. 'Black woman with striped collar' (plate 27) and 'Black girl with broad white collar' (plate 28) have the soft texture of charcoal drawings. The decorative silhouettes obliterated detail, and their off-balance, yin-yang effect was more painterly than ever before. The new lenses were helping Day to overcome the uncompromising statuesque qualities of the Nubian series. The powerful manipulation of gum printing was helping him to achieve a brilliant and perhaps surprising impressionism. The sympathetic 'Bearded old black man' (plate 26), on the other hand, still relied upon the subtlety of platinum paper for the softness of its detail.

Working with platinum was not without hazards. Shortly before moving to New York, Clarence White wrote to Day:

> *I have been discouraged – the worst in a long time – and I rather lay that to an attack of platinum poisoning that caused me much suffering. Indeed I reached the point that apparently it was impossible to make a good print.*[6]

This was a clear warning to Day to resist overexposure to the medium. Day was not well. A few cyanotypes of 1906 reveal him to be painfully thin, with puffed eyes. Giving up platinum was out of the question, however. Almost all of his technical effects depended on the graphic-arts quality of that specific tonality. He relied on platinum paper that had been aged three years to produce the close harmonies of the prints and the delicacy of their halftones. His Boston suppliers were sometimes hard put to satisfy his special requirements.

If Fred had been slow to start working again on a grand scale, his pace now quickened considerably. When he returned to Five Islands in the summer of 1906, to his own sheltering inlet known as Little Good Harbor, he was not joined by the White family, who were busy establishing themselves in Manhattan. Once again, Gertrude Käsebier had been forced to decline his invitation to holiday in Maine. Left to himself, Day returned to the previous summer's themes. It is not certain who his models were, but they became in his pictures moody, introspective pagans in dramatic chiaroscuro: 'Curly-headed youth with lyre' (plate 52) and 'Youth with staff shading his eyes' (plate 51) are both well past pubescence, more serious than sensual. In keeping with his long-held ideology, F. Holland Day was still refusing to duplicate prints. 'Youth with staff shading his eyes' appears as an octagon mounted on multiple tissue papers – white, blue, grey, and brown – as a gum-bichromate print, as a platinum print, as a gum-platinum, as a rectangle, and as an oblong. Infinite pains were taken with each of these processes.

Day's mood seemed for a time unusually somber and preoccupied with suffering. The two variations of the St. Sebastian theme appeared in this summer of 1906, Day's only return to

Octagonal version of youth with staff shading his eyes, by F. Holland Day, 1906.

the sacred subjects, and neither was an exalted version of saint-hood. If anything, they reveal a side of his personality pre-viously sublimated or disguised in the crucifixions and *The Seven Last Words of Christ*. These images were tinged with homoerotic masochistic posturing, and it is doubtful that he showed them to any of his friends. Yet another image dwelt on the theme of pain: 'Youth with scar on shoulder,' an evocative portrait produced in several different versions, seems today to be remote from Day's earlier ideology of redemptive suffering. Perhaps toward the end of the summer, he returned to the sunnier themes, to paganism embodied in nude youths pur-suing hedonistic revels. The finest of these is the distant, shim-mering 'Nude youth standing on cliff, arms raised' (plate 49).

Day was eager to have a response to these new images, and sent off some prints of the pagan series to Käsebier. Hav-ing recovered from her siege of mental strain, she was about to be exposed to more genuine strain than ever before. Her landlord had given her three days to vacate her studio because 'the man whose sub-tenant I was had not paid his rent . . .'[7] The stock market had fallen. And Stieglitz was criticizing her preoccupation with her portrait business rather than with 'pure' art. She did not know how much longer she could en-dure Stieglitz's public castigations. Finally she got around to commenting on Day's work.

The youth with scar, below, also posed for the St. Sebastian, above, by F. Holland Day, about 1906.

> *Thank you for the beautiful print. If you want a*
> *criticism it must be something sent out for that pur-*
> *pose, not a gift. Have you see [sic] the Jan. Century.*
> *Stieglitz has certainly loosed all his dogs of war on*
> *me and why I do not know. It is a poor return for*
> *my years of loyalty. Neither he nor White have been*
> *near me. How strenuous how complex life is. A*
> *happy New Year dear Mr. Day, a very happy one.*
> *Yours sincerely,*
> *Gertrude Käsebier.*
>
> *What a magic landscape you have at Five Islands. Are*
> *you ever going to have that little island I wonder?*[8]

Somehow the triumverate that Stieglitz had conceptualized had fallen upon hard times. Käsebier complained that White never came near her except to ask for favors. 'I have made a number of friendly advances to the Whites but cannot say they

are warmly received.'[9] White rarely mentioned Käsebier to
Day. He did comment adversely about Coburn, although he
was on good terms with the young man. Day continued to send
sweets to Käsebier and invitations to White. Given the circumstances, it is remarkable that Day was able to be friends with
each of the warring factions. When Day made a brief visit to
New York, he and Käsebier had a most friendly visit, reminiscent of the days before the Philadelphia Salon of 1899. 'It was
so stimulating to see you and have a free exchange of ideas
about our work,' she wrote to him, thanking him for the gift of
several Pinkham & Smith lenses. 'I do hunger for just that in-
terchange. I do not know why it is denied me here, but it is.'[10]
She was surprised to hear Day had been ill, as White had
known nothing of it. She was all motherly and friendly again.
Now that she knew Stieglitz better, she may have realized that
Holland Day had been right about the New School of American Photography. All that Day seemed to care about was stay-
ing clear of all the internecine complications.

At that time, the biggest controversy between Stieglitz and
Käsebier was whether every print a photographer produced
must be of exhibition quality. She wrote angrily to Day, 'Has
our medium not reached a phase where an account of our men-
tality must be rendered. Not only that but our spirituality our
very being is on trial.'[11] Day was to be flattered now unre-
servedly: 'The "meat" of your few prints – which you showed
me last winter – still sustains me.'[12] How the times had
changed and how Käsebier had come around.

White, meanwhile, was feeling great discouragement.
(Day had reasons of his own to be discouraged: his father was
ill, and his time was increasingly taken up with helping to
nurse the old man at Norwood.) White wrote in 1907:

> I am doing nothing with my camera and my long
> effort – since 1898 – to help the cause has about
> wound up the ball for me. I am apparently groping
> around in the dark. I hope for the little family I'll
> see daylight.[13]

Robert Demachy had already observed that a kind of lassitude
had overtaken the warriors of the New School, that nothing
new was being accomplished. White was discovering that New
York City was not especially hospitable to art photography. Nor
were the Pictorialists especially hospitable to each other.

*Indeed I am quite muddled, and become more so
when I read so much about the* wonders of photography. *But I am going to say that I see little* appreciation *of photography . . .*[14]

White was about to accept a teaching appointment in
photography at Columbia University Teacher's College. He
was desperately poor. In a characteristic act of friendship, Day
offered to pay for the entire White ménage to come and visit
Norwood, but White would not hear of it.

*I hate though to look at the future and see myself as
a dried up teacher of photography. But I guess that is
the only cog I've even started in this year's wheel.*[15]

Even more sadly, White wrote, 'The world moves – the photographic one – but I am not on the bandwagon.'[16]

It is hard to say what bandwagon he could have meant.
Certainly, neither Day nor Käsebier was on it, whatever it was.
Day had taken time off from nursing his father for a summer's
respite in Maine. In 1907 and 1908 he began another pagan
series, using several seductively handsome models. One young
man in particular he seemed to favor for nude poses on the
rocky shore or in the forest, as in 'Nude youth leaning against
boulder' (plate 46) and the stunning 'Nude youth in dappled
woods' (plate 45). The latter displays a sun-dappled scene,
with a frontal view of the nude young man standing demurely
in a narrow stream. The same model seems to have posed for
almost all of the 'Nude youth with lyre' series of summer 1907
(plates 43, 44).

One English critic named these the Orpheus series, undoubtedly because of the presence of caves, grottoes, dark forests, elongated lyres, and the soulfully sorrowing expressions on
the young man's face. Just as suitably, these could be called an
Apollo series, as the wreathed head and the lyre were equally
attributes of the Sun God. I favor the Apollo interpretation because of Day's lengthy involvement with Keats. In Keats's
hymn to Apollo, we readily find the symbols used by Day: 'God
of the golden bow / And of the golden lyre . . .'[17] Moreover,
Poussin had painted a magnificent canvas, *The Inspiration of
the Poet,* which was known to have influenced Keats's imagery.
In it, a semi-nude Apollo, wreathed in laurel leaves and holding a lyre, is depicted as the muse of a young poet, over whose

uplifted face a cupid flies with laurel wreaths. The Poussin painting is said to have inspired Keats's lines, 'To see the laurel wreath on high suspended / That is to crown our name when life is ended.'[18]

F. Holland Day was similarly preoccupied with the rewards of the artist, the laurel wreath that the god of poetry would offer. Was there a kindly god of photography who would smile upon his efforts? His father was dying; Fred himself was suffering with kidney stones, a most painful affliction. His old friend Evans suggested Turkish steam baths as a remedy, and these provided some relief. But Day knew it was only the continued inspiration of his work that would keep him free of the Clarence White sort of melancholy. For what if nothing remained to remind the world of that small band of photographers who believed in the inspiration of art? It was a frightening thought, more likely to drive Day into the escape of picturing wreathed boys with lyres or arrows than into the story of Orpheus grieving for his lost wife, even if Day had once considered himself 'married' to photography. Either interpretation could apply.

Orpheus, moreover, had never served as a motif for Keats, who sealed his letters with a gem carved with a lyre and the words *Qui me néglige me désole*.[19] Holland Day had several times visited the Keats grave in Rome, where the monument to the poet bore his desired epitaph: HERE LIES ONE WHOSE NAME WAS WRIT IN WATER.[20] It also bore the emblem of a Greek lyre with four of its eight strings broken, the symbol of a life prematurely ended. This sad vision would come to preoccupy Day as a foreboding of his own artistic future.

Perhaps his underlying melancholy drove him to seek companionship among young men whose major gifts were youth and physical beauty. The sensual model for the Apollo with the lyre series turns out to have been scarcely a god. He was an Italian boy from Chelsea whom Day had encountered on one of his many neighborhood charity excursions. Let us call him Nardo. Like Kahlil Gibran, the boy had shown evidence of artistic talent. Undoubtedly, he had been brought to Day's attention by some well-meaning settlement-house director, eager to see the boy advance in the world. Unlike Gibran, however, this protégé turned out to be illiterate, vain, a liar, and a cheat. Although we can feel some compassion for Day that he should have been taken in, the letters Nardo wrote also compel mirth.

My dearest Mr. Day –
You are making me Happy every single Day of the
week. I feel as if I had a lot of powre when you mak
me feel Happy do not thing for one moment becouse
I do not say anything to you you might thing I forget
you. . . . Often time I thing that you are to kind to
me My dearest Mr. Day – But I am sure that the day
will come when you shall fell so happy for what you
have done for me . . . for I thing there is nothing like
F. H. Day in this while while [wide wide] world for
wherever you go I shall for wherever you step I shall
step I will fowlow you through Hell if it is nessissery
I mean it so Help me god this is the trut and nothing
but the trut.[21]

Two of the lyre series by
F. Holland Day, 1907; the one
above was probably titled *The
Last Chord and Then No More.*

Day had been reading Keats's *Isabella; Or, The Pot of Basil*, a passionate but morbid poem, to Nardo; it was an odd choice. He was supporting the boy in art school, leading him into the study of Burne-Jones, and introducing him to employers for his art. He wrote a strong recommendation to William Dana Orcutt at the University Press, where Nardo was to apprentice himself in the world of commercial art. One day a week, he was to be allowed time off to attend art-school classes. But Nardo quickly let Day know he was not satisfied with such largesse. He complained that it took him so long to complete his designs that he was not getting sufficient criticism – usually rendered by Nardo as 'critixdims.' His letters ended with such phrases as, 'I am afraid yo do not get my mennings which I would like to explane to you as quick as possible . . .'[22]

Day got his 'mennings' all right, but not soon enough to discover that the boy had been using the time off from work not to attend art class, but to woo his landlord's daughter. Perhaps if Day had known the inclinations of his handsome protégé, he would not have posed him for the Apollo lyre series. Yet that is hard to say, for Day's infatuation seemed to see only the surface of things. By mid-winter of 1908, he had become somewhat disenchanted. The boy was not following the outline Day had made the year before to help him study English. Furthermore, he was doubling the amount authorized him at a fine bookstore. When Nardo went to New York that winter, pursuing a rich young girl, he shamelessly wrote asking Day for a five-hundred dollar loan. After a short delay, Day wrote back.

> *I am enclosing the loan you ask, but I want you to*
> *know that I do so out of no sort of sympathy with*
> *your distress, brought on as it is by certain disregard*
> *of the good advice you have long had and your stub-*
> *born determination to do as you please without*
> *hindrance.*[23]

That rigorous, puritanical response should have impressed
Nardo, but it did not. After a while, his spelling and syntax
considerably improved, he wrote again. This letter reveals that
their relationship had certainly bordered on the homoerotic
even if it was never consummated.

> *Many a time I think of you during the day the joy-*
> *full and happy times we had together. My life then*
> *was one joy of happness, and allways cheerful full of*
> *love life and ambition. I will never forget the day we*
> *were out to Brockton, how happy I was, I thought*
> *the world was mine. When both of us walking in*
> *through the woods together ame in ame [arm in arm]*
> *and the beautiful birds that were singing sweet melo-*
> *dies . . . What paradise it was! Tell me dear Mr Day,*
> *do you not remember the happy time we had there?*[24]

Day, of course, remembered the happy time, but he also remembered Nardo's lies. Nardo begged Day to forgive him, and
complained that the last time he had been permitted to see
Day, someone else had been in the studio and the visit had only
lasted an hour. So he threatened, 'I will leave you in piece I
will go fare away where know body will know where I am.
That is just as soon as I get enough money of my own.'[25]
    One can only hope that by this time Day was laughing at
the impertinence of the boy.

> *I wonder if you could give me a photo the figure with*
> *the lyer standing beside the big rock and the last cord*
> *that was striking and then no more do you know*
> *which one I mean the last breath . . .*[26]

It turns out that Herbert Copeland, Day's former partner,
also became involved with Nardo and with other male protégés.
Herbert had been suffering with acute alcoholism, and at that
time, unfortunately, there were no groups for psychological

Portion of Copeland's letter to
Day telling him about his
'Jimmie-Hermes,' 1909.

assistance. Alcoholics were considered pariahs, hopeless and
repugnant. Several times, Herbert was forced out of his lodgings for lack of rent money. He had been 'borrowing' from
patient Fred Day for years. When their publishing firm dis-
solved, and Day was gaining an international reputation for his
photography, Herbert had been desperate for work. He ended
up in the South, editing Booker T. Washington's *The Future
of the American Negro*. It may have been the most worthy job
he ever undertook. Soon he was back in the North, scrounging
a living. Fred put him to work as a tutor for some of his young
protégés in the slums, of whom Nardo was one.

Nardo seems to have been almost more than Herbert
could handle. On an early visit to investigate Nardo's circumstances, Copeland found himself confronted not only by
Nardo's wife but his mother, who had disapproved greatly of
her son's posing for Day.

> *The mother said – 'It's very good of you Mr. Cope-
> land to take such an interest in Nardo,' whereupon
> he remarked – 'Nobody can help taking an interest in
> me can they Mr. Copeland?' This in all seriousness!*[27]

Copeland had been having his difficulties with other
young men.

> *What have we done? Again I'm wondering . . . if it
> is right to adopt those of another class than our own.
> Your experiments have not apparently been success-
> ful, and I'll never get over my former barber and his
> buying a Buddha and candlesticks and incense . . . he
> is a very apt disciple. In other words, he has, in the
> course of our very intimate relationship, become com-
> pletely embued with my taste in theater, opera, food,
> clothes, house furnishings, and all that. Now this is
> very flattering to me, and there's no harm in his ac-
> quiring good taste. But his wife will never sympathize
> with him in all this. . . . I was desperately taken with
> him at first sight, and deliberately laid myself out to
> catch him (you know I've always wanted a disciple)
> before I knew he was married. . . . This was some
> months, and then it was too late. I tried to quit
> then – but – well, I just didn't, and our intimacy has
> steadily increased. And now, because I have got what*

I wanted, I am, as you see, 'leaving 'em.' . . . Why
can't we find the right one in all ways? What'll I do?
Nothing, I suppose . . .[28]

Herbert did not always seek disciples. On the contrary, he admitted that his interest in young men consisted primarily of
infatuation. About one young man who had been his masseur
he wrote rhapsodically to Day, although he seemed to be quite
unsure of his own taste in lovers. Likening this masseur to the
statue of the nude *Resting Hermes,* Copeland asked Day if he
would not like to photograph the new demigod. Day apparently
put Little Good Harbor and Castle Guiney at Herbert's dis-
posal for these amours, and Herbert was planning another trip.
'He really "has" me hard and I wish I might stay for a day or
two, for I'd like you to know him – though I dare say he's not
very interesting save to *me.*'[29] Finally, he wrote that the young
man would indeed join him in Maine – in the dead of the
February cold. They would arrive at Day's Boston studio in the
morning, before taking the boat.

I'm 'scared!' I'm afraid you won't like his looks . . .
I'm afraid you will think he's commonplace looking.
Maybe he is – only he has *me! And if you could see*
him in the 'altogether' I believe you would care – but
he's 'afraid' so don't speak of it.[30]

Was this the self-righteous Herbert Copeland who had once
warned Fred Day not to compromise himself by posing for
Beardsley? More than fifteen years had passed since then. Now
he seemed totally unconcerned about committing such scandalous thoughts to paper.

What Fred Holland Day thought about all this we may
never know, as the letters he wrote to Copeland during this
period seem to have disappeared. A phrase from Herbert's letter, 'And if you could see him in the "altogether" I believe you
would care . . .' has unmistakable implications for our understanding of Day's own proclivities, even without the evidence
of the Nardo episode and the increasingly sensual photographic
treatment of male nudes. Certainly, many of these youthful
models are deliberately provocative and enticing, whether or
not they were disguised as woodland deities. Unfortunately for
any biographer, Day never documented his homosexual activities in terms of physical relationships. This absence of firm
evidence might even lead to the conjecture that, given his ad-

The youth in feathered hat, left, also posed in North African costume, right, for F. Holland Day, about 1907.

miration for Balzac's chastity as providing the necessary energy for an artist's creative life, Day may have managed to sublimate rather than express his sexuality – an improbable but entirely possible supposition.

In the first decade of the twentieth century, Day's æsthetic passions fixed on the nude pubescent and adolescent male, in the manner of a true Hellene. Yet he simultaneously continued to photograph women of all ages in a most sympathetic and charming fashion, and at all times he was accepted by the Clarence White family as a gentlemanly bachelor friend with no danger of indiscretion. Numerous letters from young boys who spent time at Little Good Harbor indicate that Day always controlled his physical desires – that is, unless he had invited a willing partner to the chalet he built in 1910. Several snapshots taken after the Nardo interlude do reveal a handsome youth posed casually nude among the granite pillars of Day's Greek temple, below the chalet, in a manner more intimate than artistic.

It is conceivable, of course, that the voyeurism inherent in photography was sufficient to satisfy his fastidious soul. But Stephen Parrish noted that, after Day's death, letters to Day from Oscar Wilde and Aubrey Beardsley were discovered that confirm what we can easily suspect.[31] Meanwhile, it makes no crucial difference to our appreciation of his photographs of male nudes: some are what they seem to be, erotic posturings; others use the male body as an artistic motif, an excuse for flamboyant composition, and a vivid symbol of a physical freedom Day seemed destined never to enjoy.

The Clarence White family, all
in sailor suits, taken by Gertrude
Käsebier in Maine, about 1912.

13 Little Good Harbor

While Fred Holland Day was privately enjoying his Five Islands refuge, the public had not forgotten him. Nor had he quite given up hope of recapturing the attention that had been lavished upon his pictures in the late 1890s and especially in Paris at the exhibition of the New School of American Photography.

Between 1905 and 1912, Day experimented with different approaches to portraiture. Some, in their use of a suffused over-all light and certain compositional dynamics, were closely allied to the contemporaneous efforts of Clarence White and Gertrude Käsebier. Often, in portraits like 'Woman in veiled hat' (plate 37), he pushed the gum-platinum process to extremities of darkness. At the same time, he could transform a potentially banal subject, like 'Old woman smiling' (plate 38), by composing her delightfully off-center and subduing her wrinkles with the gum process, and make of her a decorative and utterly charming image of sturdy optimism.

A pale shimmer, often tinged with dull yellows and earthy oranges, enhanced the glow of many of these portraits. If an occasional subject seemed to mimic the repertoires of White or Käsebier, especially in a print like 'Mother nursing infant'

Clarence White's *The Readers,*
1897, at left; Day's portrait of two
girls reading, 1907, on the right.

(plate 41), Day's treatments usually were significantly different. A comparison, for example, between White's *The Readers*
of 1897 and Day's 'Two girls reading' (plate 42) of 1907 indicates how far Day could move from the decorative flat pattern-
ing of his earlier *japonisme*. Yet the firmest of japonistic verti-
cals and horizontals characterizes 'Woman in white, reading'
(plate 40), and Japanese prints appear as details in 'Child
curled up on couch' and other less rigid compositions.

Day's images continued to manifest an underlying loyalty
to Pictorialist ideals, yet the total effect was now softer, less
artificial. His female models and child subjects were no longer
the operatic actors of the 1890s, but tender, good-humored,
sympathetic, relaxed. In attempting to renew himself immediately after the 1904 catastrophe, Day had turned more and
more to family themes, inspired by the White family. We find
mothers and children sharing activities, reading together, and
playing, or charming creatures like 'Young woman with wispy
blonde hair' (plate 29) and 'Seated young girl with braids'
(plate 30). These many lovely portraits, including several such
as 'Seated woman with dark straw hat and umbrella' (plate

Day's shimmering evocations of summer, Maine, 1908 (see plates 35, 56).

31), which Day produced in many variations, disprove the canard that he was interested only in nubile young boys. It was probably the mark of a genuine empathy with women of all ages, and also of an exceptional artistic versatility.

When some visitors from Japan came to Little Good Harbor in 1909, Day did not hesitate to make it a Japanese garden, transforming local curved bridges, wooden jetties, and the ubiquitous pines into suitable decorative motifs (plate 32). He never relinquished his contacts with Oriental art dealers and Japanese floriculturists, from whom he purchased bulbs for his gardens at Norwood. Some of his handsomest portraits were of these friends (plate 33). At the same time, he dressed up some of the local boys in white sailor suits with dark blue ties, creating a series (plates 34, 35, 36) in which the shapes created by the sailor-suit collar, the dark silhouette of the tie, and the overall softness combined once again into a shimmering evocation of summer. One of the most delightful prints of this period was the fairy-tale picture of a 'Nude child on flagstone path' (plate 56) running toward the camera with arms outstretched. Pale and a lovely grey, it was an instance of the photographer's increasing joy in spontaneity, and a direct result of the long visits that the White family had resumed in 1908.

In England, meanwhile, Day's old friends, Frederick Evans and George Davison, were watching his recovery with interest. Stieglitz was also kept aware of Day's progress through correspondence with these nen and other members of the

Linked Ring. Davison described a visit from Evans, 'who
brought up to my office a portfolio of new photographs sent to
him by Holland Day,'[1] while Steichen reported that 'Evans certainly owns the best Days in existence now – but your "ebony
and ivory" is miles ahead of his.'[2] Day had presented Evans
with samples of his new work, as gifts not intended for exhibition. But Evans could not resist praising Day to Stieglitz.

> I wish you could see Holland Day's work . . . of
> which I have a large parcel, so far ahead of himself
> as we knew him before the fire, so far ahead of the
> allegorical things you have in C[amera] W[ork] this
> summer.[3]

That must have tantalized Stieglitz, who liked to be in com-
mand of any photographic situation and who always wanted to
know what his rival was producing. When Day continued to
reject his requests for prints, either for *Camera Work* or for exhibition under his own aegis, Stieglitz made Evans a most unusual offer. It brought a hasty and surprised reply.

> No, I can't sell any Holland Days things. They are
> gifts to me as his oldest English friend and he refused
> me any permission to exhibit any. . . . You'll see 'em
> and admire 'em if you can only spare me an after-
> noon or two here. I never argue with dear old Day,
> he can't be moved, even by me tho he believes in me
> a lot. . . .[4]

Stieglitz was planning a huge retrospective show of the
Pictorialists at the Albright Gallery in Buffalo, New York. In a
long letter to Heinrich Kühn dated March 1, 1909, Stieglitz
complained bitterly about the difficulties he was having assem-
bling the prints, especially criticizing Käsebier's tardiness. The
exhibition was scheduled for the fall of 1910. Clarence White
and Max Weber were both to help him hang this document of
the art photography movement. Stieglitz had even swallowed
his pride and had written to Day, asking for the loan of twenty
recent prints, but Day refused. Commenting to Kühn that 'It
would be a scandal to have an exhibit without Day,'[5] Stieglitz
decided to show five of Day's superb prints of the 1890s, from
his own collection. He was now completely enraged at what he
saw as Day's continuing intransigence, yet he never could bring
himself to confess his own guilt in the original hostilities. As

Portrait of Frederick Evans by
Alvin Langdon Coburn, 1906.

Evans observed, neither could Day be moved once he had made
up his mind.

After the exhibition opened, Evans found himself in the
middle of a nasty quarrel. He so informed Stieglitz.

> *In a letter I have just had from my dear old friend
> Holland Day, he tells me he is but very slowly re-
> covering health and strength, and I shan't be able to
> see any new or this year's work for a month or more,
> if then. . . . But what moved me to write to you
> about him is a sentence or two where he refers to
> Buffalo; he learns, only then, that early work of his
> has been exhibited, that 'not only without his appro-
> bation or consent but directly contrary to his ex-
> pressed wish.'*[6]

Stieglitz had not even bothered to send Day a catalogue of the
Buffalo exhibition. Day had no idea what was being shown,
but had learned from Clarence White that Stieglitz's prints
from his Nubian series and several early portraits of women
had been included, despite his instructions. It was the last straw.

Stieglitz's cavalier leadership, his genius for picking fights
with his most loyal supporters, his disinclination to harmonize
ideas with others, and his temper were all combining to make
membership in the Photo-Secession onerous to even its most
brilliant members. Patient Clarence White was finding the
situation insupportable.

> *Mrs K showed me a very friendly note from the* Boss
> *of 291 – 5th Ave. and it now seems as if he was try-
> ing to win back some of those that they branded as
> 'no good.' At any event, there seems to K at least a
> very changed attitude that 'photography was not mak-
> ing good and will have no shows until some work is
> produced worthy of being shown at 291.'*[7]

That seemed a gratuitous slap in the face to Stieglitz's friends.
By 1912, both White and Käsebier had resigned from the
Photo-Secession.

It was true, nevertheless, that the Pictorialists were tend-
ing to repeat themselves, all except Day and Stieglitz. More
importantly, Stieglitz had just produced a folio of his own
prints in *Camera Work* for October 1911 – masterpieces like
The Steerage and *The Aeroplane* – which indicated that the

The Aeroplane and *The Steerage,* by Alfred Stieglitz, as reproduced in *Camera Work, 1911.*

future of photography lay not in imitating the effects of other media but in direct composition from nature. Day had always considered himself an advocate of what came to be called 'straight' photography. He had never, like Steichen or Demachy, scraped and scratched negatives or prints in an imitation of etching or mezzotint. While his portraits had loosened up considerably, they were still posed, not spontaneous, not snapshots. Stieglitz was bringing to photography a new modality that was antithetical to his prior enthusiasm for Pictorialism. It was a modality well suited to the frenzied futurism of the new era. It came out of the hand-held camera and the fast dry plate, the unretouched negative and an attitude of discovering rather than invention.

Day had also been modernizing his work, in the sense that he had moved away from the ponderously posed mythological subject staged in the studio. But his energies had been seriously

Portrait of Lewis Day by his son,
shortly before his death in 1910.

weakened by his attendance upon his sick father, and by a dis-
abling attack of jaundice. Having lost both weight and strength,
he could no longer spend hours at the camera or in the darkroom. He was also distracted by the sorrows of his old friend
Louise, whose mother, like Day's father, was dying of a pro-
tracted illness. When she came home in 1908 to attend her
mother, Louise was almost completely deaf. After nursing her
mother for nearly a year, she had a severe physical breakdown,
and had to be nursed herself for six weeks before she could return to England. While in Boston, she managed to complete
the transactions for the Maine property, so that Day could finally call the Little Good Harbor landscape his own. Louise
departed from her old friend wondering if they would ever
meet again.

In 1910, Louise's mother died, Lewis Day died, and so did
Edward VII. In the photographic world, a curious paradox had
crystallized: Stieglitz was winning recognition for the Pictorialists through his major retrospective of their work at the Albright Gallery in Buffalo, and simultaneously the Photo-
Secession itself was dying. Stieglitz knew it was the end of an
era; he now concentrated on the modern painters. In that
same year, 1910, Clarence White purchased a derelict house
not far from Little Good Harbor, at a place called Seguinland.
There he opened a summer school for photographers, with Day
assisting in the criticism of students' work, the painter Max
Weber instructing in the history of art, and Gertrude Käsebier
joining in occasionally on portrait studies. It seemed now that
Fred Day would finally have about him the company he enjoyed. For despite his seeking necessarily private delights in the
wilderness around Five Islands, Day was essentially a gregari-
ous man who was never happier than when his cabin was over-
flowing with guests. He entertained not only the Whites but
Norwood neighbors, such as the Hasenfus family, and hordes
of children from the Boston slums. His father's death had left
him a millionaire. He now had the money to proceed with a
plan for a new house at Little Good Harbor. Shanty Guiney
was to be leveled, and a grand, new chalet-style summer mansion erected overlooking the water. This proved to be such an
interesting process that Day, with a small camera, made a substantial series of pictures documenting the razing of the cabin,
the bringing in – by his own barge – of the construction materials for the chalet, the gradual erection of the timbers, and the

Day's 'Royal Barge' – a converted scow used to carry construction materials from the mainland.

finishing of the interior with interesting old wood. In taking this series, he frequently attempted panoramic views, and his scrapbooks were filled with carefully matched prints glued together to show the entire operational theatre.

Below the chalet, on a projecting platform near the water, Day ordered himself an outdoor, uncovered Greek temple, complete with unfluted columns of an early Doric style, and an arborlike trestle overhead. There, when he had no other guests, he liked to pose some of his young male friends in the nude. With one or two exceptions, like the 'Greek temple with Michelangelo's slave,' most of these pictures were informal snaps totally unlike the Pinkham & Smith pagan series. He now had a surfeit of models, thanks to the guests continually arriving at the chalet, yet his summer pictures were fast becoming only haphazard records of this transience. Perhaps the long exhaustion of nursing his father, or perhaps having a house he could call his own (Anna Day being very much alive and very much in charge of the Norwood establishment), had wrought some change in his otherwise meticulous personality and professional ideals. He seemed much more relaxed and informal than ever before.

A typical 1912 excursion from Little Good Harbor found young Maynard White as the pilot of Day's boat, meeting the Hasenfus family from Norwood for a day's outing.

The highpoint of this visit to Fred Day was a picnic at Lower Mark Island. . . . Day's picnic was well planned and carried out. In the building of his Swiss chalet, Mr. Day needed a huge scow for the carrying of heavy materials and stone, for no road ran within

Formal portrait by F. Holland Day of his 'Greek Temple,' left, and a snapshot of his chalet 'Castle Guiney,' taken from the harbor, right.

a half mile of his property. Now that this scow had served its purpose as a freight barge, the imaginative publisher had converted it into what he facetiously called 'State Barge', a large awninged flatboat. The barge was towed out to Lower Mark by a motor boat, and almost thirty-five of us were aboard. . . . Lower Mark Island was a photographer's heaven, and this may have been the reason why the picnic had been planned for there . . .[8]

As Mr. Hasenfus testifies, 'Pictures by the hundred were taken by Mr. White's students.'[9]

Day had not abandoned his pagan series, and had kept up with Keatsian themes summer after summer, although not in great quantity. Some of the more remarkable pictures of the series as it progressed were various youths with lyres, or arrows, the 'Youth with shepherd's pipes' (plate 50), and several triptychs. But the best of the series is clearly one of Day's masterworks. *The Prodigal* (plate 54), signed 1909, has a softness and breadth of effect reminiscent of Puvis de Chavannes's allegorical murals. In its sustained mood, appropriateness of detail, tonality, and air of sorrowing mystery, this triptych has great power. Exhibited at the first London Salon of Photography in the fall of 1910, it moved critics like E. O. Hoppé to regret Day's long absence from the scene. *Photograms of the Year 1910* reported there was some likelihood that Day might take a studio in London and produce a one-man show.

His Prodigal . . . which hangs in the Salon, is of his older, religious, semi-mystical style, and should be

The Prodigal, triptych by
F. Holland Day, posed in Maine,
1909 (see plate 54).

*dwelt with for awhile, to realize fully the grey depths
of gloom and self-condemnation of the spirit, once
proud and wayward, now broken to the point of saying, 'I will arise and go to my father, and will say
unto him, Father, I have sinned.'*[10]

How much of this repentant mood was the result of Day's imagination, and how much represented his regrets during his
father's last illness, is hard to say. That he had once sinned
against what Bostonians considered to be good taste was still a
subject for public criticism. Ten years afterward, an anonymous
editorial in *Photo-Era* was still beating Day for the dead horse
of his sacred subjects. Nowhere mentioning him by name, the
editors remarked: 'It was but natural that his desecration of a
divine theme should bring upon him well deserved censure
and ridicule.'[11]

The second triptych was of a different mood. 'Boy embracing the Herm of Pan' (plate 53) is certainly somber paganism, but difficult to label repentant. Here the three panels
seem less inevitable than those of the *Prodigal* where the subject is enhanced by the elongated, segmented shape. Clarence
White had perhaps originated – or at least popularized – the
three-part photograph in his famous *Spring* of the late nineties,

Sailor suits dominated the portraits of 1910 to 1913; at left, boy in sailor suit, by Day; at right, snapshot of Day smoking a Russian cigarette.

where it was used to imitate a window looking out upon an impressionist garden. Käsebier, among others, took advantage of the panoramic quality of this iconic form. In Day's own work, the design of Japanese screens, which rhythmically interrupt dreamlike abstractions, had clearly influenced him.

From 1910 to 1913, Day continued not only the pagan series but the sailor-suit pictures, often using a gum platinum on a creamy paper. Sometimes the entire Clarence White menage would be posed in sailor suits. But who took the portrait of Day smoking one of his favorite Russian cigarettes? Was "F. Holland Day smoking' a self-portrait? It may have been; it is much more probable that it was snapped by one of White's students. Day in this simple sailor suit seems far away from his former foppishness. Yet it *was* slightly eccentric that he owned so many blue-and-white suits of this kind, since he never went fishing, only occasionally put out in a rowboat, and rarely sailed. He seems to have enjoyed wearing the sailor suit when sitting out on the sunny cliffs, looking toward the open sea.

During the late Edwardian years, Day seems to have indulged in nostalgia for an earlier and less complicated time. He renewed correspondence with members of his old bibliophile societies whom he had not seen in years. One such friend, Herbert A. Hess, wrote in 1909 to sympathize over the 'passing of No. 9,' meaning the apartment Day had had on Pinckney Street.

One of the last portraits of Day
at Little Good Harbor, about
1915.

*Many are the pleasant evenings I had there, never to
return again apparently. I told Bro. Copeland you
should have had a Dr. Watson to place the chronicles
of No. 9 in enduring print. He thought, sometimes
the truth is better left unsaid. Nevertheless, the walls,
doubtless if they could speak, could tell some interesting tales.*[12]

Another friend from the Club of Odd Volumes, Dr.
Charles Banks, who was in Cumberland, Maine, gossiped hap-
pily about the lost days of 'extra-illustrated books in crushed
levant, a mute monument to the crushed wallet that paid the
piper.'[13] In reminiscing, Banks remarked that Day had once
taken up the art of etching, 'and like me, dabbling in portraits.'[14] Day's 'extra-illustrating' days were long gone with the
other fads of the eighties and nineties. But he retained his great
interest in Keatsiana, and continued to collect odd bits of memorabilia as well as first editions. The Fanny Brawne letters were
still locked away.

His nostalgia was undoubtedly the direct result of his
serious illnesses between 1910 and 1913. Bedridden for part of
these years, he was unable to pursue photography during the
cold Norwood winters. Letter writing increasingly occupied his
leisure hours. Among his favorite correspondents was his cousin
Coburn, whom he had helped to establish in photography.
After a slow start, Alvin had returned to England, and by 1908
had gained quite a reputation as a portrait photographer. He
also began to serve on prestigious juries and on the Royal Photographic Society board of directors for exhibitions. In that
capacity, he was frequently in touch with Day, asking him to
contribute prints, or to give permission to Evans to lend the
Society his own Day photographs. Day was pleased that George
Bernard Shaw, a close friend of Evans, was impressed with
Coburn; and Shaw's praise undoubtedly helped to launch him
into society work. Evans was also supportive and enthusiastic,
and Coburn's letters were always full of tidbits of information
about their mutual friend. In one amusing letter of 1908, Coburn wondered if Day had heard about Evans's 'terrible tragedy
with his 80 large films being eaten by microbes . . .'[15]

Despite his good humor, Coburn never seemed especially
sensitive to Fred Day's talents. In a letter on Royal Photographic Society stationary dated March 18, 1914, Coburn dem-

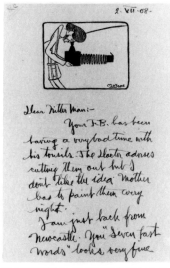

Portions of a letter from Alvin Langdon Coburn ('Fritter-Man') to F. Holland Day ('Nitter-Man'), 1914.

onstrates both boyish gratitude and an uncanny naiveté about Day's earlier achievements in photography.

Dear Nitter-Man: –
Do you remember the R.P.S. show that you arranged in 1900? That seems a very long time ago does it not. Now in 1914 they have appointed the Fritter-Boy a member of the selecting committee of this years [sic] exhibition, and we are arranging a room to be devoted exclusively to American work. Of course you know what I want! Six prints from the Nitter-Man in memory of old times in Gilhooly Street.

Do you remember what you gave me for a birthday present on the 11th of June 1901 nearly thirteen years ago? That fine fat 'Chambers' Dictionary has solved many a problem for me since then . . .

If you do not want to trouble to send, perhaps you will authorize Evans to send six of the beautiful things he has, which have never been seen in England? Yours ever,
Fritter-Boy
Otherwise known as Alvin Langdon Coburn[16]

Of course F. Holland Day remembered the Royal Photographic Society show of 1900; it remained the apex of his public career. But it had, indeed, been a very long time ago. Much had happened to him personally; much had happened in the art world. In 1913, the Armory Show in New York shook the public and artists alike. Kandinsky, Matisse, Picasso, Duchamps, and Max Weber – a good friend of Coburn and of Clarence White – were now showing the public that cubism, fauvism, and abstraction were the styles of the avant-garde. Stieglitz, thanks to Steichen's influence, had jumped on the modernist bandwagon. It must have seemed to Day that the New School of American Photography was already a hopeless anachronism.

More than art movements were about to be destroyed. On the eve of World War I, Day found himself once again too ill to travel to Little Good Harbor. There may have been some scares about boat travel to Maine now that German submarines were prowling the seas. Yet the war never came home to America in the way that Louise Guiney, Alvin Coburn, and other American expatriates began to experience it. Coburn

called it 'this brutal, unnecessary, criminally foolish war.'[17]
Louise was suffering genuine hardships, including food short-
ages. The Atlantic had ceased to be a friendly lake between
two great cities which were equally home to Day.

As soon as he had recovered sufficiently to leave Boston,
Day fled for his health's sake to Little Good Harbor in February 1915. To a friend back home he wrote:

> *I guess you'd think me well if you could see me eat –*
> *I get outside more than any of the rest of them in*
> *spite of the fact that I don't especially enjoy their*
> *fare – they don't give me beans or fish enough – and*
> *I've had but one headache since I came – I wouldn't*
> *have said that of this length of time at home – I* may
> *have gained in weight but I doubt it – Scales will*
> *tell –*[18]

This peckish letter begins to show a peculiar hypochondriacal
note, which became a symptom of his emotional distress during
his last decades. Nevertheless, it was true that he had continued
to suffer from migraines for all of his adult life. Jane White
called them his 'zig-zag' headaches,[19] and she could sympathize
with his frequent disabilities since she shared them.

The Whites were barely scraping by with Clarence's various schools in New York and at Seguinland. As always, Day
was more than generous and Jane White felt close enough to
him to ask considerable favors without fear of being rejected.
Day had become a 'good uncle' to the White boys. Maynard,
his special favorite, was now old enough to enlist in the Army
when the United States joined the Allies in 1917. Elevated to
lieutenant in the Heavy Artillery School with the American
Expeditionary Force in France, Maynard had little money to
purchase food and extras. So Jane White simply turned to Fred
Day for assistance.[20] Day later supported Maynard through
Brown University and received affectionate letters from him
until 'uncle' died.

The war years found Anna Day ill, and Fred not much
stronger. There was bad news from England about an influenza
epidemic. Always prone to bronchial infections, and weakened
by his continuing bouts with jaundice, kidney ailments, and
related illnesses, the fear of influenza contributed to Day's increasing mental fatigue. But one clue to Day's unusual despair
had nothing to do with hypochondria; it had to do with a sim-

F. Holland Day and one of
Clarence White's sons at Little
Good Harbor, about 1915.

ple but little-known fact of photographic history. Platinum, the precious metal used in the preparation of Day's favorite photographic process, came from two major sources: the Ural mountains of Russia, and Colombia, South America. As early as 1914, Willis & Clements of Philadelphia, the importers of the platinotype papers, warned Day that 'the English company continues to ship to us regularly but everything is slower since the war and we never know what vessel is bringing us supplies.'[21] When the Russian Revolution of October 1917 sealed off supplies from the Urals, the makers of platinum papers simply called a halt to production. The materials had become almost impossibly expensive.

It may be hard for anyone who is not a photographer to understand the serious shock to the Pictorialists, who had depended on the velvet smoothness, low-key harmonies, and permanence of platinum papers. Back in the 1880s, Peter Henry Emerson had sworn that if platinum papers and photogravure were no longer available, he would give up photography. His oath was carried out by at least three photographers: Frederick Evans, Robert Demachy, and F. Holland Day. Fred felt the loss of the platinotype papers so profoundly that he made sporadic efforts to recover platinum from old prints, and even trained one young man to pursue this process during the 1920s.

But the pure technique of platinotypes, and the mixed subtleties of his own gum-platinum effects, were now impossible to
achieve.

Sick at heart, weakened in body, Fred Day closed down
the chalet at Little Good Harbor in 1917, returning to it only
after his death. He had needed its curative powers; he had
relied upon its privacy and inspiration. It had provided a rare
source of companionship with the Whites, who often begged
him to reconsider his decision to give up Maine. With an
aging, frail mother who suddenly needed him to nurse her, he
must have come to believe that his personal trials would never
end. He was about to be swallowed up by the house at Norwood, with no one to share his past achievements except the
friends who occasionally came down from Boston. After the
war, he did make several efforts to communicate once again
with the outside world. He would do this by calling upon his
collection of Keatsiana for an illusion of continuing influence
and power; nothing, however, would assuage the loss of photography as a creative means of self-expression.

It could hardly have proved any consolation that his great
rival, Stieglitz, had capitulated to the times. In 1917, the year
in which Day gave up photography, *Camera Work* published
its last issue. With its disappearance, the accomplishments of
the art photographers of the Pictorialist period seemed merely
vainglorious memories. Demachy had already written an epitaph for Pictorialism: it had been too easy to imitate. The new
path was marked out by Paul Strand, whose images dominated
the last pages of *Camera Work*. It was a path at once documentary and formal, abstract and literal. In short, it was a revolution totally inimical to Day's romanticizing mysticism, totally
alien to the allegorical temperament. It was a revolution even
more powerful than Stieglitz's own.

When F. Holland Day, now white-haired and puffy in the
face, took to his bed in 1917, his Norwood neighbors went wild
with speculation. He was considered a full-blown hypochon-
driac by his doctor, a sadistic egomaniac by Amy Lowell and
other Keats biographers, and his Norwood neighbors thought
him a crazed old man likely to clutch little boys if they strayed
within his grasp.

His friends knew better. He was writing affectionate, articulate, and helpful letters to the Clarence Whites. He was
still keeping the aging Gertrude Käsebier in sweets and flowers.
With Louis Arthur Holman, of Goodspeed's Bookshop in
Boston, he was planning an edition of the Fanny Brawne letters. To his contacts in Tokyo he dispatched frequent notes
about Oriental artifacts and floriculture. His mind was utterly
clear, a fact substantiated by the very doctor who later mocked
his retreat to the upstairs bedroom.

Why should a creative man in full possession of his mental faculties make so complete a withdrawal from active partici-
pation in the world? The decision was probably unconscious,
precipitated in part by his contracting influenza in the summer
of 1918. He had been weakened by a series of ailments from

Portrait of Day in Norwood,
about 1917.

about 1908 on. His best friends, noting that he had never
looked so thin, had been worrying about his health throughout
the war. Day had the further embarrassment of hemorrhoids,
not an ailment for an exceedingly fastidious gentleman. Ever
since his adolescence, as we know, he had been stricken with
excruciating headaches; allergies, arterial problems in the brain,
and acute anxiety all have been known to trigger such pains.
Frustrated sexuality, insoluble dilemmas, and aborted creativ-
ity – all could be counted upon to exacerbate Day's illnesses.

His diagnosis in the 1920s was 'neurasthenia'; today he
might be termed severely depressed. To pleas from Herbert
Copeland or Louise Guiney that he try to go out again, he an-
swered that he was too ill. Later, he insisted that he had been
everywhere, seen everything, and that nothing had any appeal.
Perhaps he could have made the effort if the early years of the
decade had not been marked by the deaths of people extremely
important to him. The first to die was Louise Imogen Guiney.
In his last letter from her, dated April 6, 1920, her vivacity
belied an acute physical deterioration. It was a letter which
rang with the enthusiasm of the old days.

> *Sonny, my Dear – it is almost a twelvemonth! but*
> *I've been thinking furiously of you ever-so often, and*
> *wishing I knew how you got on. It is about unbear-*
> *able that you should be wilting in bed: only I des-*
> *perately hope that you aren't. Be good and tell me.*
> *And Mother Day – I want her to be better. My best*
> *love to her, and Cheerio!*[1]

Among the bits of gossip, Louise confided that 'R.A.C.' (their
old comrade of the Visionist days, Ralph Adams Cram) was on
his way to Paris for some architectural studies. 'His old spirit
and fire seem burning low,' she observed.[2] Nevertheless, Ralph
had been serving as her champion.

> *He, Ralph, tells me the Authors' Club (in Boston I*
> *suppose) gave me a pre-mortem memorial the other*
> *day, devoting an evening to me [sic] Works! and that*
> *he, being called upon, 'made a few inadequate, but*
> *tender, remarks.'*[3]

As had become customary for Fred and Louise, they were ex-
changing ideas about various schemes to create an archive of
Keats material at Lawn Bank. 'I should like a Fanny Brawne

letter or two to be kept forever in the house where they were written. Doesn't that appeal to you?'[4] Poor Louise! She went to her grave never having been granted the privilege of reading the original Brawne letters, yet she had long ago ceased to chastise Fred for that omission. Now she asked, 'Send me a line to say you are young and FAT and in fighting trim, and give much love always to a certain dear Lady, for auld lang syne.'[5] She signed the letter, 'Ever affectionately, L.I.G.' Soon after a painful alternation between insomnia and nightmares about her impoverished condition, she suffered a stroke. Louise was gone.

From his dear and faithful friend, Gertrude Savage, came words of caring. 'Just the word of real sympathy – my dear Fred – over the going from our Earth of the old friend, Louise Guiney. I am sorry.'[6] Many of their mutual friends remembered Louise as a bright and cheerful spirit.

If Fred ever felt guilty about having kept the Fanny Brawne letters from Louise, there is no direct evidence of it. For years he had been vainly seeking some way to make the letters public. Unfortunately, his ambitions exceeded his financial capabilities. He had always wanted a 'companion volume to the rare, large-paper edition of Forman's *Letters of John Keats to Fanny Brawne* (1878), the issue to be limited and privately printed.'[7] Even private publication would not have obviated a copyright suit by Brawne's heirs, who continued to disregard all pleas for release. Yet the copyright problem was possibly no more serious an obstacle than Day's own ambivalence about relinquishing his prize possession. The Brawne letters may have seemed his last ticket to immortality.

The famous poet and towering, cigar-smoking grande dame of Boston, Amy Lowell, chose this unfortuitous moment to begin what she hoped would be the definitive biography of John Keats. With Louise recently gone and Day's mother seriously ill, Day had to rouse himself to respond to her inquiries. When he hinted about knowledge of some materials concerning Fanny Brawne, Lowell discovered to her amazement and dismay that Day's Keatsiana was a far greater collection than her own. Hoping for some distinctive coup that could ensure her biography's success, she began to pursue Day by letter and telephone. The story of their tragicomic interchanges has been thoroughly documented by Rollins and Parrish, in *Keats and the Bostonians*. Fred Day kept the insistent Lowell at bay for over a year, tantalizing her with snatches from the Brawne letters, yet never revealing how or where he knew about them. Nearly mad with frustration, she cursed him as 'Jesus Christ Day,' after his self-portraits as the Messiah.

Since few had paid attention to Day's repeated newspaper reports about the letters, and almost no one remained who recalled how he had obtained them in Spain back in 1891, Lowell discovered after her biography's publication that many scholars believed the Brawne letters to be a figment of her imagination. The accusation was to drive her nearly to insanity. It was bad enough that her one personal visit to Day had proved a disaster. After trying to extract a promise from her never to use the materials – a preposterous idea – Day foiled her, and other visitors, with chit-chat about nightingales, the Japanese iris, and Virginia Woolf. As she strode around his bedroom (purposefully emptied of all chairs large enough to admit her considerable girth) and listened to Day's polite and ingenious patter from the canopied bed, Amy must have felt on the verge of committing murder or suicide. The Brawne letters remained at Norwood. She was permitted to quote from two letters, without revealing her source, and to reproduce several of Day's photographs of Keats memorabilia and the poet's haunts.

As Rollins and Parrish indicate, his confrontation with Lowell provides one of the most marvelously revealing portraits of Day as a collector, and an insight into the savagery of collectors in general. Yet Day was no more mischievously reticent than Lowell herself; she admitted freely that the greatest pleasure a collector could have was the secret knowledge of his prizes.

Curiously enough, Day was not hiding the rest of the magnificent Keats collection. In 1921, with the help of his old friend and former colleague, Francis Watts Lee, he lent enough material for a major exhibition of Keatsiana at the Boston Public Library, permitting his own name to be used. Lee was enthusiastic about the collection, but wished they had found more time to prepare the catalogue. Still, 'it was a good show and did you and us both credit . . . I am glad you are able to keep up your interest in these things and sorry I don't have a chance to see something of you these days, even though I too have seldom a chance to expose a plate.'[8]

Day may have given up active work with the camera, but not his wish to be known for his photographs. He was delighted when the Department of English and History at the Massachu-

Day's 1890 photograph, *Millfield Lane,* as reproduced in Amy Lowell's biography of Keats.

setts Institute of Technology wrote to him for the loan of whatever prints he cared to share. A Mr. Morris was to give a lecture on the Fine Arts, and felt it mandatory to include in it a display of the work of the most renowned of Boston's art photographers, F. Holland Day. In their letter of thanks, the department chairman wrote Day that the young men had been enthusiastic, especially over 'the study of a nude figure in the mist on the ledge among the Gloucester rocks.'[9] Day had apparently neglected to inform them about Little Good Harbor, the cliffs of Lower Mark Island, or even to locate the pictures properly in Maine. Gloucester's own 'Good Harbor' compounded the error.

For copies or prints from the negatives of his later work, he was still relying on the Boston firm of Pinkham & Smith for darkroom work. Their chief operator had suffered a nearly fatal accident, but was recovering sufficiently by November 1922 to return to work on Day's plates. The correspondent from Pinkham & Smith apologized for the delay, but recognized that only work of the highest quality would satisfy their famous client.

Clarence White, whose family had now moved to Canaan, Connecticut, wrote to Day that he had been unable to work on anything photographic 'except bread and butter – and I might add "school" – for it hardly belongs to the "bread and butter class." '[10] Bitterly, White talked about their old rival and former leader.

> Stieglitz too seems to be working hard getting most of the criticism (favorable) directed at photography. It seems too bad photography should be such a closed corporation.[11]

For Fred, all of this must have seemed like buzzing from a remote, long-forgotten world.

All that year his ailing mother, Anna Day, had lain sequestered in her bedroom on the second floor of the Norwood mansion. She was striving to keep up her good spirits, but kept such ladylike habits that it was difficult for outsiders to know her. In her time she had had adventurous notions; it was said that she had owned the first motorcar in Norwood. But since Fred had been her only child, she lavished on him all her motherly energies, even after he became an international figure. She also teased him, often sending him amusing clippings about his activities from the Boston papers. One was entitled, 'What Are Keats?'

> The unveiling of the American memorial of Keats in London on Monday recalls the story that a wealthy pork packer who was asked to contribute said, 'Certainly, put me down for a hundred; but, tell me, what in thunder are keats, anyhow!'[12]

The Day servants, the Tanneyhill family, kept communications going between the second- and third-floor bedrooms at Norwood. On February 8, 1922, one of the household brought two items on a tray up to Fred's third-floor hermitage: a very large lead pencil, and a tiny piece of paper from Anna's diary. It was exactly the same size and shape as that on which she had recorded the arrival of a 'little Day.' In the same cramped, tiny hand, she wrote her last joke.

Day's last portrait of his mother, Anna Day, about 1917.

My dear Teddy
I thought – as you were fond of big ~~noses~~ [sic] men
with big nose [sic] I would give you a pencil to agree
with that dispo_si_tion. Write how you like it.[13]

On this tiny scrap, Day added, 'Last note from Mother! She died
3 July 1922.'

Apparently 'men with big nose[s]' referred to Day's many
Greek, Syrian, Italian, and Portuguese acquaintances. She had
never been cured of her dislike of her son's exotic friends; he,
on the other hand, had never given them up. It had always
been a family scandal that he enjoyed the company of shock-
ingly unconventional – and nonwhite – persons. The provin-
cialism of his family and of his home town must have sorely
tried his cosmopolitan patience.

His mother's death was a little death of his own. Gertrude
Käsebier wrote sympathetically, 'You were a devoted son. You
had a wonderful mother. May you find consolation. May you
be given health and fortitude to bear the strain.'[14] Unfortunately, he had neither. The loss of both mother figures, Anna
and Louise, seems to have pushed him further into seclusion. A
close friend of Louise's recognized his grief: 'Are you all alone
in that large Norwood house? It must be *very* lonely without
your mother.'[15] It was. Only remote cousins were left of the
family. He knew he was the last of the Days.

According to one psychological theory, human beings
sometimes assume the illnesses or symptoms of lost loved ones.
It is as if this magical act can re-create the other in oneself,
keeping the other alive. A bizarre idea, but Day's doctor believed that Fred was enacting not only his mother's illness but
that of his long-dead father as well. Now Fred began to keep
fanatically detailed records of his daily physical condition: accounts of temperature, pulse, general mood, hours of sleep. He
began to resemble another famous recluse, Marcel Proust,
whose chills demanded multiple overcoats and mufflers, even
in warm weather. Visitors now found him sweatered, shawled,
swathed in blankets in mid-summer. It seems likely that Fred's
constant need for warmth was the side-effect of drugs like
opium or of Marcel Proust's own favorites, veronal and trional.

In his fascinating book, *Creative Malady,* George Pickering reports that many artists have used illness as an ally to keep
unwanted people from intruding on the creative process.[16]

Quilted, sweatered, Day reads in bed, probably 1930.

Proust had used just this device to help him create *Remembrance of Things Past*. F. Holland Day's masterworks had already been created, but he definitely wanted to prevent unnecessary intrusions. He was beginning a compulsive and uncoordinated pursuit of local history, an endeavor he had promised himself as long ago as 1887. He filled notebooks with the development of the post roads, property boundaries, family trees. His bedroom was a labyrinth of bookcases and neatly stacked boxes of correspondence. Aside from occasional visitors and the presence of his servants, the Tanneyhill family, Day's only contact with the world was in gazing down through his bedroom windows into the garden. He noted the passing flights of evening grosbeaks, cardinals, vireos, bluejays, and beyond, remotely, the comings and goings of the working people of Norwood.

After his mother's death in 1922, another death pushed him further into regression and seclusion. The Reverend Minot Simons of New York forwarded a telegram dated November 23, 1923:

> *Herbert Copeland is unconscious and probably dying in apoplexy. Nobody here knows his near relatives. Who should be notified. Can your wife supply information. Copeland is at Boston City Hospital . . .*
> *J M Morton Jr* [17]

Herbert had been a clerk at the city hospital in Boston for two years, where he had won a reputation for efficiency and courtesy. Before that, he had lived briefly in Philadelphia, hoping for rejuvenation in a job at the *Saturday Evening Post*. It was so difficult for him to get along with people, even those who meant him well, that he had lasted hardly a year. One of his last messages to Day, however, had been a note of condolence. 'I have just seen of your mother's death in the paper. You have my sympathy. You know how I feel about the matter – that after a long life Death is the Welcome Out.'[18]

Of Herbert's own death, one of his friends wrote, 'Sic transit sensitiveness and ability and humanism of a high order.'[19] Sensitivity had not served him well. It is entirely probable that he did not even recognize Copeland and Day's fine contribution to American letters, nor its historical achievement of the highest standards in typography and design. Copeland had nothing to grasp at the end. Perhaps if he had been as rich as Day, he might have ended his years as a protected alcoholic recluse.

That was not what Fred Day was – so much his doctor confirmed. The doctor who came to take charge of him in July 1923 did not seem particularly adept psychologically. He knew Day was severely neurasthenic, but suggested no other cure than to light a fire under Day's canopied bed. Today we would recognize that Day was displacing his emotional difficulties, his grief, his despair over the loss of his creative art, onto his body.[20]

According to Dr. Conrad Wesselhoeft, the physician who attended him until his death, Day actually came downstairs in 1925. Alas, he went right back upstairs again. The good doctor thought this was because he was unable to resist the 'magnetic attraction'[21] of the warm bed and blankets, where he lay snugly attended like a baby. The doctor did not know that Day's attempt to recover was aborted by the worst possible news.

He had learned that Clarence White was taking a group out of the country that summer.

> *My dear FHD –*
> *I am going to Mexico on June 20th with a few students, where I think I will find an* impetus *that should be profitable* to my own work. *If in the short stay I make I can get hold of it – I shall return to Canaan, Conn. early in August.*[22]

Day's enthusiasm for Clarence White's continuing struggle for

Portrait of Clarence White by
F. Holland Day, about 1910.

creative expression may have been the stimulus that brought
him out of bed. Also, Robert Demachy had written to White
from Paris about putting on a small exhibition of representative
Pictorialists. He wanted one or two of Day's elegant prints, and
Day agreed. Other shows may have been planned. But Clarence
was not to return to Canaan or anywhere else. On July 6 he
was stricken in Mexico City by what seemed to be a heart attack. The next day he was dead of an aneurism.[23]

That was a wrenching shock. Day's good friend was gone.
If he considered himself to have any family at all, it was the
White family – always dear, always appreciative. Now, of the
three once vaunted by Stieglitz, only Day and Käsebier were
left, and she was complaining bitterly about increasing lame-
ness and deafness. Fred was beginning to have trouble with his
eyes.

Naturally enough, Day now began to wonder how to dispose of his possessions: his costly collections, and his own

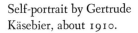

Self-portrait by Gertrude
Käsebier, about 1910.

prints. He began to make inquiries. He nearly gave his photographs to the Watertown Public Library, but Jane White sent
him news that the Library of Congress had offered to purchase
a large group of Clarence's prints, the first such purchase the
Library had ever made. Käsebier had also written that the Library of Congress had purchased one of her prints. If their work
was to reside in Washington, then so would his. The wish was
incorporated into his will.

When Bruce Rogers, a comrade of the Visionist era and
now an eminent book designer, wrote in August 1925 to ask for
a portrait Day had taken of him years ago, Day replied with a
long and pitiable letter.

> *I have been so entirely out of the world that I hardly
> seem of it in many ways. Old lines of interest, old*

haunts, and old friends – many of them have gone;
and though in a rather crippled way I try to keep
abreast [of] some movements I find it increasingly
hard so to do in any acceptable manner.[24]

Day wondered if Rogers could suggest some means of disposing of his Copeland and Day editions.

> *. . . a complete set I believe of all the C & D volumes*
> *save one – the extraordinary large paper copy of*
> *'Arabella and Araminta' my only copy of which was*
> *destroyed in the Harcourt fire. I am much averse to*
> *attempting to sell that sort of thing; but if there is*
> *any institution which you can commend which would*
> *place sufficient value upon these books to give them*
> *shelf room, it would be a great pleasure to me to*
> *make a gift of them.*[25]

Day then turned to Charles Knowles Bolton, the librarian of the Brookline Public Library and later of the Boston Athenæum, for suggestions on how to dispose of his 'stuff': 'Stuff of, by, for or about several of our mutual friends of the "perilous nineties." '[26]

As he looked ahead to his own death by beginning to prepare a complicated will, so he looked back to the history of his town, as he had promised he would do in the 'innocent eighties.' The convolutions of these genealogical studies became obsessive for him. His handwriting, cramped from arthritis, shrank so much that finally he was keeping a diary exactly like his mother's – on tiny serrated scraps of paper die-cut in a large notebook. He made arrangements to divest himself of the chalet at Little Good Harbor, and finally, in 1927 or 1928, sold the property to some Norwood acquaintances, the Otis Bakers, for a fraction of its worth. This was bound to sadden Jane White, who had loved Five Islands and their many summers there together. Maynard White, Day's surrogate son, came to visit, and Jane could observe, 'Maynard brought good reports from you and we are all hoping you'll have a good year.'[27]

The year 1929 would include long hours of gazing down the hill from the upstairs window, at those Norwood neighbors who hardly recognized him any longer or who warned their children to stay away from the crazed old man. He was compulsive and obsessive, but not crazed. Jane White and he contin-

Looking pensive, wrapped in a blanket, Day gazes at the view from the upstairs windows, about 1930.

ued to swap letters. 'How busy your days are –' she wrote enviously, 'between the books – the birds and the writing – and household!'[28]

How the economic crash of 1929 affected him is nowhere recorded; one assumes that he must have lost some of his fortune. He quietly sold off some of his rare books, which were now worth thousands of dollars. Yet the house stood intact, and he had sufficient funds to maintain the Tanneyhills as servants. He was still rich enough to send to Tokyo for artifacts and flower bulbs. He could order dozens of flowers from Max Schling's in New York City. Cosmos, poppies, French marigolds – each item was meticulously listed, with its price, in his diary.

Thus he might have gone on until his death, in pleasant surroundings and with a certain calm perseverance. But in 1931 he had yet another bout with the Fanny Brawne letters, this time with Dorothy F. Hyde, who was studying Keats and having problems with 'Harvard red tape.'[29] She had decided

that her real interest for her doctoral dissertation lay with
Fanny Brawne, neglected by Keats biographers.

> *That road has been beset with difficulties as well.*
> *The surviving descendants of the family seem very*
> *loathe to assist in any way. Why are they so anxious*
> *that 'Fanny' be shrouded in mystery?* [30]

Day, of course, knew all about that. Hyde complained that she
had searched in vain for even a scrap of a Brawne letter.

> *I meet the same reply everywhere, 'No such letters*
> *exist.' Then where did Miss Lowell find the letters*
> *she quoted from? She says 'They are the property of*
> *a gentleman who does not wish his name to be*
> *disclosed.'* [31]

All of this was irritating enough. But then Hyde came across
an faded newspaper clipping which revealed that F. Holland
Day owned the letters and that they were to be reproduced in
an edition for private distribution. After registering polite surprise and shock, she made what was to be a mistake. Relatively
wealthy herself, she offered to buy the letters. It must have
been then that Day decided Louise Guiney had been correct:
the letters must go to the Hampstead memorial in England.

Two activities seemed to give him special pleasure in his
last years: horticulture and his correspondence with the Matsuki family in Japan. Yet he confessed to one old friend that it
was not Japan that he ached to see, but China.

> *. . . which brings me to Mrs. Bucks two books* Good
> Earth *and* Sons. *Their praise isn't a bit exaggerated:*
> *their style is in places almost Elizabethan. . . . I'm not*
> *a reader of fiction at all, but these have attracted me*
> *1st because they're of* China *and quite apart than for*
> *any reason.* [32]

Why he never visited China can only be conjectured. Now, of
course, it was too late. Japan had invaded Manchuria.

In 1932 Day discovered that he was suffering from cancer
of the prostate gland, an exceedingly painful disease. By an odd
coincidence, the same disease also struck his long-time idol,
George Moore, who would die ten months before him. Made
tolerably comfortable by an emergency operation, Day labori-
ously finished a somewhat ambiguous will.

Solace of sorts came in July 1933 when a young photographer named Arthur asked to study with him. Day promptly gave him a commission: 'Platinum paper has disappeared from the market but I have uncovered the method for making it in a book so shall make some . . .'[33] In October, he wrote to Arthur once again.

> *I believe I have found an excellent method of recovering the platinum from your paper. The paper is burned and the residue treated with various acids to form the metallic platinum. The recovery can be carried a little further to produce the potassium chloroplatinate, which is the salt used in sensitizing the plate.*[34]

Alert and sounding like his old self, Day encouraged Arthur to become his protégé. If he studied hard, Day promised that eventually he could use Day's own 8 × 10 camera and the legendary lenses.[35]

What became of his photographic equipment is uncertain. The prints, six-hundred and fifty of them, did go to the Library of Congress. The remains of his fortune went to establish an historical trust in his name. The servants were to be well rewarded with property and other remunerations. Friends at Five Islands would also be remembered. And the Keats collection, including the Fanny Brawne letters, was to be donated anonymously to the Hampstead memorial in England.[36]

If you visit Norwood today, you can find two monuments to F. Holland Day, gentleman publisher and master photographer. One is the Day house, now the home of the Norwood Historical Society. The other is a Gothic Revival chapel ordered by Lewis Day in 1903 to commemorate his own father. The architect of this imposing mausoleum, specifically nondemoninational and available to the town for funeral services on that basis, had been Ralph Adams Cram. The chapel, revealing Cram's high-church mood, contains three marble tombs. In one of these lies the remains of Lewis Day; in another, those of Anna Day. The third is empty. No; 'Jesus Christ Day' did not rise from the tomb in some mockery of the Resurrection. He simply had no intention of spending eternity in Norwood.

When he died on November 6, 1933, at the age of sixty-nine, his coffin was, in fact, placed temporarily in that third marble vault. There it remained until January 12, 1934, when

Interior of Ralph Adams Cram's mausoleum–chapel for the Day family in Norwood.

Day on the bluffs overlooking
Little Good Harbor, about 1915.

he was taken to the Forest Hills crematorium near Boston and,
like George Moore, burned to ashes. Originally Day had intended that Elisha Fields, a trusted housekeeper and cook at
the Five Islands chalet, should have the honor of scattering his
ashes into the sea between Little Good Harbor and Lower
Mark Island. But as Elisha died before his employer, Day had
been forced to add a hasty codicil to his will. All that is certain
is that Day's ashes were scattered into the frigid waters off the
coast of Maine.

Why did he not choose to rest with his beloved parents in
an elegant mausoleum? Why Five Islands? Several biographers
of Louise Guiney insist that it was because he had been in love
with her, and because, in a way, they had shared a home together there. That is a better story, perhaps, than the simpler
truth: he had probably never felt completely free anywhere
else. Little Good Harbor had never mocked him, nagged him,
harrassed him, or bored him.

There were few newspaper accounts of his death. The
Norwood Messenger did carry a letter from Day's old friend,
Kihachiro Matsuki, who had known him since 1900. When
Matsuki first visited Boston on a commercial trip, his family
had posed for Day at Little Good Harbor. They had kept up a
lively correspondence over the years. Now Matsuki was shocked
to learn that Day had died utterly alone, with no surviving relatives.[37] 'He was a most kind and thoughtful person and often
sent remembrance to my family. . . . His death brought to us a
deep grief.'[38] There can be little doubt that this high opinion
of Day was shared by many families who had enjoyed his unstinting generosity and his gentlemanly temperament.

Gertrude Käsebier, the last of the triumverate, survived
F. Holland Day by one year. And in that year, 1934, a group of
Stieglitz admirers came together to publish *America & Alfred
Stieglitz*, a eulogy in which Day was mentioned not even once.
Like Keats, his name had been writ in water.

F. HOLLAND DAY
A Selection of Photographs

1. [Ethel Reed in the grand feathered hat]

2. [Girl in Moorish costume, reading]

3. [*Study of white drapery*]

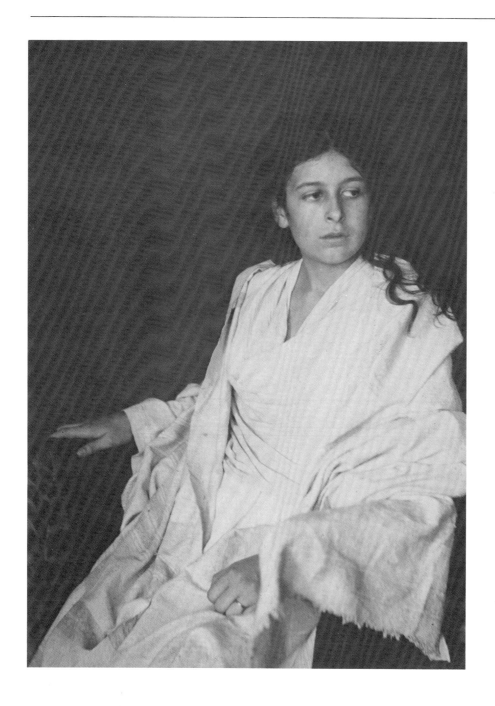

4. [*Pepita in white drapery*]

5. *The Gainsborough Hat*

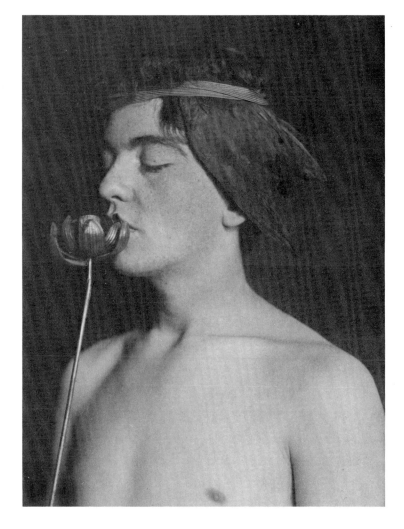

6. [*Nude in forest*]

7. *Hypnos*

8. [*Tow-headed girl in chiton*]

9. *African Chief*

10. *An Ethiopian Chief*

11. *Ebony and Ivory*

12. *The Smoker*

13. *The Vigil*

14. *Beauty Is Truth*

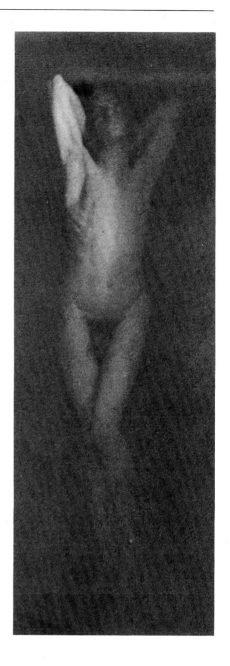

15. *The Lacquer Box*

16. *Study for the Crucifixion*

17. [*Crucifixion*]   18. [*Crucifixion with Roman soldiers*]

THE SEVEN LAST WORDS OF CHRIST   19. *Father, Forgive Them for They Know Not What They Do*

20. *Today Thou Shalt Be with Me in Paradise*

21. *Woman, Behold Thy Son, Son Thy Mother*

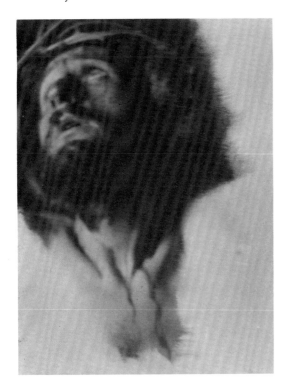

22. *My God, My God, Why Hast Thou Forsaken Me*

23. *I Thirst*

24. *Into Thy Hands I Commend My Spirit*

25. *It Is Finished*

26. [*Bearded old black man*]

27. [*Black woman with striped collar*]

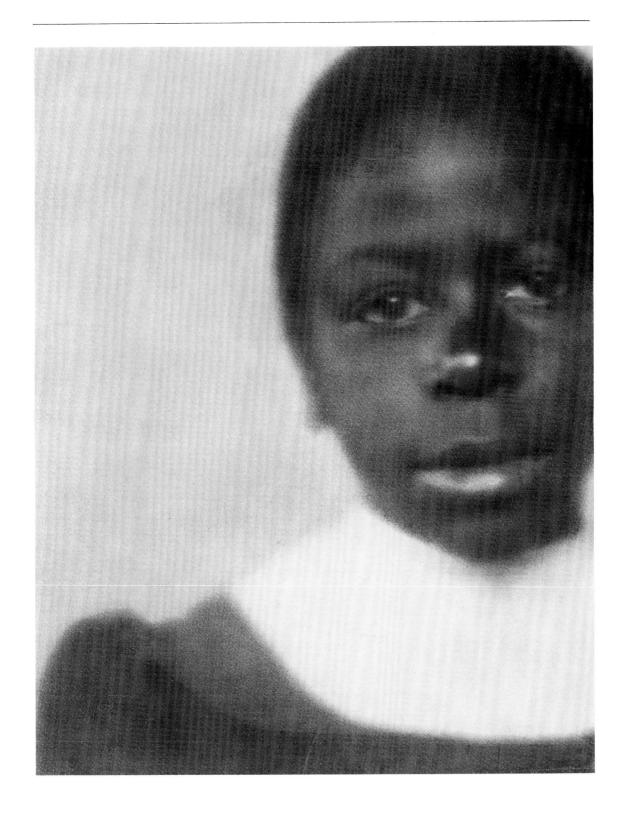

28. [*Black girl with broad white collar*]

29. [*Young woman with wispy blonde hair*]

30. [*Seated girl with braids*]

31. [*Seated woman with dark straw hat and umbrella*]

32. [Japanese bridge]

33. [Japanese man reading]

34. [*Youth in white sailor suit and cap, reclining*]

35. [Boy in white sailor suit standing in doorway]   36. [Youth in white sailor suit and broad hat]

37. [*Woman in veiled hat*]

38. [*Old woman smiling*]

39. [*Child curled up on couch*]

40. [*Woman in white, reading*]

41. [*Mother nursing infant*]

42. [*Two girls reading*]

43. [*Nude youth with lyre*]

44. [*Nude youth with lyre in grotto*]

45. [*Nude youth in dappled woods*]

46. [*Nude youth leaning against boulder*]

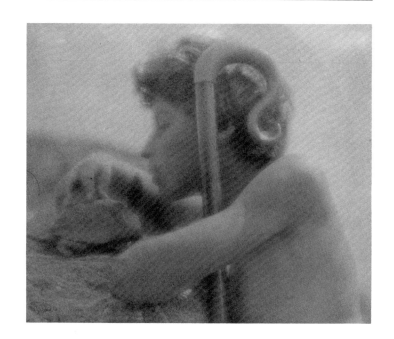

47. [*Boy with shepherd's crook
and tortoises*]

48. [*Reclining youth on boulder
with tortoises*]

49. [*Nude youth standing on cliff, arms raised*]

50. [*Youth with shepherd's pipes*]

51. [*Youth with staff shading his eyes*]

52. [Curly-headed youth with lyre]

53. *[Boy embracing the Herm of Pan]*

54. *The Prodigal*

55. *[Head of youth, looking up]*

56. [*Nude child on flagstone path*]

57. [Curly-headed youth on boulder]

58. [Silhouetted youth shooting arrow]

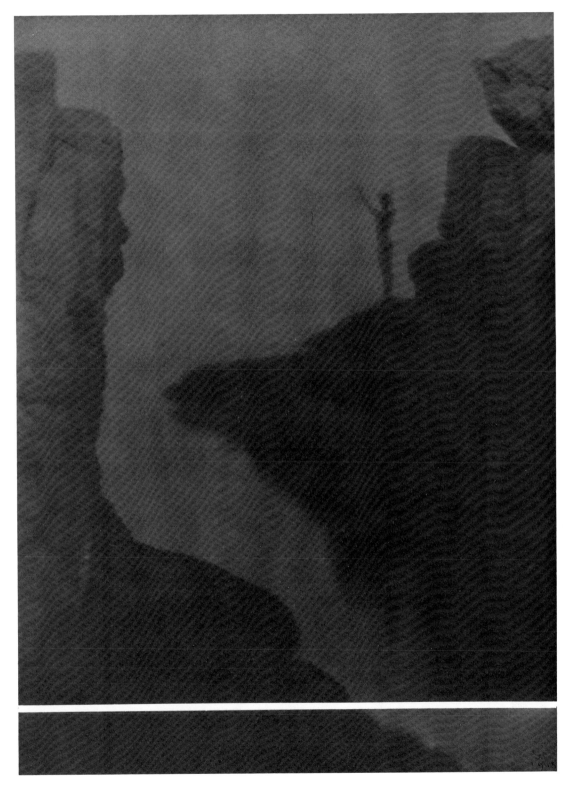

59. [*Silhouetted youth on boulder at shore*]

Notes to the Plates

As anyone who has studied the amazing array of print technologies available at the end of the nineteenth century can verify, it is almost impossible to determine with certainty the specific process by which each of Day's prints was created. At the beginning of his career Day undoubtedly worked in silver prints, but soon turned to platinum. Possibly beginning with *The Seven Last Words of Christ* (1898) he used glycerine methods of manipulating platinum prints (see the description of this process by Joseph T. Keiley in *Camera Notes,* April 1900, p. 221), and then combined platinum with gum bichromate techniques to give himself more direct control over highlights and design effects. Some of his black-tinted prints of the late 1890s resemble carbon prints more than platinum, and it is impossible to distinguish some of these cool effects from palladium-toned silver chloride.

It was therefore decided to avoid assigning arbitrary and possibly misleading processes to the prints, unless the process is unmistakable. Where platinum and gum bichromate were combined, or glycerine and mercury possibly entered into the making of the final image, the term *combination print* is used. Where the process is probably silver-based, the color of the image is indicated.

Day used both tinted papers as well as tinted gum bichromate to achieve color. Many of his post-1904 images float on a tone best described as peaches-and-cream; many have a distinct orange hue under the black platinum. To attempt to reproduce the enormous range of tints which appear in these prints was impossible, even using duotone. The reader should be advised, therefore, that the colors here represented are approximations and nothing more. The essential goal was to duplicate the softness and texture of Day's work as closely as possible.

Yet another characteristic of the original prints must be considered. Day usually was a fanatic about the mountings and mattings of his prints, almost always creating individualized tissue paper and colored paper borders set one on top of another to separate the print from the background mat. However important they were to Day, it was decided to leave them out for reproduction purposes. One reason for so doing is that Day produced unique prints, sometimes as many as thirteen from a single negative, in different croppings, processes, mountings, sizes.

Since Day infrequently signed and dated his prints, many dates given here are approximate. Sizes are rendered in centimeters, width before height. Sources are abbreviated as follows:

L C   Library of Congress
M M N Y The Metropolitan Museum of Art, New York
P C   Private collection

N O T E : Titles in brackets were assigned by the author; all others were assigned by F. Holland Day.

1. [*Ethel Reed in the grand feathered hat*]; reddish sepia; 9.3 diameter; about 1895. L C

2. [*Girl in Moorish costume, reading*]; sepia; 11 diameter; about 1895. L C

3. [*Study of white drapery*]; sepia; 18.5 diameter; about 1895. L C

4. [*Pepita in white drapery*]; black; 12 × 16.5; about 1895. L C

5. *The Gainsborough Hat;* portrait of Ethel Reed; sepia; 11.5 × 15; about 1895. L C

6. [*Nude in forest*]; black; part of the *Armageddon* triptych, which includes *An Ethiopian Chief* (Plate 10) and *Kedan* (not illustrated); platinum; 16 × 12; about 1897. L C

7. *Hypnos;* black; 12.2 × 16; about 1897. L C

8. [*Tow-headed girl in chiton*]; black; 23.2 × 18.5; about 1897. L C

9. *African Chief;* model, Alfred Tanneyhill; dark sepia; 12.5 × 17; 1897. L C

10. *An Ethiopian Chief;* Alfred Tanneyhill; platinum; 18.1 × 18.4; 1897. M M N Y

11. *Ebony and Ivory;* Alfred Tanneyhill; platinum; 18.3 × 20; 1897. M M N Y

12. *The Smoker;* Alfred Tanneyhill; platinum; 11 × 15.6; 1897. M M N Y

13. *The Vigil;* platinum; 11 × 16.2; about 1899. M M N Y

14. *Beauty Is Truth;* the upper part of Day's composite which included the *Entombment;* platinum; 1896 or 1897. L C

15. *The Lacquer Box;* platinum; 11.7 × 16.5; 1899. M M N Y

16. *Study for the Crucifixion;* sepia; 5.6 × 15.8; 1896. L C

17. [*Crucifixion*]; platinum; 4 × 16.5; 1898. L C

18. [*Crucifixion with Roman soldiers*]; platinum; 11.6 × 18.7; 1898. L C

THE SEVEN LAST WORDS OF CHRIST (plates 19–25):

19. *Father, Forgive Them for They Know Not What They Do;* combination print; 15 × 20.2; 1898. LC

20. *Today Thou Shalt Be with Me in Paradise;* combination print; 11.8 × 15.7; 1898. LC

21. *Woman, Behold Thy Son, Son Thy Mother;* combination print; 11.8 × 15.7; 1898. LC

22. *My God, My God, Why Hast Thou Forsaken Me;* combination print; 15.2 × 20.3; 1898. LC

23. *I Thirst;* combination print; 11.8 × 15.7; 1898. LC

24. *Into Thy Hands I Commend My Spirit;* combination print; 11.8 × 15.7; 1898. LC

25. *It Is Finished;* combination print; 11.8 × 15.7; 1898. LC

26. [*Bearded old black man*]; platinum; 18.7 × 23; 1905. LC

27. [*Portrait of black woman with striped collar*]; combination print; 19 × 24; 1905. LC

28. [*Black girl with broad white collar*]; combination print; 19 × 24; 1905. LC

29. [*Young woman with wispy blonde hair*]; combination print; 19.5 × 24; 1905. LC

30. [*Seated young girl with braids*]; combination print; 19 × 23.4; 1905. LC

31. [*Seated woman with dark straw hat and umbrella*]; platinum; 19.5 × 24.6; about 1906. LC

32. [*Japanese bridge*]; Day's mooring dock in Maine with Japanese visitors; platinum; 19 × 23.2; 1909. LC

33. [*Japanese man reading*]; portrait of either Kawai Kaziro or Kihachiro Matsuki, Day's visitors from Japan; combination print; 18.8 × 24; 1909. LC

34. [*Youth in white sailor suit and cap, reclining*]; platinum; 18.5 × 21.2; before 1910. LC

35. [*Boy in white sailor suit standing in doorway*]; combination print; 11 × 26; 1906. LC

36. [*Youth in white sailor suit and broad hat*]; combination print; 19.2 × 24.5; about 1910. LC

37. [*Woman in veiled hat*]; combination print; 19.2 × 24; about 1908. LC

38. [*Old woman smiling*]; combination print; 19.5 × 24.5; about 1908. LC

39. [*Child curled up on couch*]; combination print; 24.5 × 19.5; about 1908. LC

40. [*Woman in white, reading*]; combination print; 18.5 × 23.7; about 1908. LC

41. [*Mother nursing infant*]; platinum or combination; 19 × 24; 1905; signed. LC

42. [*Two girls reading*]; platinum; 18.7 × 23; 1907; signed. LC

43. [*Nude youth with lyre*]; combination print; 19 × 24.5; 1907. LC

44. [*Nude youth with lyre in grotto*]; combination print; 19 ×
23.7; 1907. L C

45. [*Nude youth in dappled woods*]; combination print; 19.5 ×
24.2; 1907. L C

46. [*Nude youth leaning against boulder*]; platinum; 18.9 × 24;
1907; signed. L C

47. [*Boy with shepherd's crook and tortoises*]; platinum; 23 ×
18.8; 1905. L C

48. [*Reclining youth on boulder with tortoises*]; platinum; 24.5 ×
19.2; about 1905. L C

49. [*Nude youth standing on cliff, arms raised*]; platinum; 19.4
× 24.4; 1906. L C

50. [*Youth with shepherd's pipes*]; platinum; 17.2 × 21.5, octagonal; 1910; signed. L C

51. [*Youth with staff shading his eyes*]; combination print; 19 ×
23.5, octagonal; 1906. L C

52. [*Curly-headed youth with lyre*]; combination print; 19.5 ×
24.2; 1906. L C

53. [*Boy embracing the Herm of Pan*]; triptych; platinum; 19.5
× 23.8; 1905 or later. L C

54. *The Prodigal*; triptych; platinum; 31.7 × 19.5; 1909;
signed. L C

55. [*Head of youth looking up*]; gum print; 18 × 12.5; 1907 or
later. L C

56. [*Nude child on flagstone path*]; combination print; 23.8 ×
18.5; 1905 or later. L C

57. [*Curly-headed youth on boulder*]; platinum; 12.5 × 20;
1905. L C

58. [*Silhouetted youth shooting arrow*]; triptych; combination
print; 18.8 × 23.3; 1905; signed. L C

59. [*Silhouetted youth standing on boulder at shore*]; combination print; 19 × 26; 1905. L C

Notes to the Illustrations

KEY TO ABBREVIATIONS

Sources

HCC   Holy Cross College, Worcester, Mass.
FL   Forbes Library, Northampton, Mass.
IMP-
GEH   International Museum of Photography at George Eastman
        House, Rochester, N.Y.
KHH   London Borough of Camden, from the collection at Keats
        House, Hampstead
LC   Library of Congress, Washington, D.C.
MMNY   Alfred Stieglitz Collection, Metropolitan Museum of Art,
        New York
NHS   Norwood Historical Society, Norwood, Mass., courtesy of
        Charles Lennon, photographer
PC   Private collection

Persons

AB   Aubrey Beardsley   LIG   Louise Imogen Guiney
HC   Herbert Copeland   GK   Gertrude Käsebier
C & D   Copeland and Day   NS   Napoleon Sarony
ALC   Alvin Langdon Coburn   ES   Edward Steichen
RAC   Ralph Adams Cram   AS   Alfred Stieglitz
FHD   F. Holland Day   CW   Clarence White
FE   Frederick Evans   OW   Oscar Wilde
BGG   Bertram Grosvenor Goodhue

NOTE: The number before each note refers to the page on which the
illustration appears. Sources are given at the end of each note.

1

AN INTRODUCTION

2. FHD in London, 1900, by ALC. (NHS)

5. Three views of FHD as publisher, 1894 or 1895; photographer unknown (NHS)

6. FHD as a French dandy, Paris, 1889; carte-de-visite by Jacques et Cie. (NHS)

7. FHD in medieval costume, 1893, by Notman Photo Co., Boston. (NHS)

9. *Solitude,* portrait of FHD by ES as published in *Camera Work,* April 1906. (IMP-GEH)

9. The first of FHD's *Seven Last Words of Christ: Father, forgive them, for they know not what they do,* 1898. (LC)

10. FHD in his London darkroom, 1900, by ALC; damaged platinum print. (NHS)

2

BIBLIOMANIAC WITH
A CAMERA

12. Lewis, Anna, and Fred Day; cartes-de-visite by Blanchard Photo Co., Boston, about 1870. (NHS)

13. The Day mansion before the renovations of 1892; photographer unknown. (NHS)

14. Etching of James Abbott McNeill Whistler; artist unknown. (LC)

14. FHD on February 8, 1878, probably by Blanchard Photo Co., Boston. (NHS)

15. *Madame Sadi Yaco with Parasol* by FHD, about 1896. She was a traveling Japanese actress. (MMNY)

15. *Portrait of a Chinese Man* by FHD, about 1896. According to Weston Naef, the Chinese sitter was identified as 'Leung Foo.' (MMNY)

16. Tintype of FHD with two young women, probably taken at Chauncy Hall, about 1880. (NHS)

16. FHD en route to Europe in 1883; photographer unknown. (NHS)

17. FHD's mother, 'Madame Day,' in 1883; photographer unknown. (NHS)

17. Offices of A. S. Barnes and other Boston book dealers, 1885, by W. Chase, Boston. (NHS)

20. Early photograph by FHD of marble bust, probably to 'extra-illustrate' a volume, about 1886. (LC)

22. Honoré de Balzac, by AB, for an edition of *Scenes of Parisian Life.* (LC)

24. Self-portrait by FHD, in the garden at Norwood, 1887. (NHS)

25. FHD's first gaslight photograph, 1887; the friends who posed have not been identified. (NHS)

3

ENTER LOUISE GUINEY
AND FANNY BRAWNE

28. LIG and FHD shelling beans on her porch, about 1889. LIG lived in Auburndale, now a subdivision of Newton, Mass. Almost certainly a double-portrait taken by FHD. (PC)

32. LIG as 'The Muse of Poetry,' wood engraving by Timothy Cole, 1921, from FHD portrait of 1888. (FL)

38. Miniature portrait of John Keats, profile, about 1819; artist unknown. (KHH, courtesy M. Trace, photographer, London)

38. Sketches of John Keats by Haydon, about 1818. (LC)

39. Miniature portrait of Fanny Brawne, 1818; artist unknown. (KHH, courtesy Errol Jackson, photographer, London)

40. FHD, probably in London, 1890; photographer unknown. (NHS)

40. Carte-de-visite by Jacques et Cie. of FHD, Paris, 1889. (NHS)

41. FHD's 'prima mater,' Anna Day, about 1890, photographer unknown. (NHS)

42. Detail from a wood engraving, 'The Crowning with Thorns,' of the Oberammergau Passion Play, as reproduced in *Harper's Weekly,* January 3, 1891, p. 8. This is the production FHD saw in the summer of 1890. (LC)

42. Rosa Llanos y Keats and her husband, Juan, by FHD, Madrid, 1891. Never before published. (KHH, courtesy Errol Jackson, London)

43. Fanny Brawne's letters to Fanny Keats at the Keats House, Hampstead. The ink is fading despite efforts to preserve these precious letters. (KHH, courtesy Errol Jackson, London)

44. Lyre-shaped brooch with strands of Keats's hair, given to FHD by Rosa Llanos y Keats, Keats's niece, in 1891. A similar brooch was given by FHD to LIG. It was a common practice to preserve snippets of hair from the newly dead. The lyre was Keats's own emblem. (KHH, courtesy Errol Jackson, London)

4
VISIONISTS, CULTISTS, DECADENTS ALL

47. Portrait of HC by FHD, about 1892. (NHS)

49. Members of the Visionists, 1892; possibly taken by FHD. (NHS)

50. William Butler Yeats, wood engraving by Robert Bryden, from William Archer's *Poets of the Younger Generation,* 1902. (FL)

51. *The Lacquer Box* by FHD, about 1899. (MMNY)

51. *The Vigil* by FHD, about 1899. The symbolism of this picture so closely matches rituals of the Golden Dawn that it seems likely FHD joined that organization, but there is no sure evidence. (MMNY)

52. Visionists and 'Knights Errant': RAC, HC, and BGG, probably taken by FHD in 1892 on the lawn of their bachelor quarters in Norwood. (NHS)

53. RAC by FHD, about 1892. (LC)

53. Cover for *The Knight Errant,* designed by BGG. (Columbia University Library, courtesy Susan Otis Thompson and The Art Museum, Princeton University)

55. RAC, HC, and BGG in Norwood, probably taken by FHD in 1892. (NHS)

55. Medieval dinner party at the Day mansion, about 1893; FHD at rear, LIG at left front with RAC; photographer unknown. (NHS)

56. Detail of ivory miniatures of the Parthenon frieze in FHD's

library, supplied by Brucciani of London. (NHS)

57. FHD's bedroom at Norwood, decorated in black and scarlet
and copied from furnishings in French chateaux; photographer unknown. (NHS)

57. Corner and upstairs alcove of FHD's renovated library; photographer unknown. (NHS)

58. The Keats corner in FHD's renovated library. Portrait of OW
by NS was sepia-toned, gilt-edged; photographer unknown. (NHS)

59. *The Decadent* by RAC, designed by BGG, the first book published by C & D, 1893. (Boston Athenaeum)

5

PUBLISHERS AND
POETS

62. FHD, publisher, about 1893; photographer unknown. (NHS)

62. BGG, designer, by FHD, about 1893. (LC)

63. HC, partner, by FHD, about 1893. (NHS)

64. Page from the Kelmscott *Chaucer,* 1896, by William Morris
from Edward Burne-Jones's designs. (LC)

64. Page from Dante Gabriel Rossetti's *House of Life,* C & D,
1894. Designed in 'the medieval look' by BGG but close to Renaissance
originals. (PC)

65. End papers by Tom Meteyard for *Songs from Vagabondia,*
C & D, 1894. (Courtesy Susan Otis Thompson)

66. Wood engravings by Robert Bryden in Archer's *Poets of the
Younger Generation.* (FL)

66. Title page by Will Bradley, with typical C & D printer's
mark, for Richard LeGallienne's *Robert Louis Stevenson,* 1895. (Columbia University Library, courtesy Susan Otis Thompson)

67. Ethel Reed, model for FHD's most frequently reproduced
portrait, *The Gainsborough Hat,* 1895, was a talented illustrator and
designer about whom not much is known. (LC)

67. Ethel Reed's poster for *Arabella and Araminta,* C & D's most
successful children's book. (LC)

69. Fred Gordon's orchids for *The Black Riders,* by Stephen
Crane, C & D, 1895. It was about this cover that Amy Lowell complained. (Columbia University Library, courtesy Susan Otis Thompson)

70. LIG and Alice Brown in walking costume for tour of England, 1895. (HCC) LIG met her when Brown was on the staff of *The
Youth's Companion* in Boston. In a letter to Edmund Stedman, October
18, 1887, LIG describes her new friend as 'a slender body, with gentle
ways, and a very great energy and spirit, and is full of human sym-
pathies, and fun, too . . .' (LC)

70. Alice Brown, possibly by FHD, about 1895. (NHS)

71. BGG's most medieval designs for LIG's *Nine Sonnets at
Oxford,* C & D, 1895. (Columbia University Library, courtesy Susan
Otis Thompson)

72–73. C & D printer's marks, many of which were designed by
BGG. Page 72, for the Yellow Hair series (Newberry Library, courtesy
Joe W. Kraus); page 72 for *Sonnets from the Portuguese* (Boston
Athenaeum); page 73. (Newberry Library, courtesy Joe W. Kraus)

6

OSCAR AND AUBREY,
SUN-GODS AND
WRAITHS

74. OW, 1882, by NS. FHD kept this portrait in the 'Keats corner' of his library at Norwood. (LC)

77. OW reclining in a smoking jacket, 1882, by NS. (LC)

78. C & D pressmark. (Newberry Library, courtesy Joe W. Kraus)

79. Tomb of Keats in Rome, by Cosmos Photograph Co., New York, probably taken in the 1920s. The lyre has only four strings, symbolizing the shortness of the poet's life. (LC)

79. St. Sebastian, one of two versions by FHD, 1906. (LC)

80. Dedication of a copy of Anne Whitney's bust of John Keats at the Hampstead Parish Church, 1894, with Edmund Gosse, FHD and LIG presiding; from a newspaper clipping. (NHS)

81. OW called this 1883 portrait of AB by FE 'a face like a silver hatchet.' (IMP-GEH)

82. Hermaphrodite by AB for a chapter heading the J. M. Dent edition of Malory's *Le Morte d'Arthur,* 1892. (Dover Archives)

82. Grotesque by AB for the *Bon-Mots* series published by Dent. (LC)

83. AB portrayed himself tied to a Herm of Pan. Called *A Foot-note,* this illustration appeared in *The Savoy,* no. 2, April 1896, preceding an excerpt from his novel, *Under the Hill.* (Dover Archives)

84. Detail from the original version of AB's title page for *Salomé* by OW. The hermaphrodite's penis was 'banned in Boston.' (LC)

85. 'The Climax' – an illustration by AB for OW's *Salomé.* The bloody head of St. John drips into lilies, and AB's emblematic signature is at lower left, a symbolic representation of ejaculation. The floating figure of Salomé and the overall decorative pattern are reminiscent of Utamara's woodblocks. (LC)

86. Two pages from *Le Morte d'Arthur,* 1892, showing the evolution of AB's 'Japanese' style, which found full expression in *Salomé.* (Dover Archives)

89. Three portraits of 'Pepita' by FHD, as reproduced in *Godey's Magazine,* January 1898, to illustrate an article by Marmaduke Humphrey [Rupert Hughes] about FHD. This publication is an invaluable source for FHD's lost portraits of women and several pagan themes. (LC)

90. Cover of the first issue of *The Yellow Book,* published jointly by John Lane and C & D, 1894. (Boston Athenaeum)

91. Lionel Johnson, recently graduated from Oxford; photographer unknown. The inscription in LIG's copy of his poems reads, 'Too pale and difficult even for speech!' (HCC)

91. OW in evening dress, by NS, 1882. (LC)

7

MR. STIEGLITZ TAKES
NOTICE

92. AS by GK, 1902, at about the time he was resigning from the Camera Club of New York and from *Camera Notes.* (MMNY)

95. *Scurrying Home,* by AS, 1894, as reproduced in *Camera Notes,* October 1899. One of many popular Dutch genre scenes taken by AS on his honeymoon. (IMP-GEH)

95. *Evening* by FHD, about 1896. Margaret Harker has traced this pose to a painting by Jean Hippolyte Flandrin. (LC)

97. Whistleresque portrait by FHD, after 1900. (LC)

99. *Hannah* by FHD, probably 1894; one print survives in poor condition at LC, and a reproduction appeared in the *Godey's Magazine* article by Marmaduke Humphrey. The model is unknown. Although this portrait won FHD election to the Linked Ring Brotherhood, very little is known about the circumstances of his submitting it, or about his first contacts with George Davison. (LC)

100. *Mrs. Potter* by FHD, 1896. Confusion exists about the identity of the sitter, who was called 'Mrs. Potter' in a private exhibition, but who is — to judge from comments in newspapers and LIG's remarks to FHD — almost certainly the actress whose name was 'Mrs. Potter Palmer.' (MMNY)

101. Young woman in Moorish headdress, by FHD, about 1894. FHD used this same metal headpiece with good effect on Alfred Tanneyhill. (LC)

102. Tow-headed girl on leopard skin, by FHD, 1895. The animal skin was used again and again by FHD, for pattern, texture, and a touch of the exotic. (LC)

103. Portrait of a young woman by FHD, 1895. (LC)

103. *Pepita,* second version, by FHD. One of his favorite models, but unfortunately not identified by her full name. (LC)

104. *Study of a Baby* by AS, as reproduced in *Camera Notes,* 1898, in a series describing glycerine and gum manipulations of prints. (IMP-GEH)

104. *The Net-Mender* by AS, as reproduced in *Camera Notes,* 1898. Also called *Mending Nets* and published in various journals; another Dutch genre scene undoubtedly taken in 1894 on AS's honeymoon. (IMP-GEH)

105. *A Study* by FHH, as reproduced in *Camera Notes,* 1898. The model has not been identified. (IMP-GEH)

8

A PURELY GREEK
POINT OF VIEW

108. *An Ethiopian Chief,* by FHD, first of the Nubian series, published in *Camera Notes,* October 1897; see plate 10 for another version which became part of the *Armageddon* triptych. (IMP-GEH)

109. *Ebony and Ivory,* by FHD, 1897. Because of production methods used in photogravure, this image sometimes appeared reversed, with the statue on the left instead of on the right. Technically, it was FHD's most difficult print, and when it was published in *Camera Notes,* FHD wrote to AS to congratulate him on a superb rendering. (MMNY)

109. *The Smoker* by FHD, 1897. Alfred Tanneyhill proved to be a majestic model. (MMNY)

110. *Hypnos* by FHD, about 1896; model unknown. The artificiality which characterized these early pagan images is epitomized by the metal poppy. (LC)

111. FHD combined the first version of *Beauty Is Truth* with one of the versions of the *Entombment;* they were exhibited together in

matched frames as a unit, which FHD later copied into one print in a more modest frame for his 1900 London show. (Collection of Molly E. Hampstead, courtesy William D. Pugh, photographer, Oxford, Penn.)

112. *In Tanagra* by FHD, about 1896, as reproduced in the *Godey's Magazine* article by Marmaduke Humphrey, 1897. No extant print has been discovered. The small plaster figure was a copy of a Greek statuette said to have inspired William Blake in his *Glad Day* watercolor. (LC)

112. Youth with urn on head, by FHD, about 1896. (LC)

115. Kahlil Gibran with book, by FHD, about 1897. Day undoubtedly bought Gibran the handsome corduroy suit. (MMNY)

116. Gibran in costume, by FHD, probably taken in 1896, as his hair is shorter here than in the pose with the book and he also seems somewhat younger. (LC)

118. Nude shepherd, by FHD, 1897. Except for an occasional tender smile or a look of amused inner concentration, these controlled pagans merited the remark by Joseph T. Keiley that they elicited 'a cold, intellectual admiration.' (LC)

119. FHD by Frederick Hollyer, about 1895, London. Not one of Hollyer's best portraits, and certainly not flattering to Day. (NHS)

9
A CROWN OF THORNS

120. Crucifixion with Mary, Joseph and saints, 1898, with FHD posing as Christ. The date for the entire sacred subjects series is generally given as 1898, but the exact sequence is unknown, and Day did begin several in 1896. What is especially confusing is the fact that the length of FHD's hair varies greatly in the series. It seems likely that he either wore a wig or let his hair grow long for the more gothic crucifixions, then had it shorn for the *Seven Last Words* and for this image. (LC)

122. 'Some of Mr. Day's Photographic Art Studies' – newspaper caption, undated clipping in FHD's albums. (NHS)

123. Newspaper clipping, undated but almost certainly 1898, in FHD's albums. (NHS)

124. Sepia art print of the Velásquez *Crucifixion,* probably purchased in Paris; badly torn and cracked. FHD was supposed to have been influenced by Guido Reni's Christs, which are more melodramatically baroque than this simple picture. The mood of the Velásquez more closely resembles the restraint of FHD's images. (NHS)

125. Two versions of LIG as St. Barbara, by FHD, 1893. The penciled halos were LIG's notion. (LC)

126. Early version of *I Thirst* by FHD, about 1898, as published in *Photogram,* February 1899. The facial make-up reproduced as realistically as LIG had predicted. (LC)

128. *The Seven Last Words of Christ* by FHD, 1898. In an architectural gilt frame hand lettered with each of Christ's last sayings, this was exhibited widely. Other versions are separate prints in sepia tone or black. (LC)

130. Page from *Harper's Weekly,* November 4, 1899, accom-

panying Charles Caffin's review of the Second Philadelphia Salon. The two prints by GK indicate how painterly her concepts were. Caffin balanced the distasteful *Entombment* with one of FHD's Nubian series, *Menelik*. (LC)

131. Page from *Harper's Weekly*, November 3, 1900. Caffin's review of the Third Philadelphia Salon comments, 'some two hundred prints were displayed; the cream skimmed off an aggregate of nearly twelve hundred submitted to the jury.' The prints by AS and FH represent the antipodes of ideology about photography at this time. (LC)

133. Tableau of the Oberammergau Passion Play, as reproduced in *Harper's Weekly,* October 27, 1900, p. 1020. (LC)

134. *It Is Finished,* early version by FHD, 1898, who was obviously experimenting with dramatic vignettes. (LC)

134. *Resurrection from the Tomb* by FHD, probably 1896, demonstrating his disregard for the presence of modern anachronisms like metal hinges on the mausoleum doors. FHD posed as Christ. (LC)

135. *Crucifixion* by FHD, gothic in conception, resembling realistic wayside crosses in Germany. (LC)

10

THE NEW SCHOOL
OF AMERICAN
PHOTOGRAPHY

136. Jury for the Second Philadelphia Salon. Frances Johnston, CW, FHD, GK and Henry Troth; photographer unknown. (PC)

138. *Spring – A Triptych* by CW, 1898. Other versions feature rounded or arched shapes, and wider separations between the three sections. (LC)

139. *Blessed Art Thou Among Women* by GK, 1899. Probably her most famous print. An unmanipulated version at LC reveals how much work went into creating these subdued harmonies, never the result of the camera unaided. (LC)

139. *The Manger* by GK, about 1898; also titled *Mother and Child,* and reproduced in both *Camera Notes* and *Camera Work.* (LC)

140. FHD by GK, 1899, at the beginning of their friendship. She made him look nervous and prim. (MMNY)

141. GK by FHD, 1899. FHD made her look thoughtful and majestic, if not relaxed. (PC)

143. Draft of a letter from FHD to AS, April 5, 1900. FHD almost always wrote out several drafts of letters before sending them, although he did not always post letters he had drafted. AS wanted to see FHD before Day left for London, whether out of a sense of guilt about behind-the-scenes machinations or in a genuine attempt to repair what seemed an irreparable break. FHD politely but firmly refused any meeting. (NHS)

144. ALC in the Mortimer Street studio, London, by FHD, 1900. The walls were decorated with Japanese objects and prints from the exhibition. (LC)

145. Display of FHD's sacred subjects as published in *Photo Era,* January 1901, p. 209. *The Seven Last Words* stretches over the combined print of *Beauty Is Truth,* which is centered on *Armageddon.* The other prints are more modestly matted and framed. This reproduction

accompanied ALC's article, 'American Photographs in London.'

146. *Lady in Black with Statuette* by CW, 1898. It is hard to believe that CW was not strongly influenced by FHD's *Ebony and Ivory,* which had appeared in CN in 1897. (LC)

147. Sadakichi Hartmann, by ES, 1903. Hartmann frequently contributed to *Camera Work, Brush and Pencil,* and other art journals. His ancestry was German and Japanese. (MMNY)

148. Zaïda Ben-Yusuf, by FHD, 1898. This is almost certainly the portrait exhibited in London which drew such sarcasm from Hartmann. Ben-Yusuf was a respected portrait and landscape photographer. (MMNY)

149. *Evening – Interior,* by CW, 1898 or 1899. (LC)

149. *Mother and Child,* by GK, about 1899. An extreme example of her posterizing effects achieved with gum bichromate. The poster revolution, itself influenced by both Japanese art and color lithography, had an impact on several of the Pictorialists. (LC)

151. ES by FHD, in Paris, 1901. (LC)

152. AS holding what was probably the first issue of *Camera Work,* by ALC, 1903. *Camera Work* was undeniably AS's greatest editorial achievement, with superb photogravures supervised by his former photoengraving firm. It is today among the rarest of photography journals. (MMNY)

II

A PHOENIX FROM

THE ASHES

155. FHD in London, 1901, by ALC. (NHS)

157. Three portraits of FHD in Algerian costume, by FE, London, 1901. (left, Museum of Fine Arts, Boston, gift of David Bakalar; center, NHS; right, damaged print at NHS)

159. LIG at forty-four, inscribed 'To L.C.M. [Louise Chandler Moulton] from L.I.G. with Christmas love, Oxford, 1905.' (LC)

161. Self-portrait by ES, 1902. (MMNY)

164. GK by ALC, 1903. ALC worked briefly with GK before he returned to England. (MMNY)

164. CW by ES, 1903. (MMNY)

165. The Day mansion in Norwood, by CW, 1905. The Lombard poplars are gone now, but the exterior of the house retains its grandeur. (NHS)

12

THE HERM OF PAN

166. Boy with Herm of Pan, by FHD, 1905. The same model identity unknown, posed for the triptych (see plate 53). (LC)

168. *The Pipes of Pan* by FHD, 1897. (LC)

168. *The Marble Faun* by FHD, 1897. (LC)

169. *Archer in Woods* by CW, 1905. (LC)

169. Nude archer, by FHD, 1905. A comparison between the two versions of the same subject reveals the increasingly strong decorative impulse in FHD's work and the softer, looser romanticism of CW at this time. (LC)

170. One of many versions of the same theme by A B for the chapter headings in *Le Morte d'Arthur*. The pubescent, quasi-innocent boy and the devilish Herm of Pan were favorite subjects of his. (Dover Archives)

172. Youth with staff shading his eyes, by F H D, signed, 1906. (L C)

173. St. Sebastian, one of two versions by F H D, about 1906. Possibly Day was inspired to attempt this theme because of the large scar on the clavicle of his model, identity unknown. (L C)

173. Youth with scar, by F H D, about 1906. Same model as in the St. Sebastian. (L C)

176. Youth with lyre, by F H D, 1907. One of the Apollo/Orpheus series; each print varied in shape and size. (L C)

177. *The Last Chord* by F H D, 1907. The title is mentioned in a letter from Nardo to F H D. (L C)

179. Letter from H C to F H D, one of a series about his 'Jimmie-Hermes' explicitly describing his infatuation with his former masseur. (N H S)

181. Youth with feathered hat, by F H D, about 1907. The model may have been Nardo. The costume headpiece, like the wings of Hermes, had been used by F H D in his Nubian series. (L C)

181. Youth in North Africa costume, by F H D, about 1907. Nardo may have been the model. (L C)

13

LITTLE GOOD HARBOR

182. The family of C W in sailor suits, by G K, taken in Maine about 1912, after White had established his school at Seguinland. F H D also took many photographs of the C W menage, often in the form of cyanotypes. (L C)

184. *The Readers* by C W, 1897. The suppression of detail into a strong formal pattern was one of the influences of *japonisme*. (L C)

184. Two girls reading, by F H D, signed, 1907. Here F H D seems to be learning from the Impressionists, including Degas. (L C)

185. Seated woman with dark straw hat and umbrella, by F H D, 1908, in Maine. F H D took several striking photographs of this model, identity unknown. (L C)

185. Nude child on flagstone path, by F H D, 1908. Taken in Maine, possibly one of the White children. (L C)

187. F E by A L C, 1906. Evans was Day's staunchest ally in England, and ultimately gave his magnificent collection of F H D's prints to the Royal Photographic Society, London. (M M N Y)

188. *The Aeroplane* by A S, as published in *Camera Work,* October 1911. (I M P - G E H)

188. *The Steerage* by A S, as published in *Camera Work,* October 1911. An acknowledged masterpiece, the picture was taken on a steamer going to Paris, not coming from Europe as is commonly assumed. A S was interested purely in the formal qualities of the crowd arrangement, and boasted that Picasso had said they were both working in a similar – cubist – vein. (I M P - G E H)

189. FHD's last portrait of his father, Lewis Day, before his death in 1910. (NHS)

190. FHD kept an album of snapshots recording the progress of construction of 'Castle Guiney.' This image of the 'Royal Barge,' his scow, consists of two prints pasted together to make a panorama. (NHS)

191. FHD's 'Greek temple' featured a life-size reproduction of Michelangelo's *Slave*. (LC)

191. Snapshot by FHD of the completed 'Castle Guiney' about 1910 as it looked from the harbor. There were apparently no public roads to the site. (NHS)

192. *The Prodigal* by FHD, 1909. From 1905 on, FHD experimented many times with the triptych form, which had appealed to both CW and GK as well (see plate 54). (LC)

193. Boy in sailor suit, by FHD, one of many variations on this theme. The white or blue sailor suits became the preferred costume for the CW menage and FHD wore them constantly. (LC)

193. FHD smoking, taken in Maine about 1910; photographer unknown. (LC)

194. FHD in blue sailor suit, smoking. At Little Good Harbor, about 1915. Day was greatly addicted to tobacco in all forms, but preferred Russian cigarettes which were long and elegant. (NHS)

195. Letter from ALC to FHD. The caricature at the top was by Marius de Zayas, one of the Stieglitz circle. The origin of their nicknames for one another is not known. (NHS)

197. FHD with either Maynard or Clarence White, Jr. at 'Castle Guiney,' before 1917; photographer unknown. (NHS)

14
FROM THE UPSTAIRS
WINDOW

200. FHD in Norwood, about 1917, photographer unknown. (NHS)

203. *Millfield Lane,* taken by FHD during his Keats mania of 1890. Reproduced as a photogravure in Amy Lowell's biography of Keats, vol. I, inserted between pp. 280 and 281. (Simmons College Library)

204. Last portrait of Anna Day by FHD, about 1917. (NHS)

206. FHD surrounded by books and papers in his canopied bed, about 1930; photographer unknown. (NHS)

208. Last formal portrait of CW by FHD, about 1910; where this was posed is not certain. (LC)

209. Self-portrait by GK. Date uncertain, but probably about 1910 when she was becoming robust again after several years' illness. (PC)

211. FHD pensively looking toward the windows of his bedroom, about 1930; photographer unknown. (NHS)

213. RAC's chapel for the Day family. Some of the lively sculptures on the exterior may have been designed by BGG. Courtesy of Charles Lennon, photographer. (NHS)

214. FHD gazing out to the sea, photographer unknown. (NHS)

Notes to the Text

Sources

BJOP	*British Journal of Photography*
HCC	Holy Cross College, Worcester, Mass.
IMP-GEH	International Museum of Photography at George Eastman House, Rochester, N.Y.
LC	Library of Congress, Washington, D.C.
NHS	Norwood Historical Society, Norwood, Mass.
YUSA	Alfred Stieglitz Archive, Collection of American Literature. Beinecke Rare Book and Manuscript Library, Yale University, New Haven, Conn.

Persons

BB	Bernard Berenson	GK	Gertrude Käsebier
ALC	Alvin Langdon Coburn	LCM	Louise Chandler Moulton
HC	Herbert Copeland	GS	Gertrude Savage
FHD	F. Holland Day	AS	Alfred Stieglitz
LIG	Louise Imogen Guiney	CW	Clarence White

I

AN INTRODUCTION

1. The first useful attempt to survey Day's life and career was by Joe Walker Kraus in his master's thesis (University of Illinois, Urbana, 1941), 'A History of Copeland & Day (1893–1899).' The specifics of the publishing firm are documented by Kraus's *Messrs. Copeland & Day, 1893–1899*, printed privately by George McManus, Philadelphia, 1979.

Stephen Maxfield Parrish's doctoral thesis (Harvard University, Cambridge, Mass., 1954), 'Currents of the Nineties in Boston and

London: Fred Holland Day, Louise Imogen Guiney and Their Circle,'
and *Keats and the Bostonians: Amy Lowell, Louise Imogen Guiney,
Louis Arthur Holman, Fred Holland Day* (New York, Russell &
Russell, 1951), written with Hyder Edward Rollins, are two major
sources of information.

Possibly the first work to concentrate on Day's photographic
achievements was Ellen Fritz Clattenburg's catalogue for the 1975
Wellesley College Museum exhibition, *The Photographic Work of
F. Holland Day*. Despite an heroic effort to pull together materials from
secondary sources, it contained errors, such as: 'Little is known about
Day's photography in Maine' (much could be found in the papers at
Norwood Historical Society); 'When Day did exhibit, as in the Albright
Show in 1910, he rarely submitted anything but his early work' (Day
refused to exhibit in the Albright Show under Stieglitz, and gave
Stieglitz explicit instructions forbidding the use of his early work). Her
notes on the photographs, however, are excellent.

Weston Naef also allowed a number of errors to creep into his
useful volume, *The Collection of Alfred Stieglitz: Fifty Pioneers of
Modern Photography* (New York, Viking, 1978). Naef's is the only
recent source of any significance that establishes Day's reputation
within the photographic milieu at the turn of the century and permits us
some glimpses of the stature of Day vis-à-vis Stieglitz.

2

BIBLIOMANIAC
WITH A CAMERA

1. Papers of Anna Day, NHS. The diary entry is on a tiny scrap
of paper; apparently the diary had separable small sheets.

2. FHD to Lewis Day, April 16, 1879, NHS.

3. Notes in his copybooks for 1932–33, NHS.

4. Lewis Day to FHD, July 7, 1879, NHS.

5. *Commercial Bulletin,* Saturday, February 16, 1884, n.p.; from
scrapbook, NHS.

6. FHD lent his talents to raising money for the Unitarian–
Universalist Church of Norwood, which had been razed by fire. He
gave talks 'illustrated with a stereopticon' (January 21, 1885) despite
a long illness. The *Norwood Review* for January 30, 1885 noted that
the stereoscopic slides had been outstanding, and that Mr. Black of
Blacks', Boston, came out 'to throw the views in person.' Blacks' was a
major supplier of stereographs. Scrapbooks, NHS.

7. FHD to Charlotte Porter, Philadelphia, August 11, 1886, NHS.

8. FHD to Miriam Robinson, February 10, 1885, NHS. His address is given as 32 Bromfield Street, Boston.

9. FHD to unidentified correspondent, n.d., 1886, from the new
address of 24 Boylston Street, Boston, NHS. 'Trinity' is H. H. Richard-
son's magnificent Trinity Church at Copley Square, completed in 1875.
It was at the cultural center of the city, facing the Museum of Fine
Arts, which later moved to its present location on Huntington Avenue,
and the Boston Public Library. Day would have been well pleased by
the windows designed by the Pre-Raphælite Edmund Burne-Jones and

executed by his partner, William Morris, among other stained-glass achievements in the church.

10. FHD to Philip Savage, October 24, 1888, NHS.

11. FHD to 'Charles,' March 5, 1885, NHS.

12. FHD to Edgar Evertson Saltus, December 30, 1886, NHS. Saltus had written an introduction to Balzac's complete works, as well as a brief and diverting biography. Day collected Saltus's works, and seems to have been especially impressed with *The Philosophy of Disenchantment* (1885). An interpretation of the pessimism of Schopenhauer, its primary message was to live and let live, because the only meaning in a scientific world emptied of God and 'First Design' was the meaning we ourselves imposed on the universe. Day's letters often reveal sympathy with such a view.

13. FHD to 'Jno. Gilmer Speed, Esq., c/o Dodd, Mead, New York,' September 14, 1886, NHS.

14. FHD to BB, December 6, 1887, NHS.

15. FHD to Madame Helena Modjeska, March 31, 1888, NHS. The novella was Balzac's *Duchesse de Langeais*.

16. Katherine Prescott Wormseley, *A Memoir of Honoré de Balzac,* (Boston, Roberts Bros., 1894), p. 271.

17. FHD to GS, July 23, 1889, NHS. This letter also describes his enthusiasm about the Psychical Society in Paris.

18. *Anthony's Photographic Bulletin,* advertisement, 1885, n.p.

19. FHD to 'Aunt Liddy,' from Boston, December 22, 1886, NHS. The exact identities of Day's relatives have been extremely difficult to ascertain. *Aunt* was used for friends of his mother, according to the custom of the time, but it seems that both his mother and father had sisters living in Massachusetts.

20. FHD to GS, September 4, 1886, NHS.

21. FHD to GS, September 13, 1886, NHS.

22. FHD to unidentified Dedham official. Draft of letter, September 14, 1886, NHS. Norwood was considered part of Dedham at that time.

23. FHD to 'Aunt Lydd,' July 19, 1887, NHS.

24. FHD to 'Isabella,' June 24, 1887, NHS.

25. FHD to 'Isabella,' September 16, 1887, NHS.

26. FHD to GS, September 17, 1887, NHS.

27. FHD to Ada Langley, October 5, 1887, NHS.

28. FHD to 'Annie,' December 16, 1887, NHS.

29. 'A New Era in Instantaneous Photography,' *Anthony's Photographic Bulletin,* October 22, 1887 (vol. 18, no. 2), p. 609.

30. FHD to LIG, March 22, 1888, NHS.

31. *Fourth Annual Exhibition of Photographers of the United States* (catalogue, New York, 1891), from the preface. The board of judges included the painter Thomas Moran, the designer Will H. Low, and the photographer Edward Bierstadt, brother of the painter Albert Bierstadt.

32. *Ibid.*

33. 'The Largest Negative in the World,' *The Amateur Photog-*

rapher (England), September 17, 1886, p. 140. The camera was home-made by 'Mr. Burnham,' and the lens was 'No. 8 Euryscope, largest of that class.' (Burnham was awarded a silver medal at Philadelphia.) A single sheet of Morgan's albumen paper, 36″ × 60″, was used, with an exposure of 20 seconds.

34. 'The Exhibit of Apparatus at Boston,' *Anthony's Photographic Bulletin*, September 14, 1889 (vol. 20, no. 17), p. 530.

35. Joseph T. Keiley, 'The Philadelphia Salon: Its Origin and Influence,' *Camera Notes*, January 1889 (vol. 2, no. 3), pp. 116–17.

3
ENTER LOUISE GUINEY AND FANNY BRAWNE

1. FHD to 'Maggie,' June 2, 1886, NHS.

2. *Ibid.*

3. FHD to LIG, November 12, 1887, NHS.

4. FHD to LIG, November 17, 1887, NHS.

5. FHD to LIG, January 21, 1888, NHS.

6. FHD to LIG, December 21, 1888, NHS.

7. FHD to LIG, December 29, 1888, NHS.

8. FHD to LCM, December 29, 1888, NHS. One of Day's minor eccentricities was to repeat, almost verbatim, salutations and whole paragraphs from letter to letter.

9. LIG to LCM, March 5, 1888, LC. The two Louises carried on a long and ardent correspondence until Moulton's death. It was Guiney who tired first of the endless emotional demands made by her god-mother. Guiney was dependent on much charity from Moulton, and wrote to her with affection and gratitude from wherever she was in England or Boston. The dark side of Guiney revealed itself in several curious letters to Moulton written in 1885, where, after addressing Moulton as 'My Liege Lady,' and signing herself 'Louise the Less,' she meticulously drew a skull and crossbones under her name. The drawing bears no resemblance to the conventional symbols for poison or piracy; rather it resembles the symbol of death which painters have placed at the foot of the cross at Calvary. Other indications of poor self-image, coupled with a fascination with death, occur frequently in the Guiney–Moulton correspondence. Louise was not always gay and witty.

10. FHD to LIG, n.d., 1888, NHS.

11. LIG to FHD, n.d., 1888, LC.

12. See *William James on Psychical Research*, Gardner Murphy and Robert O. Ballou, eds. (New York, Viking, 1960). James's account of his experiences with Mrs. Piper appeared as 'Certain Phenomena of Trance' in the *Proceedings of the Society for Psychical Research* (London), 1890 (vol. 2, part 17). Mrs. Piper was well known on both sides of the Atlantic.

13. FHD to LCM, April 2, 1889, NHS.

14. FHD to LIG, April 1, 1889, NHS.

15. LIG to FHD, n.d., 1889, LC.

16. FHD to LIG, n.d., 1889, NHS.

17. FHD to LIG, from New York, March 28, 1890, NHS. Louise

had other 'Sonnies,' as evidenced in her collected letters; among these she definitely included Lionel Johnson. Day never signed 'Sonny' except for a few letters written before they went abroad in 1889. Louise teased him by calling him 'M. Frederic Hollande du Jour,' and other playful nicknames. Sometime in the mid 1890s, she became 'Quinck,' and that remained his favorite name for her. Even her last letters to him, however, were addressed to 'Sonny.'

18. Mary F. Sandars, *Honoré de Balzac: His Life and Writings* (New York, Dodd, Mead, 1905), p. 89.

19. See Alice Brown, *Louise Imogen Guiney* (New York, Macmillan, 1921), p. 6.

20. FHD to LIG, April 5, 1889, NHS.

21. Oscar Wilde, 'The Tomb of Keats,' quoted in Richard Ellmann, ed., *The Artist as Critic* (New York, Random House, 1968), p. 69.

22. LIG to FHD, May 2, 1889, HCC. In this letter Guiney speculates at length on the question of the color of Keats's eyes. Her enthusiasm for the poet exceeded even Day's.

23. Henry G. Fairbanks, *Louise Imogen Guiney* (New York, Twayne, 1973), p. 53.

24. *Ibid.*

25. *Boston Evening Transcript*, Saturday, December 14, 1889; clipping in Day's scrapbook. A draft of the letter he sent to the various newspapers is at NHS:

> *My Dear Sir —*
> *If you have engaged with no European correspondant for the Summer & Fall I would much like to send you letters from Great Britain & France during that time. Not being at liberty to refer you to my previous press correspondence I should wish to stipulate that the agreement be left practically open till the first letter has been recieved [sic] and accepted by you. Also that a semi-agreement be made now as to amt of matter required in each article & remuneration etc. and that payment be made on the 25th of each month for the four (or five) letters of that month, and deposited here as I may direct. The range of subjects could be wide, embracing — Travel, of necessity, Literature, Art, Drama and some of the moves made by Americans in Europe. I should also wish my identity kept between us as all matter would be signed with a nom-de-plume. As I leave Boston on Wednesday, please direct immediately to P.O. Box 1374 Boston . . .*
> *F. H. Day.*

Day's hero worship of Balzac led him to pursue his subject to the grave site, and to his house; much of the *Transcript* correspondence indicates the depth of his knowledge of Balzac's life and career. He also noted several pictures of Balzac, and remarked, 'The daguerreotype by Gavarni, it is true, was broken by the Prussians, but not before a photographic reproduction had been made of it, a copy of which is in my own possession.' He saw this at the Vicomte de Lovenjoul's collection.

26. *The Critic,* June 14, 1890; clipping in Day's scrapbook, NHS. Day kept much of the Balzac information to himself. A good reason for his silence was that he had promised the Vicomte de Lovenjoul, '*Assurement, je ne donnerais jamais au public ni le portrait de la main de Balzac ni aucune des autres choses précieuses que vous avez eu la bonté de me presenter, sans votre parfaite permission.*' [Assuredly, I will never give the public either the picture of Balzac's hand or any of the other precious things which you have had the goodness to present to me, without your complete permission.] Photocopy of letter dated January 25, 1891, NHS.

27. FHD to GS, October 16, 1889, NHS. In an earlier letter, dated August 12, 1889, FHD tells GS,

> *I wish you could see me at this minute. It is 11 a.m. and I am sitting beside my table and wearing a very peculiar garment purchased in the Cairo department of the Exposition. It is dark bottle green, shrimp pink, and navy blue striped with white. Trimmed with a sky blue silk braid and buttons of the same shade also in silk. . . . My mother has pestered me for years to wear a dressing gown and now I've got one though it has been wove by some old Turk a century ago.*

Day apparently purchased a number of costumes at the Cairo Department of the Paris Exposition of 1889, using these later in his Moorish portraits in addition to wearing them in his studios.

28. FHD to GS, November 6, 1889, NHS.

29. *Boston Advertiser and Review,* Saturday, December 21, 1889. The clipping from Day's scrapbooks (NHS) includes a description of him as 'special European correspondent to the *Boston Transcript.*'

30. LIG to LCM, December 6, 1889, LC.

31. *Boston Courier,* Sunday, June 15, 1890; clipping in Day's scrapbooks, NHS.

32. Marie Adami, *Fanny Keats* (London, Murray, 1937), p. 232.

33. FHD to Herbert V. Lindon, October 23, 1890, NHS. The letter was posted from 18 Tavistock Street, Bedford Square, London.

34. Fairbanks, *Louise Imogen Guiney,* p. 57.

4

VISIONISTS, CULTISTS, DECADENTS ALL

1. FHD to GS, n.d., 1889, NHS.

2. FHD to GS, August 1889, NHS.

3. FHD to GS, September 20, 1889, NHS.

4. Philip Henry Savage to FHD, September 8, 1889, NHS.

5. See Joe Walker Kraus, 'A History of Copeland & Day,' p. 38, for a variety of opinions: Louise Guiney found Copeland 'nice . . . a very sound judgement on art matters'; Mitchell Kennerley said, 'Herbert Copeland was a charming, dissipated, ineffectual person'; Gelett Burgess recalls him as a 'lean, lithe, witty chap, enthusiastic, dry.'

6. Ralph Adams Cram, *My Life in Architecture* (Boston, Little, Brown, 1936), p. 91.

7. *Ibid.*, p. 92.

8. *Ibid.*, p. 93.

9. Karl Beckson, 'Yeats and The Rhymers' Club,' in Robert O'Driscoll and Loring Reynolds, eds., *Yeats and the 1890s* (Yeats Studies, no. 1, Irish University Press, 1970), p. 29.

10. Arnold Goldman, 'Yeats, Spiritualism, and Psychical Research,' in George Mills Harper, ed., *Yeats and the Occult* (Macmillan of Canada, 1975), p. 149.

11. *Ibid.*

12. FHD to William Butler Yeats, February 5, 1892, NHS. With an earlier letter dated April 2, 1891, Day had sent Yeats a catalogue of Blake's work from an exhibition. Blake had been deeply influenced by Swedenborgian mysticism, and was considered one of the progenitors of the spiritualist movement among poets. Blake's famous visions encouraged a belief that he dealt in magic. Madame Blavatsky's position on black magic was somewhat ambivalent, but the story goes that Yeats actually built a cabalistic bonfire and attempted to cast spells. See note 13.

13. See Ellic Howe, *The Magicians of the Golden Dawn: A Documentary History of a Magical Order, 1887–1923* (London, Routledge & Kegan Paul, 1972), for a complete index to the symbols of the Golden Dawn. Day's *The Vigil* is so remarkably close to those symbols that it is likely he had become a member, or that someone, perhaps Yeats, had shared information about the rituals with him. Given Day's self-imposed mock crucifixion of 1898, the temptation is strong to decide he was a member of the Golden Dawn, but, for obvious reasons, that is difficult to verify. See also Virginia Moore, *The Unicorn* (New York, Macmillan, 1954), pp. 149–50, for details of the symbolic crucifixion.

14. FHD to Yeats, February 5, 1892, NHS.

15. HC to FHD, February 8, 1892, NHS.

16. *Ibid.*

17. Francis Watts Lee to FHD, November 7, 1892, NHS.

18. 'The Quest: Being an Apology for the Existence of the Review Called The Knight Errant,' *The Knight Errant*, no. 1, 1892, p. 2.

19. Bertram Grosvenor Goodhue, 'The Final Flowering of Age-End Art,' *The Knight Errant*, no. 4, 1893, p. 106. The idea that the medieval period had been the golden ages was based on the notion that craftsmen–artists then were inspired, dedicated, and happy. Certainly, in the nineteenth century, industrialization was creating an unhappy populace alienated from the fruits of its own labors by factory technologies.

20. *Boston Courier*, August 14, 1892. Clipping at NHS.

21. *Ibid.*

22. *Boston Journal*, May 20, 1893. Clipping at NHS.

23. FHD to unidentified correspondent, November 21, 1893, NHS.

24. Ralph Adams Cram, *The Decadent, or, The Gospel of Inaction* (Boston, Copeland and Day, 1892), p. 10. There is much description here of the books which might well have been in Day's library, 'great folios and quartos in ancient bindings of vellum and ivory and old calf-skin . . .' etc.

25. *Ibid.,* p. 41.

5
PUBLISHERS
AND POETS

1. LIG to Bertram Grosvenor Goodhue, February 16, 1893, LC.

2. LIG to Richard Garnet, *Letters,* Grace Guiney, ed., (New York, Harper, 1926), (vol. 2), pp. 46–47.

3. From 'Vagabondia,' Bliss Carman and Richard Hovey, *Songs from Vagabondia* (Boston, Copeland & Day, 1895), p. 4.

4. Quoted in Kraus, 'A History of Copeland and Day,' p. 42.

5. From 'Speech and Silence,' Bliss Carman and Richard Hovey, *More Songs from Vagabondia* (Boston, Copeland and Day, 1896), p. 26.

6. From 'Three of a Kind,' *More Songs from Vagabondia,* p. 40.

7. Quoted in Kraus, *Messrs. Copeland and Day,* p. 24.

8. William Archer, *Poets of the Younger Generation,* with 33 full-page portraits from woodcuts by Robert Bryden (London, John Lane, 1902), p. 251.

9. *The Book Buyer,* December 1895 (vol. 12), p. 716.

10. See Victor Margolin, *The Golden Age of the American Poster* (New York, Ballantine, 1976), p. 17. Bradley was called the American Beardsley. See also the parody of Bradley's 'The Twins' by Will Denslow, in Margolin.

11. LIG to FHD, probably January 28, 1896, LC. Louise was never reticent. In writing to FHD about *Attila,* a book under consideration, she found it 'a *very* dull and foolish piece of verbiage, quite excuseless. While I do not think it *very nasty* – I think many people would – and we could not claim fine execution as an excuse for it, as we can for Beardsley and other *queer* things.' LIG to FHD, 1895, NHS.

12. LIG to Herbert Clarke, January 21, 1896. *Letters* (vol. 1), pp. 95–96.

> *Thank you for not liking the stories. I hate 'em. . . . You don't know how they [the stories] were dragged out of the obscurity I thought best for them. The publishers, Herbert Copeland . . . and Fred Day . . . are great old friends of mine, and simply badgered me into printing them.*

The question remains: why, if she hated them so much, did she show them to FHD and HC in the first place?

13. Jessie B. Rittenhouse, *The Younger American Poets* (Boston, Little, Brown, 1913), p. 259.

14. Quoted in John Berryman, *Stephen Crane* (New York, Sloane, 1950), p. 92.

15. Kraus, *Messrs. Copeland and Day,* p. 27.

16. *Ibid.*

17. William Butler Yeats, 'The Wanderings of Usheen,' quoted in Archer, *Poets,* p. 536.

18. Archer, *Poets,* p. 63.

19. Quoted in Archer, *Poets,* p. 63.

20. LIG to Charles Warren Stoddard, February 19, 1895, LC. Louise commented: 'I began my modern world with Stevenson, and I have ended it with him.'

21. Parrish, 'Currents of the Nineties,' p. 230.

22. Gertrude Smith to FHD, October 1, 1898, NHS. The letter is amusingly angry:

> *My dear Mr. Day —*
> *You said there would be royalty money due me in Sept. for*
> *Arabella and Araminta, when you last wrote to me. Will you*
> *please send it me, I need it, and please tell me when the*
> *next is due? I do not understand our contract! (I know I*
> *am stupid but I don't!)*

6

OSCAR AND AUBREY,
SUN GODS AND WRAITHS

1. LIG to FHD, March 21, 1892, LC. This was a direct response to Day's adulation of Moore in a book review for *The Mahogany Tree,* March 19, 1892, p. 188 ff. The difference in tastes between these two was strong: Guiney favored Robert Louis Stevenson, Edmund Spenser, Herrick, and Longfellow. Day was steadfast in his admiration for the French writers, especially Balzac, Hugo, Sainte-Beuve, Daudet, Maupassant, and George Sand.

2. Introduction by Floyd Dell to George Moore, *Confessions of a Young Man* (New York, reprinted by Scholarly Press from the Modern Library ed., 1970), p. xi. Moore, of course, may have circulated this rumor about himself to enhance his diabolist pose.

3. LIG to FHD, July 12, 1892, LC. In this letter Louise describes a meeting with a stranger who reminded her vividly of FHD: she had encountered a Chinese gentleman on Atlantic Avenue, 'dressed in your identical upper garment! freshest lavender, gilt buttons, and all, but accompanied by Philistine dark blue trousers. I was in a great rush, but I had to look twice and grin.'

But it was not Wilde's — or Day's — flamboyant æstheticism that bothered Louise. What made her choke over Wilde was his advocacy of inaction: 'Don't talk about action,' he had written. 'It is a blind thing dependent upon external influences, and moved by an impulse of whose nature it is unconscious. It is a thing incomplete in its essence, because limited by accident, and ignorant of its direction, because always at variance with its aim. Its basis is the lack of imagination. It is the last resource of those who do not know how to dream.' Quoted in Philippe Jullian, *Oscar Wilde* (New York, Viking, 1969), p. 176. Jullian's book on Wilde is by far the best in the field at present.

4. Refrain from W. S. Gilbert's lyrics for the operetta *Patience.*

5. Lloyd Lewis and Henry Justin Smith, *Oscar Wilde Discovers*

America 1882 (New York, Harcourt Brace, 1936), p. 122. Wilde further commented, 'As I look about me, I am impelled for the first time to breathe a fervent prayer, "Save me from my disciples."' See p. 125.

6. FHD, 'Books,' *The Mahogany Tree,* no. 10, March 5, 1892, p. 153. Wilde and Day met again in London in 1889. At a dinner party given by Lady Mary Seton to honor Louise Chandler Moulton, Day was among the guests who included 'Mr. and Mrs. Oscar Wilde and Lady Wilde.' From an unidentified Boston newspaper clipping, NHS. He then met Wilde at the Rhymers' Club and other gatherings of poets and writers. A letter dated March 25, 1895, indicates that Day dined at least once with both Wilde and Lord Alfred Douglas in 1894. The draft of the letter (at NHS) to Douglas reads, 'I have often thought of ~~that~~ [sic] the ~~pleasant~~ [sic] evening at Gobbet Park and the dinner which followed in Soho with much pleasure; I have not been in England since that time.' The dinner may have been on the occasion of the dedication of the Keats Memorial.

7. LIG, inscription on the inside front cover of her copy of Lionel Johnson, *Reviews and Critical Papers* (New York, Dutton, 1921), HCC.

8. Kraus and others remind us that Copeland and Day combined the printer's marks used by two sixteenth-century English printers, Richard Day and Robert Copeland. See Kraus, *Messrs. Copeland and Day,* pp. 63–68 for a survey of the variety of colophons they used.

9. The lily was an almost ubiquitous symbol in the 1890s. The Brussels symbolists employed it extensively, sometimes oppressively, in paintings of religious intent, and the following poem by Lionel Johnson sums up the duality of the symbol:

FLOS FLORUM

Lily, O Lily of the Vallies!
Lily, O Lily of Calvary Hill!
White with the glory of all graces,
Earth with the breath of thy pure soul fill:
Lily, O Lily of the Vallies!
Lily, O Lily of Calvary Hill!

Quoted from Guiney's copy of the *Religious Poems of Lionel Johnson,* p. 29, HCC.

When the firm of Copeland and Day closed, LIG wrote a bitter epitaph: 'Sicut lilium inter spinas: i.e., to be choked up, prickled, strangled, and overlaid by the world's unworthiness.' LIG to FHD, November 2, 1903, LC. But this fantasy about crass materialism putting their publishing career to an end was foolish, for she had already noted to FHD the year before, 'I don't think you love Partner as you once did, my fickle child.' LIG to FHD, October 3, 1898, LC.

10. Quoted in Richard Ellman, ed., *The Artist as Critic, Critical Writings of Oscar Wilde* (New York, Random House, 1968), p. 5. Wilde wrote an elegy to Keats which once again refers to him as 'Sebastian,' in a Keatsian vein of masochistic sensuality:

The youngest of the martyrs here is lain,
Fair as Sebastian and as foully slain.
  No cypress shades his grave, nor funeral yew,
  But red-lipped daisies, violets drenched with dew,
And sleepy poppies, catch the evening rain. . . .

11. Quoted in Fraser Harrison, ed., *The Yellow Book: An Anthology* (New York, St. Martin's Press, 1974), p. 7.

12. Quoted in Roy McMullen, *Victorian Outsider* (New York, Dutton, 1973), p. 146.

13. The story has it that Dent was searching for someone who could fake the William Morris–Kelmscott Press look by using the newly perfected photographic technology of the line engraving, a process not only much faster than Morris's and Burne-Jones's laborious woodcuts, but much cheaper. Dent needed someone who could use pen and ink to good effect. It was Frederick Evans who suggested Beardsley.

14. FHD to Dent, May 20, 1893, NHS.

15. FHD to Dent, June 21, 1893, NHS.

16. Quoted in FHD to HC, August 1893, NHS.

17. FHD to HC, August 1893, NHS. The book in question was Wilfred Scawen Blunt's *Esther,* which they published in 1895.

18. Quoted in Fraser Harrison, *The Yellow Book,* p. 5.

19. HC to FHD, May 11, 1894, NHS.

20. HC to FHD, June 25, 1894, NHS.

21. HC to FHD, June 3, 1894, NHS.

22. HC to FHD, June 25, 1894, NHS.

23. HC to FHD, June 1894, NHS.

24. HC to FHD, June 25, 1894, NHS.

25. John Milner, *Symbolists and Decadents* (London, Studio Vista, n.d.) p. 41.

26. Harrison, *The Yellow Book,* p. 42.

27. Quoted in Stanley Weintraub, ed., *The Yellow Book: Quintessence of the Nineties* (Garden City, N.Y., Anchor, 1964).

28. Philippe Jullian's *Oscar Wilde* contains an excellent account of both the genesis of the trial and its aftermath.

29. LIG to FHD, March 25, 1898, LC. On April 25, 1898 (LC), she wrote, 'Just too late, arrived my second asked-for English letter: from the priest who received A.B. into the Church, Fr. David Bearne. It is almost as beautiful as Lionel's. I will give it to you to read. The boy was a saint; that seems to be the long and the short of it.' See Brigid Brophy, *Beardsley and His World* (New York, Harmony Books, 1976), p. 88, for a picture of Marc-André Raffalovich, and p. 104 concerning Beardsley's duplicity: simultaneously, he wrote pious letters to his wooer and bawdy, profane, and totally irreverent letters to the publisher of his *Rape of the Lock.* In March 1897, Beardsley capitulated to Raffalovich.

30. Jullian, *Oscar Wilde,* p. 378.

31. *Ibid.,* p. 371.

32. See the *British Journal of Photography,* October 26, 1900,

p. 677, for its reminder of the æsthetic craze and George DuMaurier's scathing satires on Wilde. Wilde had by no means been forgotten.

7
MR. STIEGLITZ
TAKES NOTICE

1. Helmut Gernsheim, *Creative Photography: Æsthetic Trends, 1839–1960* (New York, Bonanza Books, 1962), p. 119.

2. FHD, 'Art and the Camera,' *Camera Notes*, July 1898 (vol. 2, no. 1), p. 5.

3. *Ibid.*

4. FHD to GS, August 1889, NHS.

5. FHD to LIG, Easter Sunday, 1890, NHS.

6. Herbert Whyte Taylor, 'F. Holland Day: An Estimate,' *Photo-Era*, March 1900 (vol. 4, no. 3), p. 78. On p. 77 of this article, Taylor describes the visit of Elbert Hubbard, an æsthetic publisher of the late nineties, to Day's Boston studio: 'Mr. Day wore a fez and turned-up Turkish slippers, worshipped a squat number ten joss, and wrote only by the light of thirteen candles.' Taylor then modifies this caricature with his own observations (p. 78):

> *Although Mr. Day has gained such recognition, both in America and abroad, as places him on the highest plane among amateurs, we found him personally a modest man. It seemed as though, while he was pleased to give pleasure to his friends by throwing open his doors, no one could accuse him of exulting over his less brilliant fellow-photographers. Mr. Day was perhaps the first amateur photographer to come prominently before the public with just this style of work; but now we find hosts of imitators, men and women who are filling the magazines and exhibitions with more or less successful Dayisms. . . . Our artist is the leader of a new cult, admittance to which demands long, hard, and intelligent study.*

7. *Ibid.*, p. 78.

8. Marmaduke Humphrey (Rupert Hughes), 'Triumphs in Amateur Photography, II – F. H. Day,' *Godey's Magazine*, January 1898 (vol. 12, no. 21), p. 16.

9. *Ibid.*, p. 13.

10. *Ibid.*, p. 16. 'His studio is a simple square room. It has not the usual top-light, but has instead both a northern and a southern exposure. This permits him strong values that can be modified at will.' Day's studio was also mocked as being 'Beardsley-esque' by Elbert Hubbard. His collection of Orientalia was apparently considered unconventional, even bizarre.

11. LIG to FHD, January 1895, LC.

12. *Boston Journal*, May 4, 1906, clipping at NHS.

13. Sadakichi Hartmann, 'Portrait Painting and Portrait Photography,' *Camera Notes*, July 1899 (vol. 3, no. 1), p. 15.

14. *Boston Journal*, May 4, 1906, clipping at NHS.

15. Platinum paper was almost a prerequisite for this group of photographers. It was the basic guarantee of a superior graphic-arts quality.

16. Quoted in Helmut and Alison Gernsheim, *The History of Photography* (New York, McGraw Hill, 1969), p. 464.

17. George Davison to AS, June 12, 1895, YUSA.

18. Rudolph Eickemeyer to AS, June 28, 1895, YUSA.

8

A PURELY GREEK
POINT OF VIEW

1. *The Record*, Philadelphia, October 22, 1899. Clipping in the Second Philadelphia Salon album, 1899, IMP-GEH.

2. 'W. M. M.', 'F. H. Day's Exhibition of Prints,' *Camera Notes*, July 1898 (vol. 2, no. 1), p. 22.

3. *Camera Notes* used photogravure for several reasons: it was the most beautiful of all the reproduction processes, used by Emerson and others for conceptualizing original work, and it was the only medium that could transmit the subtleties of lighting epitomized by Day's photographs.

4. FHD to AS, letter #42, 1898, YUSA.

5. Joseph T. Keiley, 'The Philadelphia Salons,' *Camera Notes*, January 1899 (vol. 2, no. 3), p. 125.

6. 'W. M. M.,' 'F. H. Day's Exhibition of Prints,' p. 22.

7. *Ibid.*

8. *Ibid.*, p. 21.

9. *The Photo Beacon*, November 1901 (vol. 13, no. 11), p. 330.

10. Joseph T. Keiley, 'The Salons,' *Camera Notes*, January 1900 (vol. 3, no. 3), p. 163.

11. *Ibid.*

12. *Ibid.*

13. Peter Henry Emerson's *Naturalistic Photography for Students of the Art* (London, 1889) was probably the most important single influence on Stieglitz's school of straight photography, in the sense that Emerson urged going back to nature and avoiding artifice. See Nancy Newhall's superb biography of Emerson for details of the Stieglitz–Emerson interaction, as well as the fascinating story of Emerson's recantations of his own theories.

14. A. Horsley Hinton, 'Both Sides,' *Camera Notes*, January 1899 (vol. 2, no. 3), p. 78. Hinton's mention of the relationship between music and 'feeling' should be noted: it was a prime tenet of Æstheticism, as articulated by Walter Pater, that all the arts aspired to the condition of music. Hinton is therefore praising Day more than is evident on the surface.

15. LIG to FHD, n.d., 1897, LC.

16. LIG to FHD, May 13, 1898, LC.

17. Copy of letter to FHD from Miss Beale, November 25, 1896, NHS. The original is missing.

18. LIG to FHD, January 10, 1919, LC. Gibran's *The Prophet* continues to sell millions of copies. It is firmly based on Mæterlinck's philosophies.

19. LIG to FHD, January 10, 1919, LC.

20. LIG to LCM, n.d., LC. Rollins and Parrish, in *Keats and the Bostonians,* p. 11, comment: 'Miss Guiney called him "The best mortal extant." ' Day was extremely generous to her, but the fact is that Guiney used similar terms to describe Lionel Johnson and Robert Louis Stevenson. She was obviously a victim of her own penchant for hyperbole.

21. Marmaduke Humphrey, 'Triumphs in Amateur Photography,' *Godey's Magazine,* January 1898, p. 20.

22. George Davison, 'The London Exhibition,' *American Amateur Photographer,* November 1895, p. 489.

9
CROWN OF THORNS

1. According to Helmut Gernsheim's *Creative Photography: Æsthetic Trends 1839–1960* (New York, Bonanza Books, 1962), pp. 133–34, the American Lejaren à Hiller and L. Bovier in Belgium had both staged crucifixions—'extraordinary aberrations of taste when arranged for exhibition purposes.' See p. 134 for Hiller's *Deposition from the Cross* of about 1910, staged totally indoors and with none of the æsthetic transformation Day achieved in *The Seven Last Words,* if nowhere else.

2. Clattenburg, *Photographic Work of Day* (exhibition catalogue), p. 31. Clattenburg quotes much of an interview Day granted *The Boston Herald* on 'Sacred Art Modernized,' Tuesday, January 17, 1899, p. 1.

3. FHD to 'Jack' (John Bemis of Worcester), June 3, 1886, NHS.

4. Clattenburg, *Photographic Work of Day,* p. 31. From the same interview.

5. FHD to AS, summer 1898, YUSA.

6. FHD to LIG, November 29, 1890, NHS.

7. FHD to 'Folsom,' May 1891, NHS.

8. LIG to FHD, May 9, 1892, LC.

9. See advertising, for example, in *Harper's New Monthly Magazine,* April 1893, p. 29 of ad inserts.

10. 'Carbons' were carbon-process prints, a guarantee of permanence; the impermanence of silver-chloride prints was still within the memory of the 1890s generation.

11. HCC owns a fine transparency, framed, of Guiney in the 'look-up' pose for St. Barbara. It is a far better image in this form than in the enlarged prints.

12. LIG to FHD, March 1893, LC.

13. *Ibid.*

14. *Ibid.*

15. LIG to FHD, March 31, 1893, LC.

16. The clipping, undated, is from a London newspaper; it describes a lecture by Sir Wyke Bayliss at the Society of British Artists,

'The Likeness of Christ from the First to the Nineteenth Century.'

17. LIG to FHD, September 22, 1898, from Five Islands, Maine, LC. In this letter, encouraging Day to continue his misguided sacred subjects, she remarks that he would do well because he had so many fine models among his friends: 'Lee [Francis Lee] would be an admirable figure for the Christ; he has the true enthusiast look, but you must be careful not to let him be fierce, and William-Morris-socialistic, instead of divinely democratic.'

18. LIG to FHD, n.d., September 1898, from Five Islands, Maine, LC.

19. *Ibid.*

20. *Ibid.*

21. *Ibid.*

22. Printed invitation, NHS. Also in LIG correspondence, LC.

23. *Ibid.*

24. Typewritten explanation by Frederick Evans, in a box of prints which he produced in 1912, IMP-GEH.

25. 'Sacred Art and the Camera,' *The Photogram*, April 1899, p. 98.

26. Keiley, 'The Philadelphia Salons,' *Camera Notes*, p. 118. Keiley is quoting from the catalogue of the exhibition, which continued: 'For the first time in this country is presented a photographic exhibition confined exclusively to such pictures rigidly selected by a jury, whose certificate of acceptance is the only award.'

27. *Ibid.*

28. *Ibid.*, p. 120.

29. *Ibid.*

30. *Ibid.*, p. 126.

31. *Ibid.*, p. 128.

32. Charles H. Caffin, 'Philadelphia Photographic Salon,' *Harper's Weekly*, November 5, 1898, p. 1087.

33. *Ibid.*

34. Charles H. Caffin, 'Philadelphia Photographic Salon,' *Harper's Weekly*, November 4, 1899, p. 1118.

35. [Charles H. Caffin], 'The Philadelphia Photographic Salon,' *Harper's Weekly*, December 7, 1901, p. 1119.

36. Sadakichi Hartmann, 'A Decorative Photographer, F. H. Day,' *The Photographic Times*, March 1900 (vol. 32, no. 3), p. 102.

37. *Ibid.*

38. *Ibid.*, p. 105.

39. *British Journal of Photography*, October 26, 1900, p. 678.

40. Frederick Evans, letter to the editors, *BJOP*, November 2, 1900, pp. 702–3.

41. *Ibid.*

42. *BJOP*, November 2, 1900, p. 702.

43. 'Tacoma,' letter to editors, *BJOP*, November 9, 1900, p. 718.

44. 'Tuck,' letter to editors, *BJOP*, November 9, 1900, p. 718.

45. J. J. Vezey, letter to editors, *BJOP*, November 9, 1900, p. 719.

10
THE NEW SCHOOL
OF AMERICAN
PHOTOGRAPHY

1. AS to FHD, March 31, 1899, YUSA.

2. GK to FHD, April 29, 1899, NHS.

3. Sadakichi Hartmann, 'Clarence F. White,' *The Photographic Times,* January 1900 (vol. 32, no. 1), p. 22.

4. GK to AS, August 21, 1901, YUSA.

5. Hartmann, 'A Decorative Photographer,' *The Photographic Times,* p. 106.

6. Quoted in Sadakichi Hartmann, 'Gertrude Käsebier,' *The Photographic Times,* May 1900 (vol. 32, no. 5), p. 195.

7. *Ibid.*

8. *Ibid.*

9. GK to FHD, April 29, 1899, NHS.

10. GK to FHD, April 12, 1899, NHS.

11. GK to FHD, n.d. (July?), 1899, NHS.

12. GK to FHD, July 3, 1899, NHS.

13. *Ibid.*

14. This two-page opus is so uncharacteristic of the image GK presented to the world that it is pleasantly surprising to learn she could unbend. The poem begins, 'Dear family Lee, dear Mr. Day / What can we do, what can we say, / Your spiritual message to repay?' One of their favors to her was helping her find a misplaced trunk at the railroad station.

15. GK to FHD, September 23, 1899, NHS.

16. FHD to AS, letter #12, 1898, YUSA.

17. FHD to AS, letter #56, YUSA.

18. Quoted in White catalogue, YUSA.

19. GK to FHD, December 14, 1899, NHS.

20. FHD to AS, n.d. (1899?), YUSA.

21. *Ibid.*

22. *Ibid.*

23. Edward Steichen, *A Life in Photography* (Garden City, Doubleday, 1963), p. 3.

24. Alvin Langdon Coburn, 'American Photographs in London,' *Photo-Era,* January 1901 (vol. 6, no. 1), p. 209.

25. 'The English Exhibitions and the "American Invasion",' *Camera Notes,* January 1901 (vol. 4, no. 3), p. 163. This is a quote from 'Thos. Bedding, Editor of the BJOP.' Bedding held nothing back. In his view, the New American School was a series of 'deplorable travesties of photographic work which a handful of American photographers, encouraged by the adulatory writings of neurotic "appreciators," were deceived into believing were "artistic" or "pictorial." ' The 'appreciator' was the critic Sadakichi Hartmann.

26. *Ibid.*

27. *Ibid.,* p. 165. Quoting E. J. Wall, editor of the *Photographic News,* London.

28. *Ibid.*

29. *Ibid.*

30. *Ibid.,* p. 166.

31. *Ibid.,* p. 169.

32. Originally in Hartmann, 'A Decorative Photographer,' quoted in *BJOP*, October 26, 1900, p. 677. The writer who quoted this gossip took it as an invitation to explode:

> *So now we have the essential part of the formula for the very newest kind of American photograph. You must believe yourself something out of the ordinary; sit under a shelf near the ceiling; smoke a water pipe; and make a 'clucking' noise – which is what a brooding hen does.*

A simple typographic error (or error of copying) had given rise to a permanent calumny. Day often behaved outlandishly, like an adolescent seeking attention by whatever means, but this kind of 'clucking' was not his style.

33. Hartmann, 'A Decorative Photographer,' p. 103. Quoted again by Thomas Bedding and used in the *Camera Notes* summary, January 1901, p. 163.

34. 'The English Exhibitions and the "American Invasion",' p. 163.

35. Edward Steichen to FHD, n.d., 1900, NHS.

36. FHD, 'The New School of American Photography,' (an address delivered before the Royal Photographic Society on October 10, 1900), *BJOP,* November 20, 1900, p. 760. In the address, Day notes that the aged Whistler had attended the exhibition and had cordially praised Clarence White's *Girl with the Pitcher.*

37. 'Argus,' 'Mr. H. Day's Cryptograms,' *BJOP*, December 7, 1900, p. 772. Argus warns: '. . . let Mr. Day learn at once that the educated British public will not stand for a moment his unblushing effrontery, egotism, and braggadocio, though it will welcome some of his best photographs.'

38. 'Granpa's Little Talk on Fuzzography,' *Photo-Era,* June 1902 (vol. 8, no. 6), p. 473.

39. Edward Steichen to FHD, n.d., 1901, NHS. Written from 83 Boulevard Montparnasse.

40. Robert Demachy, 'The American New School of Photography in Paris,' *Camera Notes,* July 1901, p. 41.

41. *Ibid.*

42. *Ibid.,* p. 33, from the introductory paragraphs signed 'The Editor' – i.e., Stieglitz. To preface an article by a recognized leader of the Pictorialist movement was unconscionable interference with Demachy's opinions.

43. Steichen, *A Life in Photography,* n.p. Steichen notes, 'F. Holland Day was the first man to assemble a collection consisting exclusively of the work of men and women later recognized as leaders in the most important American movement in pictorial photography. Among the pioneers he was in a class with Alfred Stieglitz.'

44. Among the works repeated by Stieglitz were Käsebier's *The Manger, Blessed Art Thou Among Women,* and *Red Indian.* True; the reproductions (or replications, if you prefer) were photogravures of the highest order, and much improved over the *Camera Notes* repro-

ductions. But they were still the same pictures. *Camera Work* was not so much a revolution in image making or in organization as in technologies of photographic reproduction.

I I

A PHOENIX FROM
THE ASHES

1. FHD to unidentified correspondent, July 8, 1921, NHS.

2. *Ibid.*

3. *Ibid.*

4. *Ibid.*

5. *Ibid.*

6. Alvin Langdon Coburn, *An Autobiography,* Helmut and Alison Gernsheim, eds. (New York, Praeger, 1966), p. 18.

7. *Ibid.*

8. LIG to FHD, April 30, 1901, LC. This letter includes several revealing comments on her attitudes toward religion. 'I dread a peace founded on fatalism. A muddy Teuton cheer, a Latin frivolity, are preferable to me. It is really because I am entirely susceptible to that sort of fascination which the East can exercise that I wish never to see, hear nor think of it. But you who are the Great Immune, will notice only the charm there, and get only the profit.' There was a strong streak of fatalism in Day.

9. FHD to 'Mar—,' June 1901, NHS.

10. *Ibid.*

11. *Ibid.* Mary Devens was a protégée of Day's, a young and very talented photographer from Cambridge, Mass. She worked in the closest of tonalities with textures resembling charcoal drawings. Day raved about her work to everyone from Stieglitz to Demachy. She accompanied Day and Steichen to a dinner at Demachy's house in Paris, and they were all good friends.

12. LIG to FHD, n.d., 1900, NHS. It was typical of Day to send her Mæterlinck; he was very proud that the famous playwright and theosophist had been pleased with Day's portrait of him, taken on a visit with Steichen.

13. Quoted in the preface to LIG, *Letters.*

14. Papers of FHD, NHS.

15. Printed invitation, NHS.

16. Steichen, *A Life in Photography,* p. 3.

17. *Ibid.*

18. J. Newton Gunn to FHD, July 27, 1904, NHS. Curtis Bell was essentially a landscape photographer, but also produced sentimental genre scenes. He had helped to organize the Salon Club of America in 1903. Sadakichi Hartmann remarked, in 'The Salon Club and the First American Photographic Salon at New York,' reprinted in his *Valiant Knights of Daguerre* (Berkeley, University of California Press, 1978), p. 118 ff: 'A duel between Messrs Alfred Stieglitz and Curtis Bell would prove indeed a great attraction. . . . It will stir up the stagnant waters of pictorial photography – they surely need it . . .' (p. 126). Having cut himself off from the Stieglitz circle, Day may have felt he

had no alternative to joining what quickly proved to be a mediocre organization, far beneath his standards.

19. Curtis Bell to FHD, July 19, 1904, NHS.

20. *Ibid.*

21. GK and ALC to FHD, telegram, November 14, 1940, 'Fire folder,' NHS.

22. GK to FHD, November 14, 1904, NHS.

23. CW to FHD, November 1904, NHS.

24. Curtis Bell to FHD, November 16, 1904, NHS.

25. Curtis Bell to FHD, May 25, 1905, NHS.

26. GK to FHD, May 11, 1905, NHS.

27. GK to FHD, July 6, 1905, NHS.

28. CW to FHD, January 8, 1905, NHS.

12

THE HERM OF PAN

1. Quoted in Ian Jack, *Keats and the Mirror of Art* (Oxford, Clarendon Press, 1967), p. 105. From a letter addressed to the painter Haydon by Keats in March 1818.

2. Day had been praised for his poetic themes before the pagan series, yet the Maine symbolism was much more lyrical than his previous work. The idea that photography can be like a poem — a compressed formal statement conceptual in nature — and that it shares this characteristic with painting in the famous phrase *ut pictura poesis* was beginning to be accepted in the critical vocabulary of photography.

3. James Hall, *Dictionary of Subjects and Symbols in Art* (New York, Harper and Row, 1974), p. 153.

4. CW to FHD, September 9, 1905, NHS.

5. FHD to AS, draft of letter dated November 30, 1906, NHS.

6. CW to FHD, June 17, 1906, NHS.

7. GK to FHD, December 7, 1907, NHS.

8. GK to FHD, December 28, 1907, NHS.

9. GK to FHD, January 26, 1907, NHS.

10. *Ibid.*

11. GK to FHD, May 9, 1907, NHS.

12. *Ibid.*

13. CW to FHD, January 5, 1907, NHS.

14. CW to FHD, May 7, 1907, NHS.

15. CW to FHD, February 11, 1908, NHS.

16. CW to FHD, March 17, 1908, NHS.

17. Quoted in Ian Jack, *Mirror of Art*, p. 180.

18. *Ibid.*, as caption to plate XXIV, a reproduction of the Poussin.

19. *Ibid.*, p. 101.

20. The poet's friend Severn had sketched out the design for the grave sometime before 1820.

21. 'N' to FHD, January 7, 1907, NHS.

22. 'N' to FHD, October 5, 1907, NHS.

23. FHD to 'N,' February 17, 1909, NHS.

24. 'N' to FHD, August 8, 1909, NHS.

25. *Ibid.*

26. 'N' to FHD, June 16, 1912, NHS.

27. HC to FHD, January 24, 1910, NHS.

28. *Ibid.*

29. HC to FHD, February 4, 1909, NHS.

30. HC to FHD, February 24, 1909, NHS.

31. Wilde's and Beardsley's letters were sold as part of Day's estate, through Goodspeed's of Boston. It would be a boon to biographers if the owner of these letters would make them available for publication.

13

LITTLE GOOD HARBOR

1. George Davison to AS, January 31, 1908, YUSA.

2. Edward Steichen to AS, letter #239, leaf 2 (1908?), YUSA.

3. Frederick Evans to AS, December 31, 1908, YUSA.

4. Frederick Evans to AS, February 2, 1909, YUSA.

5. AS to Heinrich Kühn, March 1, 1909, unpublished letter, collection of Dorothy Norman. Brought to my attention by Robert Doty.

6. Frederick Evans to AS, letter #88, 1910, YUSA.

7. CW to FHD, November 13, 1911, NHS.

8. Nathaniel J. Hasenfus, *We Summer in Maine,* 2nd ed., photographs by Clarence H. White, Jr. (West Roxbury, Mass., Sagadahoc Publishing, 1947), p. 19. Although this is not generally a reliable source for information concerning Day, since many years had elapsed and Hasenfus did not investigate beyond hearsay from his parents and his own boyhood memories, occasional descriptions of activities at the chalet ring true. Waldo Hasenfus, ordained a priest in 1912, built a charming summer home called Marycliff a stone's throw from Day's harbor, in the style of a small Greek temple. It is now used by a religious order.

9. *Ibid.,* p. 20.

10. *Photograms of the Year 1910,* p. 46. The editors commented: 'We congratulate the London Salon, the photographic world, and ourselves upon the re-emergence of Holland Day after ten years of total abstinence from exhibiting.' It was probably his father's death and his own illnesses of that period which prevented the London visit and the establishment of a new studio there.

11. *Photo-Era,* February 1910 (vol. 24, no. 2), p. 79.

12. Herbert A. Hess to FHD, April 25, 1909, NHS. Hess was a photographer in the Royal Photographic Society exhibit of 1900.

13. Charles E. Banks to FHD, April 24, 1912, NHS. Dr. Banks notes in his letter that Day continued to be ill.

14. *Ibid.*

15. ALC to FHD, July 2, 1908, NHS.

16. ALC to FHD, March 18, 1914, NHS.

17. ALC to Max Weber, August 19, 1914, American Archives of Art.

18. FHD to unidentified correspondent, February 10, 1915, NHS.

19. Jane White to FHD, March 18, 1918, NHS.

20. Jane White to FHD, n.d., 1918, NHS.

21. Willis & Clements, Philadelphia, to FHD, October 26, 1914, NHS. Gernsheim, in *The History of Photography*, p. 461, comments that 'Evans was a firm believer in pure technique, and gave up photography when his favorite platinum paper became unobtainable during the First World War.' Day's local supplier of platinum paper in Boston was Benjamin French & Co., but they purchased their materials from Willis & Clements. Willis of Willis & Clements was related to the William Willis of London who had invented the platinotype paper in 1873 and established the first company in 1879. For a time during the war, Satista Paper was substituted; it was a combination of platinum and silver, and was a soft brown paper.

14
FROM THE UPSTAIRS
BEDROOM

1. LIG to FHD, April 6, 1920, LC.

2. *Ibid.*

3. *Ibid.*

4. *Ibid.*

5. *Ibid.*

6. GS to FHD, November 17, 1920, NHS.

7. Rollins and Parrish, *Keats and the Bostonians*, p. 19.

8. Francis Watts Lee to FHD, March 10, 1921, NHS.

9. H. L. Seaver to FHD, April 25, 1922, NHS.

10. CW to FHD, December 18, 1922, NHS.

11. *Ibid.*

12. Undated clipping from Boston paper, enclosed in 1894 letter from Anna Day to FHD, NHS.

13. Anna Day to FHD, February 8, 1922. The company which manufactured Mrs. Day's diaries must have stayed in business for a very long time; either that, or she had purchased a large number of the tiny separable 'day-sheets.' The paper seems identical to that used by her to record FHD's birth. Day then started to use the same kind of paper for his diary.

14. GK to FHD, August 31, 1922, NHS.

15. 'S.A.L.' to FHD, n.d., 1922, NHS. This woman friend, as yet unidentified, wrote Day about a hundred letters; during the early 1920s, one letter reveals that Day had been gravely ill during the influenza epidemic and that he had nursed his mother through an attack of that dread disease.

16. George Pickering, *Creative Malady: Illness in the Lives and Minds of Charles Darwin, Florence Nightingale, Mary Baker Eddy, Sigmund Freud, Marcel Proust, Elizabeth Barrett Browning* (New York, Oxford University Press, 1974).

17. Telegram from Reverend Minot Simons, New York, November 23, 1923. HC file, NHS.

18. HC to FHD, July 4, 1922, NHS.

19. Unidentified correspondent to FHD, December 3, 1923, NHS.

20. See Pickering, *Creative Malady*. By an odd coincidence, one of Day's many literary idols, Maurice Mæterlinck, also went through a prolonged period of neuresthenia, from about 1906 to 1910. The diagnosis was exhaustion. See also R. M. Goldenson, *Encyclopedia of Human Behavior: Psychology, Psychiatry, and Mental Health* (1970), p. 584.

21. Parrish, 'Currents of the Nineties,' p. 324, quoted in Kraus, *Messrs. Copeland & Day*.

22. CW to FHD, June 5, 1925, NHS.

23. Maynard Presley White, Jr., 'Clarence H. White: A Personal Portrait,' doctoral dissertation (University of Delaware, 1975), p. 241. Clarence White was only 54 when he died.

24. FHD to Bruce Rogers, draft of letter dated August 17, 1925, NHS.

25. *Ibid.*

26. FHD to Charles Knowles Bolton, September 6, 1926, NHS.

27. Jane White to FHD, January 4, 1928, NHS.

28. Jane White to FHD, n.d. 1928, NHS.

29. Dorothy F. Hyde to FHD, November 31, 1931, NHS.

30. *Ibid.*

31. *Ibid.*

32. FHD to 'Bustin,' October 14, 1932, NHS.

33. FHD to 'Arthur,' July 15, 1933, NHS.

34. FHD to 'Arthur,' October 10, 1933, NHS.

35. *Ibid.*

36. Although the gift was made anonymously, the curators of the Hampstead Memorial immediately realized that there could be only one individual who had made such a collection of Keats editions and memorabilia, as well as numerous glass-plate negatives and prints: Day. Thereupon the executors of the will allowed that it had been Day, and the gift was accepted in his name. Recent correspondence with the curators of the memorial reveal that bombings during the Second World War destroyed so much documentation that it is probably impossible to reconstruct the Day gift. The closest we can come is to use the 1921 catalogue of the Keats collection which Day exhibited at the Boston Public Library.

37. Some of Day's cousins are still alive, among them the Winslows.

38. 'Japanese Merchant Writes of Fred Day,' *The Norwood Messenger*, Friday, February 9, 1934, p. 1. Matsuki owned the Shobisha Print Shop, Tokyo.

Bibliography

MONOGRAPHS

Adami, Marie. *Fanny Keats*. London: Murray, 1937.

Amaya, Mario. *Art Nouveau*. London: Studio Vista, 1966.

Archer, William. *Poets of the Younger Generation*. London: John Lane, 1902.

Beardsley, Aubrey. *Illustrations for Le Morte D'Arthur*. Reproduced in facsimile from the Dent edition of 1893–94, arranged by Edmund V. Gillon, Jr. New York: Dover, 1972.

Berryman, John. *Stephen Crane*. New York: Sloane, 1950.

Boardman, John. *Greek Art*. New York: Praeger, 1964.

Brawne, Fanny. *Letters of Fanny Brawne to Fanny Keats, 1820–1824*. Edited with a biographical introduction by Fred Edgcumbe. New York: Oxford University Press, 1937.

Brophy, Brigid. *Beardsley and His World*. New York: Harmony Books, 1976.

Brown, Alice. *Louise Imogen Guiney*. New York: Macmillan, 1921.

Bry, Doris. *Alfred Stieglitz: Photographer*. Boston: Museum of Fine Arts, 1965.

Bush, Douglas. *John Keats, His Life and Writings*. New York: Collier, 1966.

Clattenburg, Ellen Fritz. *The Photographic Work of F. Holland Day*. Wellesley, Mass.: Wellesley College Museum, 1975.

Coburn, Alvin Langdon. *An Autobiography*. Edited by Helmut and Alison Gernsheim. New York: Praeger, 1966.

Cram, Ralph Adams. *My Life in Architecture*. Boston: Little, Brown, 1936.

Davidson, Donald, ed. *British Poetry of the Eighteen-Nineties*. Garden City, N.Y.: Doubleday Doran, 1937.

Doty, Robert. *Photo-Secession: Stieglitz and the Fine-Art Movement in Photography*. New York: Dover, 1960.

Ellman, Richard, ed. *The Artist as Critic: Critical Writings of Oscar Wilde*. New York: Random House, 1968.

Fairbanks, Henry G. *Louise Imogen Guiney*. New York: Twayne, 1973.

Frank, Waldo, et al., eds. *America & Alfred Stieglitz: A Collective Portrait*. New York: The Literary Guild, 1934.

Gaunt, William. *The Æsthetic Adventure*. New York: Schocken, 1967.

————. *The Pre-Raphælite Dream*. New York: Schocken, 1966.

Gernsheim, Helmut. *Creative Photography: Æsthetic Trends, 1839–1960*. New York: Bonanza Books, 1962.

————, in collaboration with Gernsheim, Alison. *The History of Photography*. New York: McGraw-Hill, 1969.

Gibran, Jean, and Gibran, Kahlil. *Kahlil Gibran, His Life and World*. Boston: New York Graphic Society, 1974.

Green, Jonathan, ed. *Camera Work: A Critical Anthology*. Millerton, N.Y.: Aperture, 1973.

Hall, Hames. *Dictionary of Subjects and Symbols in Art*. New York: Harper & Row, 1974.

Harker, Margaret. *The Linked Ring: The Secession in Photography, 1892–1910*. London: Heinemann, 1979.

Harper, George Mills, ed. *Yeats and the Occult*. Macmillan, 1975 (Yeats Studies Series).

Harrison, Fraser, ed. *The Yellow Book: An Illustrated Anthology*. New York: St. Martin's Press, 1974.

Hartmann, Sadakichi. *The Valiant Knights of Daguerre*. Edited by Harry W. Lawton and George Knox. Berkeley, Cal.: University of California Press, 1978.

Hasenfus, Nathaniel J. *We Summer in Maine*, 2nd ed. West Roxbury, Mass.: Sagadahoc Publishing, 1947.

Hilton, Timothy. *The Pre-Raphælites*. New York: Abrams, 1970.

Homer, William Innes. *Alfred Stieglitz and the American Avant-Garde*. Boston: New York Graphic Society, 1978.

Homer, William Innes et al. *A Pictorial Heritage: The Photographs of Gertrude Käsebier*. Catalogue of the exhibition cosponsored by the University of Delaware and the Delaware Art Museum, 1979.

————, ed. *Symbolism of Light: The Photographs of Clarence H. White*. Catalogue of the exhibition cosponsored by the University of Delaware and the Delaware Art Museum, 1977.

Howe, Ellic. *The Magicians of the Golden Dawn: A Documentary History of a Magical Order, 1887–1923*. London: Routledge and Kegan Paul, 1972.

Jack, Ian. *Keats and the Mirror of Art*. Oxford: Clarendon Press, 1967.

Jay, Bill. *Robert Demachy, 1859–1936; Photographs and Essays*. New York: St. Martin's Press, 1974.

Jullian, Philippe. *Dreamers of Decadence: Symbolist Painters of the 1890s*. New York: Praeger, 1971.

————. *Oscar Wilde*. New York: Viking Press, 1969.

————. *The Symbolists*. New York: Dutton, 1977.

Kraus, Joe Walker. 'A History of Copeland & Day (1893–1899) with a Bibliographical Checklist of Their Publications.' master's thesis, University of Illinois, Urbana, 1941.

————. *Messrs. Copeland and Day*. Philadelphia: George S. Mc-
      Manus, 1979.

LeGallienne, Richard. *The Romantic '90s*. Garden City, N.Y.: Double-
      day Page, 1925.

Lewis, Lloyd and Smith, Henry Justin. *Oscar Wilde Discovers America
      (1882)*. New York: Harcourt Brace, 1936.

Lövgren, Sven. *The Genesis of Modernism*. Uppsala: Almqvuist and
      Wiksells, 1959.

Lowell, Amy. *John Keats*. Boston: Houghton Mifflin, 1925 (2 vols.).

Lucie-Smith, Edward. *Eroticism in Western Art*. New York: Praeger,
      1972.

————. *Symbolist Art*. New York: Praeger, 1972.

McMullen, Roy. *Victorian Outsider: A Biography of J. A. M. Whistler*.
      New York: Dutton, 1973.

Madsen, S. Tschudi. *Art Nouveau*. New York: McGraw-Hill, 1967.

Margolin, Victor. *The Golden Age of the American Poster*. New York:
      Ballantine, 1975.

Margolis, Marianne Fulton. *Camera Work: A Pictorial Guide*. New
      York: Dover, 1978.

Maurois, André. *Prometheus: The Life of Balzac*. New York: Harper
      & Row, 1965.

Milner, John. *Symbolists and Decadents*. London: Studio Vista, 1971.

Moore, George. *Confessions of a Young Man*. New York: Scholarly
      Press, 1971.

Moore, Virginia. *The Unicorn*. New York: Macmillan, 1954.

Morris, William. *Ornamentation and Illustrations from the Kelmscott
      Chaucer*. New York: Dover, 1973.

Naef, Weston J. *The Collection of Alfred Stieglitz: Fifty Pioneers of
      Modern Photography*. New York: Viking, with the Metropolitan
      Museum of Art, 1978.

Newhall, Nancy. *P. H. Emerson, The Fight for Photography as a Fine
      Art*. Millerton, N.Y.: Aperture, 1975.

O'Driscoll, Robert and Reynolds, Loring, eds. *Yeats and the 1890s*.
      Yeats Studies, no. 1, Irish University Press, 1976.

Parrish, Stephen Maxfield. 'Currents of the Nineties in Boston: Fred
      Holland Day, Louise Imogen Guiney and Their Circle.' doctoral
      thesis, Harvard University, 1954.

Pelles, Geraldine. *Art, Artists and Society: Origins of a Modern Di-
      lemma*. Englewood Cliffs, N.J.: Prentice Hall, 1963.

Pickering, George White. *Creative Malady: Illness in the Lives and
      Minds of Charles Darwin, Florence Nightingale, Mary Baker
      Eddy, Sigmund Freud, Marcel Proust, Elizabeth Barrett Browning*.
      New York: Oxford University Press, 1974.

Reade, Brian. *Aubrey Beardsley*. New York: Bonanza, 1967.

Rittenhouse, Jessie B. *The Younger American Poets*. Boston: Little,
      Brown, 1913.

Rollins, Hyder Edward and Parrish, Stephen Maxfield. *Keats and the
      Bostonians: Amy Lowell, Louise Imogen Guiney, Louis Arthur*

Holman, Fred Holland Day. Cambridge, Mass.: Harvard University Press, 1951.

Ross, Marjorie Drake. *The Book of Boston: The Victorian Period, 1837–1901.* New York: Hastings House, 1964.

Sandars, Mary F. *Honoré de Balzac: His Life and Writings.* New York: Dodd, Mead, 1905.

Santayana, George. *The Last Puritan: A Memoir in the Form of a Novel.* New York: Scribner's, 1936.

———. *The Sense of Beauty: Being the Outline of Æsthetic Theory.* New York: Scribner's, 1896.

Steichen, Edward. *A Life in Photography.* Garden City, N.Y.: Doubleday, 1963.

Thompson, Susan Otis. *American Book Design and William Morris.* New York: Bowker, 1977.

Watkinson, Ray. *William Morris as Designer.* New York: Reinhold, 1967.

Weintraub, Stanley, ed. *The Yellow Book: Quintessence of the Nineties.* Garden City, N.Y.: Anthology Books, 1964.

White, Maynard Presley, Jr. 'Clarence H. White: A Personal Portrait.' doctoral thesis, University of Delaware, 1975.

Wormseley, Katherine Prescott. *A Memoir of Honoré de Balzac.* Boston: Roberts Bros., 1894.

Yeats, William Butler. *Essays and Introductions.* New York: Macmillan, 1961.

PUBLISHED ADDRESSES
AND ARTICLES BY
F. HOLLAND DAY

'Art and the Camera,' *Camera Notes,* October 1897.

'Art and the Camera,' *Camera Notes,* July 1898.

'Art and the Camera,' *Lippincott's Monthly Magazine,* January 1900.

'The New School of American Photography,' *British Journal of Photography,* November 20, 1900.

'Opening Address' (to the Royal Photographic Society), *Photographic Journal,* October 21, 1900.

'Photography Applied to the Undraped Figure,' *American Annual of Photography,* vol. 12, 1898.

'Photography as a Fine Art,' *Photo-Era,* March 1900.

'Portraiture and the Camera,' *American Annual of Photography,* vol. 13, 1899.

'Sacred Art and the Camera,' *The Photogram,* vol. 6, February 1899.

'William Morris,' *The Book Buyer,* vol. 12, November 1895.

ARTICLES ABOUT
F. HOLLAND DAY

Caffin, Charles H. 'Philadelphia Photographic Salon.' *Harper's Weekly,* November 5, 1898.

———. 'Philadelphia Photographic Salon.' *Harper's Weekly,* November 4, 1899.

————. 'The Philadelphia Photographic Salon.' *Harper's Weekly,*
December 7, 1901 (unsigned).

Coburn, Alvin Langdon. 'American Photographs in London.' *Photo-
Era,* January 1901.

Demachy, Robert. 'The New American School of Photography in
Paris.' *Camera Notes,* July 1901.

'The English Exhibitions and the "American Invasion."' *Camera Notes,*
January 1901.

Hartmann, Sadakichi. 'Clarence H. White.' *The Photographic Times,*
January 1900.

————. 'A Decorative Photographer: F. H. Day.' *The Photographic
Times,* March 1900.

————. 'Portrait Painting and Portrait Photography.' *Camera Notes,*
July 1899.

————. 'The Salon Club and the First American Photography Salon
at New York.' In his *Valiant Knights of Daguerre,* Berkeley: University of California Press, 1978.

Hazell, Ralph C. 'A Visit to Mr. F. Holland Day.' *Amateur Photographer,* October 27, 1899.

Hinton, A. Horsley. 'Both Sides.' *Camera Notes,* January 1899.

Humphrey, Marmaduke (Rupert Hughes). 'Triumphs in Amateur
Photography, II, F. H. Day.' *Godey's Magazine,* January 1898.

Keiley, Joseph T. 'The Philadelphia Salon: Its Origins and Influence.'
Camera Notes, January 1899.

————. 'The Salons.' *Camera Notes,* January 1900.

Puyo, Constant. 'L'Exposition de F. H. Day et de la "Nouvelle Ecole
Americaine."' *Bulletin du Photo-Club de Paris,* April 1901.

Taylor, Herbert Whyte. 'F. Holland Day: An Estimate.' *Photo-Era,*
March 1900.

'W.M.M.' F. H. Day's Exhibition of Prints.' *Camera Notes,* July 1898.

MANUSCRIPT SOURCES

Norwood Historical Society, Norwood, Mass.
Archives of F. Holland Day: his ledgers and copybooks, unpublished correspondence to Day, miscellaneous catalogues, newspaper
clippings, albums, drafts of his letters.

Library of Congress, Washington, D.C.
Letters and miscellaneous clippings from Louise Imogen Guiney
to F. Holland Day; correspondence between Louise Chandler
Moulton and Louise Imogen Guiney.

Holy Cross College, Worcester, Mass.
Archives of Louise Imogen Guiney, including letters and her personal library, photographs, and miscellanea.

Beinecke Rare Book and Manuscript Library, Yale University, New
Haven, Conn.
Archives of Alfred Stieglitz, including correspondence between
Day and Stieglitz, as well as letters by and to other Pictorialists.

Index

SLAVE TO BEAUTY

has been set in Linotype Fairfield by Yankee Typographers. Designed by the distinguished typographer and wood engraver Rudolph Ruzicka in 1938, Fairfield is sharply cut, as though the letters came from the artist's graver rather than from his pen. Sprightly and personal, it is an 'original' old-style face combining high readability with economy of set width.

The display type is Auriol, supplied by Solotype Typographers. Designed by George Auriol along with an extensive series of ornaments, it was originally cast in foundry metal and issued in 1902 by the renowned Paris typefounders G. Peignot et Fils.

The orchid motif used in this book is taken from Fred Gordon's design for The Black Riders *by Stephen Crane, published by Copeland and Day.*

The book has been printed on Warren's Patina and bound by The Alpine Press. The jacket and folio plates were printed in duotone by Mercantile Printing Company on Cameo Dull.

The book was designed by Ann Schroeder.